Ahmadiyya Islam and Muslim Diaspora

This book is a study of the UK-based Ahmadiyya Muslim community in the context of the twentieth-century South Asian diaspora. Originating in late nineteenth-century Punjab, the Ahmadis are today a vibrant international religious movement; they are also a group that has been declared heretic by other Muslims and one that continues to face persecution in Pakistan, the country the Ahmadis made their home after the partition of India in 1947.

Structured as a series of case studies, the book focuses on the ways in which the Ahmadis balance the demands of faith, community and modern life in the diaspora. Following an overview of the history and beliefs of the Ahmadis, the chapters examine in turn the use of ceremonial occasions to consolidate a diverse international community; the paradoxical survival of the enchantments of dreams and charisma within the structures of an institutional bureaucracy; asylum claims and the ways in which the plight of asylum seekers has been strategically deployed to position the Ahmadis on the UK political stage; and how the planning and building of mosques serves to establish a home within the diaspora.

Based on fieldwork conducted over several years in a range of formal and informal contexts, this timely book will be of interest to an interdisciplinary audience from social and cultural anthropology, South Asian studies, the study of Islam and of Muslims in Europe, refugee, asylum and diaspora studies, as well as more generally religious studies and history.

Marzia Balzani is Research Professor of Anthropology at New York University Abu Dhabi, United Arab Emirates.

Routledge/Asian Studies Association of Australia (ASAA) South Asian Series

Edited by Duncan McDuie-Ra

The University of New South Wales, Australia

Published in Association with the Asian Studies Association of Australia (ASAA), represented by Ernest Koh, chair of the ASAA Publications Committee, Monash University, Australia.

Founded in 1986 to publish outstanding work in the social sciences and humanities, the SAPS entered a new phase in 2010 when it joined with Routledge to continue a notable tradition of Australian-based research about South Asia. Works in the series are published in both UK and Indian editions.

SAPS publishes outstanding research on the countries and peoples of South Asia across a wide range of disciplines including history, politics and political economy, anthropology, geography, literature, sociology and the fields of cultural studies, communication studies and gender studies. Interdisciplinary and comparative research is encouraged.

For more information about this series, please visit: https://www.routledge.com/ RoutledgeAsian-Studies-Association-of-Australia-ASAA-South-Asian-Series/ book-series/ASAASAS

Ahmadiyya Islam and the Muslim Diaspora

Living at the End of Days

Marzia Balzani

Routledge
Taylor & Francis Group

LONDON AND NEW YORK

First published 2020
by Routledge
2 Park Square, Milton Park, Abingdon, Oxon OX14 4RN

and by Routledge
605 Third Avenue, New York, NY 10017

First issued in paperback 2022

Routledge is an imprint of the Taylor & Francis Group, an informa business

© 2020 Marzia Balzani

Publisher's Note
The publisher has gone to great lengths to ensure the quality of this reprint but
points out that some imperfections in the original copies may be apparent.

British Library Cataloguing-in-Publication Data
A catalogue record for this book is available from the British Library

Library of Congress Cataloging-in-Publication Data
A catalog record for this book has been requested

ISBN: 978-1-03-240073-0 (pbk)
ISBN: 978-1-138-71585-1 (hbk)
ISBN: 978-1-315-19728-9 (ebk)

DOI: 10.4324/9781315197289

Typeset in Times New Roman
by Apex CoVantage, LLC

For Nick Allen

Contents

Acknowledgements

No ethnography could come to fruition without the support, knowledge and patience of many individuals. This one is no different, and I only hope that this book does justice to the many people over many years who have opened their homes to me, shared their time and their insights, invited me to events and answered my questions with understanding and good grace. Without the members of the Ahmadiyya *jama'at* UK and their willingness to allow me to attend functions both large and small, join in with family celebrations and take part in committee meetings as well as be granted the opportunity to learn about some of the 'backstage' organization necessary to manage the incredible amount of work required to maintain the *jama'at*, this ethnography would not have been possible.

I first found out about the Ahmadiyya Muslims living, working and worshipping in my neighbourhood in London in 2003 and soon thereafter began to take my first tentative steps towards a full-fledged ethnographic study. For much of the time since then I have worked towards this book as and when other commitments made it possible to do so. While it was often frustrating not to be able to devote a long stretch of time solely to the ethnography the slow build-up of knowledge and the opportunities this has afforded me to watch the *jama'at* grow, change and respond to events local and global has, I hope, deepened and enriched my understanding of Ahmadiyya Islam in the diaspora. It has also allowed me to watch some of the children and young people I first met years ago grow into thoughtful and considerate adults, and in some cases even to see them start families of their own. Over time friendships have developed, and I now cannot imagine a return trip to the UK without visiting people who started off as my informed consent-giving 'interlocutors' and who have now come to mean much more to me than this official sounding twenty-first-century research term would suggest. Among the very many people I wish to thank are Anni Rehman, Fauzia Mirza, Maha Khan, Maryam Karim, Qudsia Mirza, Aneela, Sara, Naheed and the very many other women who did not wish to have their names appear in print. I also wish to thank Asif M. Basit, Curator, Ahmadiyya Archive and Research Centre, London for our conversations over the years and the permission to reproduce the photographs in the book. To Usman Ahmad, who shared his memories and formidable store of knowledge about the history, official and personal, of the *jama'at* and who helped in the intensive final stages of the manuscript preparation picking up errors that had slipped into the text, thank you. I am indebted also to Naseer Dean secretary of the Ahmadiyya Muslim Association Liaison Committee, one of his many roles in the *jama'at,* for inviting me to countless official functions, for answering my never-ending questions and for keeping me informed of developments in the *jama'at* even after I left the UK. To the many individuals and volunteers who give up their time and expertise to keep the *jama'at* functioning and for whom talking to interested outsiders is just part of what they take in their stride, I cannot begin to express my gratitude for all your help, advice and diplomatic efforts to help me learn from you.

Beyond this I am grateful to all the conference and workshop participants who asked the sometimes difficult but always necessary questions which helped me to rethink, extend and improve on my ideas and work. Earlier versions of chapters of the book were presented at the 2003 conference of the Association of American Anthropologists in Chicago, USA (an early set of ideas for Chapter 1); at the Association of Social Anthropologists, Durham UK, in 2004 (now incorporated into Chapter 4); at the Second International Conference on New Directions in the Humanities, Prato, Italy also in 2004, on diasporic faith communities; in 2006 at the European Association of Social Anthropologists (EASA) conference in Bristol UK, on urban ethnography (Chapter 5); in 2008 at the European Conference of Modern South Asian Studies, Manchester University, UK, where part of Chapter 4 was first presented; and at the 2010 EASA conference in Maynouth, Ireland, where another section of Chapter 4 was first discussed. In 2010 at the Contemporary South Asia Seminar, Oxford University, part of Chapter 3 on dreams was presented; in 2014 a revised version of Chapter 1 was read to the Association of Social Anthropologists, Edinburgh, UK, and in the same year in Tallin, Estonia, at the EASA conference a revised section of Chapter 5 was presented and benefited greatly from the lively discussion which followed. Mosque building in the diaspora was the focus of a paper presented at the 2014 conference at the Asia-Europe Institute, Kuala Lumpur Malaya, Malaysia, and by 2015 Chapter 1 was reaching its current shape when presented at the International Union of Anthropological and Ethnological Sciences (IUAES), conference in Bangkok, Thailand. The following year, at a conference on Islam in the diaspora held at Waseda University, Tokyo, this chapter was further refined. Part of Chapter 4 was presented in 2017 at the IUAES conference in Ottawa, Canada, and I am grateful to Leonardo Schiocchet for an invitation to present a near final section of this at the Institute of Social Anthropology in Vienna, Austria, in 2019.

I thank David Henig for permission to reproduce a revised and extended version of an article first published in *History and Anthropology* in Chapter 3. I am also grateful to the editors of *Laboratorium* for permission to reprint sections of a 2015 article on mosque building in London. I am additionally indebted to Alexandra de Brauw, my editor at Routledge, for her considerable patience and continued support as events in my life delayed the delivery of the manuscript on more than one occasion. And I thank Nadia Balzani Zamir for her design skills in turning my diagram of the *jama'at* men's organization, the *majlis anasarullah* and the *lajna's* (women's organization) forms into print-worthy material.

Lastly, and most certainly not least, I thank Paige Mitchell for never giving up hope that this book would eventually see the light of day, and most especially I would like to thank Shamoon Zamir for living through the experience of field-work with me and learning about the Ahmadiyya community alongside me over the years. Shamoon attended many functions with me, helped translate materials from Urdu to English, hosted Ahmadi visitors in our home, and his incisive questions, comments and editorial suggestions have made this book far better than it would otherwise have been.

It goes without saying that any remaining misunderstandings or misinterpretation are entirely of my own making.

Note on transliteration, translation and quotation

Text within quotations has been reproduced exactly as in the original, including diacritics and spellings throughout the book. This means that there may be more than one spelling for a single word in the book – for example, Aḥmadīya in some quotations as well as Ahmadiyya in the main text. The English grammar found in some quotations has not been altered as long as the meaning is clear. In the main text I have chosen, for the sake of readability, not to use diacritical marks other than for the *'ayn* (') and *hamza* ('), but I have included the diacritical marks in the glossary.

Proper nouns, including place names, titles and individual names, have been transliterated and standardized using the most common spelling in English (save in quotations, as noted earlier). Wherever it has been possible to discover the information, I have used the spelling of a name that the person chose to use on official documents, such as English language passports. The real names of my interlocutors have not been used. The names which appear in the book are ones that are already in the public domain, either because the person is too well known for it to make any sense to attempt to render the individual anonymous or because I am quoting or referring to material published, broadcast or uploaded by the person who is named as the author.

Terms with common English spellings (e.g. Qu'ran) have been used wherever this seemed most appropriate and plurals of Urdu/Arabic terms are indicated by the addition of a 's' to the singular form, as in khalifa (singular) and khalifas (plural). Wherever possible, I have sought to quote from already existing English language translations of Ahmadi materials and where these are not available I note this. All dates follow the Common Era.

Abbreviations

AHRC	Asian Human Rights Commission
AIKC	All-India Kashmir Committee
AIMS (card)	Ahmadiyya Information Management System
AMA	Ahmadiyya Muslim Association
AMSA	Ahmadiyya Muslim Student Association
APPG	All Party Parliamentary Group. All Party Groups are informal groups of members of both houses of the British Parliament who share a common interest in particular issues.
BBC	British Broadcasting Corporation
CO	Colonial Office
COI/CPIN	Country of Origin Information report/Country Policy and Information Notes
DFID	Department for International Development
DO	Dominions Office
FCO	Foreign and Commonwealth Office
FIR	First Information Report
IHRC	International Human Rights Committee
IRB	Immigration Review Board
IRF	International Religious Freedom
HO	Home Office
HRCP	Human Rights Commission for Pakistan
IO	India Office
MCB	Muslim Council of Britain
MP	Member of Parliament
MTA	Muslim Television Ahmadiyya
PHRG	Parliamentary Human Rights Group
SACRE	Standing Advisory Councils on Religious Education
TLP	Tehreek-e-Labbaik Party (Pakistani Barelvi Political Party)
UKBA	United Kingdom Border Authority
UNHCR	United Nations High Commissioner for Refugees
USC	United States Congress
USSD	United States State Department

Illustrations

Figures

Tables

Preface

On 24 March 2016, Maundy Thursday, Asad Shah, the owner of a newsagents and convenience store in the Shawlands area of Glasgow, was discovered outside his shop with knife wounds to his head. Only two days earlier, three nail bombs had exploded in Brussels and the initial suspicion in the British media was that Mr. Shah had been the victim of a retaliatory Islamophobic attack. It then emerged that the day before the attack, Mr. Shah, who had moved to Glasgow from Pakistan 20 years earlier and was a respected member of the local community, had posted an Easter greeting to all his customers on his Facebook page. Speculation shifted to the possibility that the attack had been carried out by a Muslim and had been motivated by a perception of Mr. Shah as a Christian sympathizer. When the killer was finally apprehended, it became clear that Mr. Shah had been murdered for being an Ahmadi Muslim. In an incoherent but surprising public confession, Tanveer Ahmad explained that he had killed Mr. Shah because he 'disrespected' Islam and because he 'claimed to be a prophet' (Carrell 2016). This was an inaccurate characterization of Mr. Shah's conduct and beliefs shaped by modern anti-Ahmadi Islamic orthodoxy, and a garbled version of the Ahmadi faith, though many equally negative understandings of Ahmadiyya Islam are widely shared in the Muslim community. In the media coverage that followed Tanveer Ahmad's confession, a handful of essential facts were put together by journalists, but the real focus of the coverage was not the Ahmadi community but the rising threat of Islamic extremism within British borders.

The murder of Mr. Shah made clear just how little is generally known about the Ahmadis in the United Kingdom, a community that has some 25,000 members and that has its origins in late nineteenth-century India. It also potentially brought into view the complex position the Ahmadis occupy within the contemporary Muslim diaspora and within the histories of the subcontinent that continue to shape this diaspora. And lastly, it made all too painfully evident the perils faced by a religious minority as it tries to negotiate sectarian orthodoxies, theological debates and disagreements, and Western perceptions of Islam.

This book is a study of the Ahmadis in the United Kingdom and of the complex nexus of religious, social and political forces within which they maintain their faith and community. As the fate of Mr. Shah unfortunately illustrates, to study the Ahmadis and the realities of the world they occupy is also to undertake a study of contemporary diasporic Islam.

Ahmadiyya Islam was founded as a new religious movement within Islam towards the end of the nineteenth century in colonial Punjab, India, by Mirza Ghulam Ahmad, a charismatic religious leader. The movement was, in part, a response to British colonial rule, and though in many respects Ahmadi beliefs and practices are indistinguishable from those of mainstream traditions of Islam, the Ahmadis consider their founder to be both the *mahdi* and the promised messiah and themselves to be the true Muslims. It is these claims, or at least the ways in which they have been understood, that have led to the exclusion of Ahmadis from the fold of Islam. They have been declared heretics and apostates by orthodox Muslim groups all over the world and have often been subjected to legislative discrimination and both state and non-state persecution. Many Ahmadis moved to Pakistan after the partition of India in 1947 and established the centre of their community in the town of Rabwah near Lahore. But the community has been subjected to increasingly aggressive forms of persecution in Pakistan, and as a result the leader of the Ahmadiyya Muslims, the khalifa, left the country in 1984 and now lives in exile in the UK, which is now the de facto global headquarters of the sect.

Unlike most new religious movements that do not usually survive the death of a charismatic leader, the Ahmadis have not only endured but have thrived and become a global community. It is in part precisely because they are a persecuted minority faith group that the Ahmadis have had to organize to defend their faith and find new and effective ways to protect their members and to sustain and grow their community. They have sent proselytizing missions across the world and now have mosques in over 150 countries. The dispersed Ahmadi communities form a well-integrated network supported by an efficient bureaucratic system, and through the use of innovative and advanced technological means, including television channels that broadcast in a number of languages.

Although the Ahmadiyya faith rests on a call for a return to the true Islam fashioned as a response to a millenarian belief in the imminent 'end of days', the Ahmadis are in fact a complex modern Islamic sect, simultaneously religiously conservative but also in some respects socially progressive. It is, for instance, because they support education and certain leadership roles for women, because they campaign for peace ('love for all, hatred for none' is the Ahmadi official motto and was the slogan of a recent publicity campaign across the United Kingdom) and because they declare a commitment to abide by the laws of the countries in which they reside that the Ahmadis are sometimes invoked by the British media and the political establishment as exemplary citizens and 'good' Muslims. But the media, politicians and the public are, as often as not, more interested in using the Ahmadis to highlight the dangers of growing extremism and radicalization among the Muslim communities of the United Kingdom than in fostering a better understanding of the Ahmadis or of the diversity of British Islam. It is also the case that widespread misunderstandings about the Ahmadis have allowed some sections of the Muslim community to demonize the Ahmadis as a means of consolidating their own positions, and, as the case of Ahmad Shah indicates, on occasion to instigate sectarian violence.

There are then many reasons why a study of the Ahmadi community in the UK is timely. Designed as a fine-grained exploration of the complex and multiple

interactions between Ahmadis and others in local, national and international contexts, private, official, political and social, this study is the first detailed ethnography of the Ahmadis themselves in the UK, but it also extends into a comparative
examination on how Muslim sects in the diaspora position themselves and work
towards achieving their local goals. The particular location of Ahmadiyya Islam
within the histories of the subcontinent and within the Muslim global diaspora
make of the community an especially sharp lens through which to look at the
ways in which Muslim groups position themselves, and are positioned by others,
not only in relation to each other but also in relation to non-Muslim groups and
the wider polity.

The book is based on fieldwork conducted over several years in the UK in a
range of formal and informal contexts. I have attended committee meetings, public functions, internal discussion groups and community religious events. I have
conducted numerous interviews and also worked with groups and institutions that
are required to deal with the Ahmadis, such as the local councils in areas where
the Ahmadis have their mosques. In addition, I have been fortunate to have ben-
efitted from access to the UK national women's organization. While primarily an
ethnography, the study draws heavily on historical scholarship and records, as
well as on discussions in urban planning and South Asian Studies, and on theori-
zations of place and diaspora.

The book begins with a detailed historical, religious, social and political overview of who the Ahmadis are and how they came into existence in a period of
rapid social change and as a consequence of the religious and social dislocations
caused by modernity in nineteenth-century India. The rest of the book is designed
as a series of interlocking case studies. Each of the remaining chapters focuses
on one key aspect of Ahmadi thought, practice and organization. This case study
approach provides an understanding of a selected aspect of Ahmadi thought and
practice in its own terms, and offers the reader different ways to understand what
it means to be Ahmadi. Each chapter also makes use of different anthropological, theoretical and conceptual materials to analyze the Ahmadi data. While it
might be possible to read each chapter as a stand-alone analysis of one aspect of
Ahmadi organization and experience, together the chapters offer multi-layered
and constellated analyses of who the Ahmadis are, how they came to be what they
are today, how they represent themselves and are represented by others, and what
the consequences of these representations are. In keeping with contemporary ethnographic practice, the case studies approach acknowledges that it offers insights
into some important aspects of Ahmadi life and experience but does not claim to
provide a comprehensive overview or complete account.

Several topics also run throughout the book and link the chapters thematically.
These include the place of Ahmadis in the Muslim world, and how Ahmadis served
and continue to serve distinct and particular political and religious agendas in the
complex historical and contemporary sectarian divides in Islam; what it means to
be a minority, both in Muslim majority countries and in countries where Muslims
are a minority population; what it means to self-define as Muslim in the West, particularly post 9/11 and in the context of more recent acts of terrorism; the religious

uses of technology from the printing presses of the nineteenth century to the use of Twitter and blogs today to create a Muslim public sphere; the complex notions of time in Ahmadi thought in terms of the ways in which Ahmadis creatively merge their historical origins with the origins of Islam itself; and how historical events are re-worked and re-presented by today's Ahmadis to create a history in accord with the contemporary Ahmadi historical and eschatological vision.

1 Sameness and difference
Situating the Ahmadis

A people out of place

A recent Islamic studies textbook for sixth graders, serving the requirement for compulsory faith education and prepared in accordance with the guidelines 'given by the Federal Ministry of Education, Pakistan', characterized the history and beliefs of the Ahmadi Muslims for its readership of 11-year-olds as follows:

> The British hatched numerous conspiracies during the freedom movement to delink Muslims from their faith. They were keen on mitigating the love of the prophet (PBUH) from the hearts of Muslims. In 1891, under the patronage of the British, Mirza Ghulam Ahmad of Qadian, a liar, made a false claim to prophethood. His disciples too falsely pose to be Muslims. Accordingly, after the establishment of Pakistan, on December 7, 1977 (*sic*, for 7 September 1974), it was legislated by the Islamic Republic of Pakistan that no Qadiani can deceive the Muslims by calling himself a Muslim, because anyone who believes anyone to be a prophet after the Holy Prophet (PBUH) becomes an infidel (*Kafir*).
>
> (AHRC and IHRC 2015:138)

Although the message here seems quite unambiguous, the 'instructions for teaching staff' drive it home by explaining that, 'having got the lesson', the students 'should become aware of the evil of Qadianis [Ahmadis]' (AHRC and IHRC 2015:138).

Generations of Pakistanis have grown up with and absorbed one version or another of this account of Ahmadi history and theology, especially those whose lives have been shaped by the ever greater Islamicization of Pakistan over the last 50 years. It is accounts like these that have been repeated, embroidered and legitimized in schools and madrassas, in the popular media, in sermons and in state discourse. And these accounts are today widely disseminated globally, throughout the Muslim diaspora and its presence on online social media.

A UN report on education and religious discrimination in Pakistan found evidence in 'interviews with public school and madrassa teachers . . . that they had limited awareness or understanding of religious minorities and their beliefs, and were divided on whether a religious minority was a citizen'. The report further concluded that 'views expressed by teachers about Ahmadis, Christians, and Jews often were very negative. Interviews showed that these biased sentiments were transmitted and held by the students' (in Hussain, Salim and Naveed 2011:11). During the rule of Zia ul Haq (1977–1988), the number of madrassas doubled and the education system was reformed to 'implement the Islamic principles and protect the Pakistani ideology', which required a review of secondary and tertiary level teaching materials to ensure that they complied with this 'Pakistani ideology'. During this time:

> [n]ational history was presented as a string of events leading to the idea of creating an Islamic state. In libraries, secular and purely scientific books that were unrelated to religion were gradually replaced by religious literature. The study of Arabic and Islamic history and traditions was given impetus. The authorities simultaneously reduced allocations for secular education.
>
> (Belokrenitsky and Moskalenko 2013:284)

The extract from the *Islamiat for Class VI* textbook confirms the findings of the UN report and offers a telling example of the ways in which Ahmadis have been positioned within narratives of national history and state building, and of the role they have been made to play as scapegoat in the project of consolidating an orthodox and increasingly intolerant community of faith. And to the extent that the text follows not only the guidance of the Ministry of Education but also the pronouncements of many religious leaders, it allows us a glimpse into the role played by state, cultural and religious institutions in determining the fate of the Ahmadis of Pakistan. These are the concerns of this introductory chapter.

The origins of the animus directed at the Ahmadis by other Muslims reside in the ways in which the claims of prophethood made by Ghulam Ahmad, the founder of Ahmadiyya Islam, have been understood and misunderstood over many years. During the late years of the nineteenth century, Ahmad claimed to be a *mujaddid* (renewer of the faith), *masih mau'ud* (the promised messiah) and the *mahdi* (the rightly guided one who will appear at the end times together with the messiah). For many Muslim individuals and institutions, the Ahmadi attempts to reconcile these claims with the belief in the finality of Muhammad's prophethood, a core tenet of Islam, are merely forms of sophistry designed to disguise what they see as heresy. Grasping these differences and disagreements is essential for understanding the place of the Ahmadis in the Muslim world (and I return to the issue of prophethood in more detail shortly). But focusing on doctrinal differences obscures from view what is a no less important social and cultural sameness. From this perspective, the vehemence of the demonization of the Ahmadis in the textbook extract quoted at the start of the chapter can be read not so much as a statement of the obvious but as an anxious effort to make visible what may not otherwise be visible. After all, the Ahmadis in many respects behave like good Muslims, observe the same rituals and practices, study the same religious texts and, in Pakistan, they eat the same food, wear the same clothes and speak the same languages as other Pakistanis. And it is precisely here that the fear enters of the outsider who can pass as an insider, the enemy within, and hence the justification and need for ever finer and more precise definitions of who is a genuine insider and the lurking suspicion that even this is not enough to ensure that everyone is clearly and unambiguously classified.

In addition to the forms of their daily lives and many of their beliefs and ritu-als, the relocation of the Ahmadis to Pakistan at partition, and then migration to the UK mirrors in many respects the transnational migration patterns of many South Asians over the last century, moving from one nation to another in the subcontinent or Africa before heading west to Europe or North America. Yet Ahmadis, rather than being studied for the many similarities they share with other South Asian groups, including shared experiences of colonialism, migra-tion and sectarian and communal conflicts, have often been studied in terms limited to their distinctive beliefs and the socio-political consequences of their adherence to these beliefs. Past studies have, inevitably, focused on what is dif-ferent about the Ahmadis, and this often then serves as some kind of self-evident explanation, almost as though it were natural, as to why Ahmadis have been targeted by other Muslim groups, leading to the apparently inevitable political, social and religious forms of persecution they have been subject to in South Asia, and increasingly also in other Muslim majority states such as Indonesia and Algeria.

Here, while not ignoring or playing down some of the clearly distinctive features of Ahmadi Islam, I seek to understand just what is the same about the Ahmadis and other Muslim sects and minorities, so that their exclusion from Islam in the Pakistan government's declaration that Ahmadis are not Muslim in 1974 has to be explained and not simply accepted as self-evident and inevitable. Further, given that exclusion from the fold of Islam does not necessarily have to lead to automatic social and political discrimination or justify the use of violence, this too needs to be explained.[1] Ahmadis are not marginalized, scapegoated and persecuted *simply* because they have been declared non-Muslim but because of their complex social and political contextual location in colonial India, post-colonial Pakistan and in today's globalized society. Understanding the logic of the processes that led to the exclusion of Ahmadiyya Muslims from Islam in Pakistan also serves to out-line the similar processes that have resulted in the marginalization of Hindus and Christians and the sectarian violence against Shi'a Muslims, which has also taken place in Pakistan over recent decades. Pakistan, contrary to the explicitly stated intent of its first governor-general, is based on a modern conjunction of religion and state, a vision of the state as Islamic defined so as to limit the rights of, and over time increasingly exclude, all those who do not meet the officially mandated definition of Muslim. The Islamic state project that is Pakistan, through state pro-cesses which have, among other things, curtailed forms of Sufi traditional practice and made a narrow and ideological form of Islamiat education compulsory in state education, has made it possible for those who can identify as Sunni Muslim to be 'citizens who belong' and for all others to be rendered citizens who 'belong less' (Geschiere 2009:100; Ewing 1983; Leirvik 2008). And, in brief, it is these processes that go some way to explain why the almost 23% non-Muslim religious minority population of Pakistan in 1947 declined to a mere 3% by 2013 (Ispahani 2013; Hadi 2015).[2]

It is in the particularities of the sameness and difference of Ahmadi Muslims to other Muslim groups and other minorities,[3] and how these have changed over time and across national territorial space that makes it possible to begin to understand how one group that shares, in many respects, the features of many other similar Muslim groups is singled out for particular scrutiny and treatment. This scrutiny and treatment have not remained the same since the foundation of Ahmadiyya Islam some 130 years ago. Just as the Ahmadis themselves have developed institutionally and reacted to change, so too have those who seek to curtail their influence and destroy them.

I am here drawing upon Appadurai's suggestion that some minorities may be subject to violence from a majority not because of their differences but because of their similarities, or more precisely, because they blur the boundaries between groups, being both ' "us" and "them", here and there . . . loyal and disloyal . . . [and are] unwelcome because of their anomalous identities and attachments' (Appadurai 2006:44). Appadurai is, of course, drawing upon Douglas' (1984) insight that dirt is matter out of place and results from a given system of classification. And recognizing a group as metaphorical 'dirt' that does not fit the system requires that everyone be classified as belonging clearly and unequivocally to one category or another. Those who are then in the majority group may displace social anxieties on to the minority group, but this group may be particularly problematic to locate if distinguishing between them and the majority is not always straightforward.

The kind of overlapping and mixed identities described by Appadurai raise questions about possibly divided loyalties, and in the case of the Ahmadis these have been described in terms of what some have called their 'state within a state', a reference to Rabwah, the town they built in Pakistan after partition, as well as a suggestion that their loyalties are primarily to governments and ideologies located outside Pakistan (e.g. Zaheer 1984).[4] The processes needed to turn a numerical minority such as the Ahmadis into such a significant threat to the state that it has to be eliminated then becomes one that requires, as Appadurai notes, 'regularly mobilized and reawakened . . . powerful campaigns of . . . political propaganda' (Appadurai 2006:54). Such campaigns constitute 'a remarkable feat of active ideological and political engineering. Even in themselves they could be seen as evidence of the effort required to build a successful national consensus in favour of the campaign against' a minority such as the Ahmadis (Appadurai 2006:55). In Pakistan, this sustained effort against the Ahmadis has necessitated the active involvement of state institutions such as the Punjabi Auqaf Department[5] (religious affairs), which funds public anti-Ahmadi media campaigns, including sponsoring billboards and patronizing organizations that distribute 'pamphlets calling upon Muslims to kill Ahmadis everywhere indiscriminately' (Hamdani 2012). It is also visible in the government offices displaying posters with slogans incorporating language Ahmadis consider offensive such as the term 'Qadiani' derived from the birthplace of Ghulam Ahmad in Qadian, India. Such slogans include 'he who is a friend to Ahmadis is a traitor' or 'when a Muslim befriends a Qadiani, he causes anguish to the spirit of the Holy Prophet (PBUH)' (Hamdani 2012). In Appadurai's terms, it is the social uncertainty of the modern world coupled with the high level of 'doctrinal certainty' that comes from the education system itself that supports the hostility towards the Ahmadis and which focuses social, political and economic uncertainties on a single group who can then become the visible scapegoat and target of the majority population which takes on a predatory identity in the process (Appadurai 2006:91).

What follows is neither a history of the Ahmadis nor an account of Ahmadi theology: both are already available elsewhere (e.g. Friedman 1989; Lavan 1974). It is, rather, a set of episodes and fragments that engage with some aspects of history and belief as a way of situating the Ahmadis in ways that will, I hope, help frame the ethnographic studies of Ahmadi life in the diaspora that make up the subsequent chapters of this book.

Prophethood and communities of faith in the colony

In 1889, Mirza Ghulam Ahmad, claiming descent from the Prophet Muhammad through his paternal grandmothers and from noble ancestors of Persian origin, founded the Jama'at Ahmadiyya (Dard 2008).[6] As a young man, Ghulam Ahmad had witnessed the end of the Mughal empire in India.[7] Bhadur Shah Zafar, the last Mughal emperor, had suffered a crushing defeat at the hands of the British in 1857 and had been sent into exile the following year. Many Indian Muslims at the time experienced these events as disempowerment, and as both consequence and evidence of 'Muslim decline'. As Sevea (2012:4) notes:

> The late nineteenth and early twentieth centuries . . . proved to be a 'time of great ferment in the history of Muslim India'; one in which the perceived challenges to Islamic institutions, practices and traditions were more urgent and the responses more varied.

These responses included 'extensive adoption of print technology' and 'the emergence of new Muslim educational institutions – both religious and secular' but also 'the bourgeoning of Muslim movements that competed in the public arena to provide the "true" Islamic perspective on a host of socio-political issues'. Although Ghulam Ahmad's family were Muslim Punjabi landholders who claimed Mughal descent and supported the British – for which they were rewarded – it is impossible to see his discovery of his messianic calling and the founding of Ahmadiyya Islam as anything but a response to the cultural and political crisis experienced by Indian Muslims in the aftermath of the end of Mughal rule.

Seven years earlier, in 1882, Ghulam Ahmad had 'announced that he had received a divine command that he was to be a *mujaddid* (renewer of the faith)' (Jones 2008:116). 'The formal foundations for the Ahmadiyya as a distinct religious community were laid in 1888, when Ghulam Ahmad published an *ishtihar* (literally, 'advertisement') declaring himself the renewer of the age' (Sevea 2012:32). But it was on 12 January 1889, the day on which his son was born, that

Ghulam Ahmad proclaimed the conditions under which he would grant initiation through the Sufi institution of *bai'at* to his followers.[8] In the following years he published texts in which he set out his claim to be both the promised messiah (*masih mau'ud*) and also the *mahdi* (Jones 2008:116).

While this book does not deal in any detail with the theological underpinnings of Ahmadiyya Islam, it would be impossible fully to understand the history and politics of Ahmadiyyat and the Ahmadis in the subcontinent and in diaspora without some knowledge of Ghulam Ahmad's claims to prophethood. To put these claims in context, I draw on the exemplary work of Yohanan Friedmann (1989), who sets the prophetic claims of Ghulam Ahmad in the context of Ahmad's biography, the medieval theological background to his claims, and in particular the Sufi and Shi'a understandings of prophecy within Islam.[9]

A key aspect of Ahmad's claims was that while Muhammad was the last of the law-bearing or legislative prophets, prophecy itself did not cease with his death. Rather, prophets could continue to be sent, as they had always been, to the peoples of the world, and this included the people of India (Friedmann 1989:122–123). Thus it was possible for Ghulam Ahmad to claim not only that India had been granted prophets such as the Hindu god Krishna in the past, but that he was himself 'from the viewpoint of the spiritual essence' Krishna in his own day (Friedmann 1989:124). This was, in form, the same as Ahmad's claim also to resemble Jesus as both he and Jesus were sent to complete prophetic chains – Jesus as the last prophet of the Jews and Ahmad for Muslims (Friedmann 1989:120–121).

Not all prophets and prophetic experiences, however, are equal. One key difference concerns the manner by which the prophet comes to his vocation. Some are considered independent prophets who received their vocation directly from Allah, while others achieve prophethood by following closely a prophetic predecessor. Another difference between prophets, as briefly mentioned earlier in relation to Muhammad, is that only independent prophets are entrusted with founding new communities by bringing divine laws to their people (Friedmann 1989:125). The prophetic charge of those who closely follow a prophetic predecessor is 'shadowy' or a 'reflection' (*zilli*) and constitutes a 'manifestation' (*buruz*) of the prophet who serves as the model for prophethood (Friedmann 1989:124). These latter prophets have great power as they are able to gift their derived, 'shadowy' or 'reflective' prophecy to their followers. This is the kind of non law-bearing prophet Ghulam Ahmad considered himself to be (Friedman 1989:132). For Ahmad, all Muslim prophets after Muhammad can only be non law-bearing because they follow him faithfully and thus they owe their prophethood to him (Friedmann 1989:127). The continuation of prophecy after the death of Muhammad was proof, for Ahmad, that Islam was a living faith and that Muslims had not been abandoned by Allah.

One significant aspect of this view of prophethood and prophecy in Islam required that Ghulam Ahmad reinterpret the contemporary orthodox meaning of Muhammad as 'seal of the prophets', which was taken to mean 'last of the prophets'. The means by which Ahmad did this, as Friedmann shows, was in part to accept that Muhammad was indeed the last of the legislative prophets and that after him no new divine laws were to come. In part, it was also to suggest that while the prophet had no biological sons, he was nonetheless the father of spiritual sons, men who would follow his example (Friedmann 1989:129–130). Ahmad accepted some early and no longer orthodox interpretations of the meaning of 'seal of the prophet' and rejected, following established Muslim precedent, that anything that is 'last' could also be best (Friedmann 1989:52ff). Instead, Ahmad took the term 'seal' to mean that Muhammad had been confirmed as 'owner of the seal' – in other words, that he had been granted divine revelations and given the seal of the prophets, not that prophecy would end with him (Friedmann 1989:130). Ahmadis, for their part, do not consider that Ahmad reinterpreted the meaning of 'seal of the prophets', thus his perspective on the matter was in keeping with Islamic understandings of the phrase.

Yet Ghulam Ahmad did not begin his prophetic career by claiming that he was a shadowy or reflective prophet but rather by making a lesser claim, in 1882, that he was the *mujaddid*, or renewer of the faith, for the fourteenth century AH and tasked with reviving Islam in a period when Muslims no longer followed an Islamic way of life. As *mujaddid*, Ahmad's vocation was to save Indian Muslims from the proselytizing of Christian missionaries and bring them back to Islam. Ahmad's claim to be *mujaddid* was complicated, however, by his understanding that *mujaddidun* were 'prophet-like people', a position that may have been influenced by the work of the Indian Muslim Sufi Shaykh Ahmad Sirhindi on *tajdid* (renewal of Islam) and by that of some Sufis who considered *mujaddidun* to possess subsidiary prophetic perfections. Thus by ascribing some prophetic qualities to an otherwise non-deviant claim to *mujaddid* status which might not, however, have been accepted by others, Ahmad deviated from orthodox understandings of the *mujaddid* (Friedmann 1989:105–129).

Ahmad, however, soon went beyond his claim to be a *mujaddid* by additionally claiming to be a *muhaddath* (one spoken to by Allah or an angel). A *muhaddath* receives divine messages, and once more Ahmad's understanding of this was informed by Sufi tradition (Friedmann 1989:110). In Sufi literature and some Shi'a traditions, the boundary between those who are *muhaddath* and the prophets may become somewhat blurred, with Sufi authors such as al-Hakim al-Tirmidhi writing about *muhaddath* of different ranks as possessing different degrees of prophethood. For Ibn al-'Arabi, one of the sources of inspiration for Ghulam Ahmad's thought, the *muhaddath* differs from a prophet because he brings no new divine laws. Similarly, Sirhindi considered there to be an affinity between the *muhaddath* and the prophet (Friedmann 1989:86–92). Sunni thinkers, for their part, denied or diminished the notion of prophetic qualities and affinity between the *muhaddath* and the prophet. For some Sunni thinkers, for example, angels speak to *muhaddath* in the heart, meaning that unlike the prophet they do not see the angel and thus, while *muhaddath* may speak the truth, they are not prophets.

Over time, Ghulam Ahmad's claims to prophethood came to include his belief that Allah spoke to him as he had done to the prophets in the past. This honour was given to him because he so closely and completely followed Muhammad that in effect it culminated in his 'self-annihilation'. As Friedmann (1989:134) states:

Seen from a different vantage point, it constitutes the second coming of Muḥammad, which is said to have been predicted in Sūra 62:3: 'And others from among them who have not yet joined them'. . . . This being the case, his [Ghulām Aḥmad's] prophethood should arouse no envy: it emerges not from Ghulām Aḥmad's own self but rather from the prophetic fountain of Muḥammad. And being so totally dependent on the spirituality of Muḥammad, it does not interfere with the Prophet's status as *khātam-al-nabiyyīn* [seal of the prophets].

The remaining claims to prophethood by Ghulam Ahmad, that he was both *mahdi* (rightly guided one) and *masih* (messiah), may also have arisen, in part, from his desire to counter the missionizing of Christians in India. In this context Ahmad's denial of Jesus's death on the cross, his resurrection and his return at the end of days were designed to undermine the Christian missionary argument that the Christian god was alive in heaven and waiting to return, unlike the Muslim prophet who, as a mortal man, was dead and gone. By reinterpreting Muslim traditions about Jesus, Ahmad was able to maintain that the second coming of Jesus, the messiah of the latter days, should not be understood as a literal return of Jesus but rather a return in the form of a person who resembled Jesus. That person was Ghulam Ahmad, and his role was revealed to him by Allah. Ghulam Ahmad thus believed that he came to share 'absolute affinity with Jesus' (Friedmann 1989:111–117).

From this brief outline of Ghulam Ahmad's revelations about his prophetic status, it should be clear that it took several years for him to proclaim the prophetic vision of his role to its fullest extent. His revelations and prophetic claims became greater and more wide-ranging with the passage of time and the growth in the number of his followers. It should also be clear that while Ghulam Ahmad's religious mission was informed by the colonial and religious context in which he lived, his revelations and reinterpretations were derived from his reading of Sufi, Shi'a and Sunni religious thinkers. While informed by his religious study, the complex and nuanced claims made by Ahmad could not but be controversial.

Initially, Ghulam Ahmad attracted followers from the literate classes in the region and soon thereafter others who came from the less educated and more rural areas of the Punjab, leading to what Jones describes as a 'bipolar' pattern of recruitment to the new faith.[10] All, however socially heterogeneous, were seeking a return to the 'true' fundamentals of the faith, and in the religiously charged and turbulent years at the end of the nineteenth century they found, in Mirza Ghulam Ahmad, a charismatic leader who inspired a devotion which was, in Weber's words, 'born of distress and enthusiasm' (Gerth and Mills 1946:249).[11]

Many of the spiritual claims made by Ghulam Ahmad were not in themselves unique. Others had made similar claims and these were made drawing on recognized Muslim traditions, including Shi'a and Sufi ones.[12] The Punjab itself was, and is, a place where Sufi Islam is widespread and where Sufi *pirs* (saints) established themselves and attracted devotees over the centuries. Indeed, under Mughal rule in India close interactions between Sufis and the Mughal emperors were far from unknown.[13] Royal lineage and religious authority were thus often intermingled, adding a culturally established support to Ghulam Ahmad's claims as the somewhat impoverished scion of noble ancestry and divinely inspired pious Muslim renewer of the faith.[14] This was not a position that was wholly in the realm of doctrinal Islam but rather what Moin, describing the case for the Mughal and Safavid rulers, notes was one where:

> what may appear as 'heresy' from a doctrinal point of view was, in many cases, a ritual engagement with popular forms of saintliness and embodied forms of sacrality that were broadly and intuitively accepted by much of the populace as morally valid and spiritually potent.
>
> (2012:6)

And Friedmann (1989:142–146), who has demonstrated the influence of Sufi thought of Ibn al-Arabi in Ghulam Ahmad's writings, concludes that:

> the essential elements of Ghulam Ahmad's prophetology were not unknown among medieval Sufi thinkers. There is no doubt that medieval Sufi thought is an important source of inspiration for the Ahmadi movement and that the prophetology of Ghulam Ahmad is not substantially different from that of [these earlier] Sufi thinkers.

Indeed, many of the Ahmadis I have spent time with over the years consider their faith and some of their religious practices to be derived at least in part from, and oriented towards, South Asian Sufi forms of Islam.[15]

Not only were many of Ghulam Ahmad's individual spiritual claims ones that had a long history in Islam and in India, they were also, together with his prolific writing on Islam, ones that for a time at least were given serious attention and carefully evaluated by members of the intellectual elites of Muslim South Asia. Muhammad Iqbal (1877–1938), poet and activist intellectual, was one such man who 'initially expressed optimism about the aims of the movement' (Sevea 2012:121), going so far as to describe Ghulam Ahmad, in 1900, as 'probably the profoundest theologian among modern Indian Muhammadans' (Iqbal 1900:239). It is likely that Iqbal's father and his brother were Ahmadis and that he may himself have joined and remained active in the movement until 1913.[16] This may explain his initially sympathetic understanding of the movement. But Iqbal later came to fear that Ahmadi Islam 'would split the unity of Islam and that it presented a theology which sought to reconcile Muslims with disempowerment' (Sevea 2012:121).[17] In 1934, in his article on 'Qadianis and Orthodox Muslims', Iqbal reverted to the issue of prophethood as the source of this threat:

> Any religious society historically arising from the bosom of Islam, which claims a new prophethood for its basis, and declares all Muslims who do not recognise the truth of its alleged revelation as Kafirs, must, therefore, be regarded by every Muslim as a serious danger to the solidarity of Islam. This

must necessarily be so; since the integrity of Muslim society is secured by the
Idea of the Finality of Prophethood alone.

(in Shamloo ed. 1944:94)[18]

Iqbal did not, however:

call for the proscription or persecution of the Ahmadiyya; he called for them
to be recognized as a separate religious community beyond the fold of Islam.
As he felt that the Ahmadis would never voluntarily declare themselves to
be a separate religious community, he looked to the [British] government to
classify them officially as such. He pointed to the example of the Sikhs, who
were classified as a separate religious community from the Hindus in the early
twentieth century, as a precedent that should be applied to the Ahmadiyya.

(Sevea 2012:171)

Iqbal recognized in Ahmadiyyat 'not a sudden manifestation of a new religious
order but one of the outcomes . . . [of] the decline of Islam in India' (Lavan
1974:172).

Iqbal's reflection on and shifting views of Ahmadi Islam indicate the ways in
which issues of theology have helped shaped debates about Islam, nationalism
and modernity, and the ways in which the presence of religious minorities has
troubled the efforts of the Muslims of the subcontinent to fashion a unified community of faith. Iqbal's ideas were later taken up and developed by the younger
and more conservative Maududi, the founder of the Jama'at-i-Islami (1941), in his
own writings and political campaign to bring about an Islamic state in Pakistan
(Ahmad, I. 2010). And a key part of Maududi's vision necessitated a definition of
Islam and of Muslims that had no place for divinely inspired charismatic leaders
who could amass large followings and hence potentially challenge his more aus-
tere vision of the faith in which there was little space to accommodate diverse and
differing perspectives (Raja 2010:135; Sevea 2012:57–60, 203–204).[19] Maududi's
attacks on the Ahmadis and his efforts to contain them were, of course, to a large
extent continuations of the anxieties about and hostility towards the Ahmadis
expressed by orthodox Muslims in colonial India. We cannot properly understand
the fate of the Ahmadis in Pakistan unless we have some sense of the degree
to which the new Muslim nation state inherited and reshaped the religious conflicts of its own colonial origins. Here, the struggles between the Ahmadis and the
Majlis-i-Ahrar-i-Islam-Hind (henceforth the Ahrar), a Deobandi Sunni association founded in 1929,[20] how the Ahrar and the Ahmadis engaged with each other
in colonial India, how they competed in political and social arenas and, in the
Punjab in the early decades of the twentieth century, how they both constituted
distinct but viable responses to British colonialism in the wake of the disruptions
and weakened position of Muslims in India after 1857, can serve as an illustration.

Both Ahmadis and the Ahrar leaders could, each in their way, be described
as forging 'a synthesis between the divergent forces of modernity and tradition'
(Awan 2010:vii). Many were attracted to the Sunni Deobandi Muslim identity

offered by the Ahrar for the same reasons that many others converted to Ahmadi Islam: both offered prospects of faith and collective strength for the future at a time when Islam was felt to be in retreat in the subcontinent, and when, post 1857, Muslims were marginalized and excluded from positions of responsibility in the official hierarchies of state. There were, however, clear differences, both religious and political, between the Ahrar and the Ahmadis. While the more Sufi-oriented groups in the Punjab were, in broad terms, supportive of the idea of Pakistan, those inclined to a more Deobandi religious outlook were not. The Ahmadis, with a leadership that was rooted in landownership and hence a more elite social position, initially favoured continued British rule but came eventually to support the idea of an independent Muslim state. The Ahrar, whose leadership was drawn from Punjabi activists, often from 'humble economic backgrounds' who are inspired by socialist ideals and had been involved in movements such as the Khilafat Movement,[21] sought complete independence from the British but were, nevertheless opposed to the idea of an independent Pakistan. The membership of the Ahrar consisted of the 'educated lower and middle classes' including shopkeepers and artisans as well as Muslim youth inspired by the Khilafat Movement. Other significant sources of membership for the Ahrar included religious scholars, 'ulama, and workers belonging to the Deobandi school of thought' (Awan 2009:242; Awan 2010:14–18; Kamran 2013:471).[22]

Political and faith differences rooted in class distinctions combined to pit Ahrar against Ahmadi and the distrust between the two came into the open over the Kashmir issue in the early 1930s. The Muslims in Kashmir were ruled by a Hindu prince, and although a significant numerical majority in the state, they were subjected to discrimination, deprivation and human rights abuses (Copland 1981:233–235; Kamran 2013:472; Chawla 2011; Shahid 2018a). Many had migrated to the Punjab and the North-West Frontier Province seeking a better life for themselves and their families. In response to the plight of the Muslims in Kashmir, some Muslims in India came together in 1931 to form the All-India Kashmir Committee (AIKC) to try to seek redress for Kashmiri Muslims. The second Ahmadi Khalifa, Bashir-ud Din Muhammad Ahmad, was the AIKC's president and another Ahmadi, Abdul Rahim Dard, its secretary. The central office of the AIKC was in Qadian and the Ahmadis also funded the AIKC campaign (Copland 1981:237; Kamran 2013:473).

The Ahrar, for their part, were suspicious of the Ahmadi interest in Kashmir, arguing that the Ahmadis were collaborators with the British and that they could not trust the Ahmadi president of the AIKC on these grounds (Chawla 2011:92). They also considered that the Ahmadis were interested in Kashmir because they believed that Jesus had lived and died there and that they had located his final resting place in Srinagar (Copland 1981:236).[23] The Ahrar agitated against the Ahmadis in the Punjab to have the Ahmadi Khalifa removed from his position as President of the AIKC and argued that they should also be expelled from the 'fold of Islam as was demanded by the *ulama* of Ludhiana in 1925, whose *fatwa* had declared Ghulam Ahmad to be a *kafir* (infidel)' (Awan 2010:39). In 1931, at the Round Table Conferences, another Ahmadi, Sir Zafrulla Khan, was one of the delegates who discussed the Kashmir issue with the secretary of state for India. Following the Round Table Conference, the secretary of state for India wrote to the president of the AIKC to inform him of his correspondence with the ruling Prince of Kashmir and of the reforms that were to be introduced. The Ahrar were resentful of the Ahmadi control of the AIKC as the Kashmir issue was viewed as one that could be used to promote their own party (Copland 1981:238). They were also aggrieved by the failure of an Ahrar delegation which had gone to Kashmir but had not received the cooperation of the Kashmiri leaders. Part of the failure of the Ahrar delegation was down to the Ahmadi secretary of the AIKC who, while publicly appealing to Muslims to help the Ahrar, privately encouraged Ahmadi leaders in Kashmir not to cooperate with them (Chawla 2011:95; Awan 2010:47).

Accordingly, the Ahrar began to hold parallel public meetings to those of the AIKC and agitated for Iqbal, who was on the AIKC committee, to resign. He did so in mid-1933. By May 1933 the Ahrar agitation had become so divisive that Bashir-ud Din Muhammad Ahmad was left with little option but to resign as president of the AIKC. The post of president of the AIKC was, following an election, taken by Iqbal and the Ahrar, busied by other matters, ceased to be as interested in the AIKC. Neither the Ahrar nor the Ahmadis succeeded in their political or religious goals in Kashmir, and both retreated from the fray with little to show for their efforts. The Ahrar's political ambitions had been thwarted (Copland 1981:253). The Ahmadis for their part ended by promising that they would not 'do any propaganda for Ahmadiyyat among the Muslims [of Kashmir] for two years, nor . . . hold any religious discussions with other Muslims' (Copland 1981:249).

The Ahrar had been so concerned that the Ahmadis would use their position in the AIKC to reach the Muslim masses and to encourage the latter to adopt a pro-British position that they used their meetings in the Punjab on behalf of the Muslims of Kashmir to launch anti-Ahmadi attacks (Kamran 2013:468; Awan 2010:43).[24] They also organized a *Tabligh* conference at Qadian, which attracted some 12,000 people and so set the precedent for the Majlis Tahaffuz Khatm-e-Nabuwat (organization for the finality of prophethood, henceforth Khatm-e-Nabuwat) conferences that continue to this day at Rabwah (Awan 2010:83; Copland 1981:254; Sayeed 2017). Already in 1933 the Ahrar were calling for the expulsion of Ahmadis from schools, colleges and Muslim institutions as well as for a boycott to prevent Ahmadis getting seats in 'central and provincial assemblies, municipal committees and other local boards'. A few years later, in 1936, they were demanding that Ahmadis be expelled from the All India Muslim League (Awan 2010:81, 110). They also, provocatively, sought to raise funds to pay for land in Qadian on which to build a mosque (Awan 2010:84). These are tactics that were later taken up in Pakistan with respect to land in and around Rabwah and have also been used by Khatm-e-Nabuwat during election campaigns in England to prevent the election of Ahmadi candidates (Sayeed 2017; Dawn 9 March 2018; Balzani 2015).[25]

Over time the Ahrar became increasingly sectarian and communalist but remained opposed to the idea of Pakistan, even going so far as to pass an anti-Pakistan resolution at a Youth Conference in 1940. It softened its position in the following years but still insisted that if there were to be a Pakistan it would have to be one that enforced Qur'anic laws, unified Muslims and excluded Ahmadis (Kamran 2013:477–478; Awan 2010:127–130). As late as 1946 the Ahrar stood in the elections on a platform which remained anti-Pakistan and as expected, anti-Ahmadi. On this occasion the Ahrar were routed and failed to gain any seats in either Punjab or Bengal (Awan 2010:132–133). By 1947, then, the Ahrar had lost political support in elections and were marginalized and rendered irrelevant when partition became inevitable.[26]

In other respects, however, the Ahmadis and the Ahrar were both of their time and had similar modernizing outlooks and approaches to some social matters. They both, for example, permitted and encouraged the involvement of women in their organizations. Both set up women's sections and encouraged women to be active members while continuing to require women to remain segregated, observe *parda* (veiling, seclusion) and to work within the limits of what was considered to be respectable. Women raised funds for the Ahrar and were even occasionally nominated for elections. Both organizations also encouraged girls and women to receive formal education in schools and colleges as long as this did not conflict with Islamic tradition (Awan 2010:60, 74–75, 153). In relation to the wider population, both Ahmadis and Ahrar also engaged in emergency relief charity work which helped people in times of need. The Ahrar, for example, provided much needed assistance following the Quetta earthquake in 1935, and at partition in 1947, irrespective of faith (Awan 2010:75, 135–136). Such charity work continues to be a core aspect of Ahmadiyya Islam today and is often directed through their charity Humanity First.[27] And both Ahmadi and Ahrar appealed to followers who were seeking guidance in complex times to their questions about faith, the social order and politics. Both the Ahrar and Ahmadis provided answers, rooted in traditional forms of oratory and based on Islam, to the vexing issues of the times in organizations that could offer order, support and a space in which their members could feel they were working towards and contributing to shaping their own futures. Both Ahmadi and Ahrar drew on traditional forms of knowledge and organization while also developing and championing new technologies such as print media, and encouraging the uptake of new opportunities such as Western formal education. Ultimately, the decision about whether to support the Ahrar or join the Ahmadis may have come down, for many, to a combination of class position, a preference for a Sufi-oriented or Deobandi Islam, political stance on the British in India, and a host of connections with individuals and groups that mattered locally in the Punjab. In short, while very different in some key respects, it may be precisely because they were, in effect, competing for support from overlapping constituencies and grappling with the same concerns, as Muslims dealing with marginalization and disempowerment, that the hostilities between the Ahmadi and Ahrar were so pronounced. And these hostilities, played out in colonial India as they competed against each other for victory over the Kashmir issue, continued and were modified to meet changing political contexts resulting in the difficulties faced by the Ahmadis in post-partition Pakistan.

Until partition then the Ahmadis remained just one, albeit rather active, minority within a minority in British India, as a Muslim sect at odds with other Muslims in a majority Hindu nation. It is fair to say that when Ghulam Ahmad died in 1908 he left a numerically small, deeply committed and socially heterogeneous sect of followers who found in him a divinely inspired charismatic leader, while his Muslim detractors considered him divisive, misguided and an apologist for colonial rule.[28] But it is also the case that Ahmad's religious claims, formulated in reaction to the issues of his day and derived from Islamic texts and locally accepted religious practices, became Ahmadiyya Islam. Individually most of his claims can be shown to have a history shared with other South Asian Muslims and so in that sense to be 'the same', even when those who shared some of the same ideas as Ahmad's may have reached them by very different means or used them to different ends. When each of these claims is combined into Ahmadiyya Islam, the result is a new perspective on Islam suited to the needs of the age in which it was developed. Had this been where Ahmadiyya Islam ended, as is so often the case with charismatic movements that cease soon after the death of their founder, then Ahmadiyya Islam would be no more than an interesting historical case study of one among many religious reform movements which emerged in reaction to colonialism. The reason why the Ahmadis have continued into the present as a Muslim sect, playing a not always willing part in the way the nation state of Pakistan has developed, and have become a focus for much study and interest in the years since the death of their founder, has much to do with how Ahmadiyya Islam has been constructed and viewed by those who reject it as much as by those who support it, and what it has come to stand for in Pakistan. It also has to do with the active proselyting missions of the Ahmadis which centred on the West, initially primarily in the UK and the US, and with the routinization of charisma that transformed Ahmadiyya Islam into a global hierarchical religious institution of a type unknown in Sunni Islam,[29] established by their second khalifa and eldest son of Ghulam Ahmad, Mahmud Ahmad.

It is as well to remember that despite the current dogma that Ahmadis are heretics and outside the fold of Islam and have always been considered so, this position was not so self-evidently true to all Muslims during Ghulam Ahmad's lifetime, nor for some years following. To give just one example, Prince Faisal of Saudi Arabia accepted an invitation from the Ahmadis in the 1920s to be their guest of honour and to open their new purpose-built mosque in London. On this occasion he travelled to England but withdrew from the opening of the mosque, sending his apologies via telegram, at the very last minute (Basit 2012; Noakes 2018:34). By the 1970s the situation had so changed that the Saudis were calling 'for the excommunication of the Ahmadis and began denying them Haj visas' (Jalal 2014:203). The change in how Ahmadis were perceived and treated, though some had always considered them unorthodox, has much to do with how the world changed around them from the end of colonialism in South Asia in the 1940s to the rise of global Islam several decades later.[30]

National self-fashioning and the religious minority

After his death in 1908, Ghulam Ahmad was succeeded by his companion, Noor-ud-Din, and thereafter in 1914 by his son, the second Ahmadi Khalifa, Bashir al-Din Mahmud Ahmad, who led the Ahmadis until his own death in 1965. Where Ghulam Ahmad had been a charismatic leader able to inspire his followers, his son served the cause of Ahmadiyyat with his organizational skills and thus ensured the continuation of Ahmadi Islam by setting it on a secure bureaucratic and financial foundation. From his base in the town of Qadian in the Punjab, he also engaged in Indian politics, actively involving himself, as noted earlier, in the Kashmir issue in the 1930s (Copland 1981; Awan 2010:38ff; Lavan 1974:145–160; Khan 2012), and again in discussions over partition in the 1940s along with other members of the Indian Muslim elite, some of whom were also Ahmadi and included politicians of international stature such as Sir Zafrulla Khan.[31] When it became clear that Qadian was to remain in India and not become part of the new nation of Pakistan, Mahmud Ahmad left 313 men, given the title of Dervishes,[32] to protect the birthplace of Ahmadi Islam, and oversaw the migration of the majority of Ahmadis to Pakistan (Spate 1947; Tinker 1977; *Qadian: a test case* in 1947 DO:142–323; Ahmad, I. 1999:148).[33] Pakistan at this time was a secular Muslim state and the Ahmadis were able to purchase land from the government on which to build their new hometown, Rabwah, meaning 'higher ground' or place of refuge, near the city of Lahore.[34]

Despite the explicit declaration made by Jinnah, founder of Pakistan, first governor-general and first president of the Constituent Assembly, that all would be equally free to practice their faith as full citizens in the new Pakistan, the political and religious developments in Pakistan since 1947 have made this an unrealizable goal.[35] Religio-political groups hostile to the Ahmadis from pre-partition India as well as those who simply saw in the Ahmadi issue a strategic opportunity, produced and used available opportunities to advance their own political and religious ends at the expense of the Ahmadis. In 1953 this led to riots in the Punjab, sparking fears of an imminent civil war, which compelled the government of the day to impose martial law for the first time in the new nation state (Minattur 1962; *Report of the Court of Inquiry into the Punjab Disturbances of 1953*, 1954, henceforth *Report of the Court of Inquiry*). In 1974, during Bhutto's premiership and following violence which began at the train station in Rabwah between Ahmadi men and the student wing of the Jama'at-i-Islami[36] and then spread across the Punjab, the Ahmadis were declared a non-Muslim minority (Malik 2002:14ff; Khan 2003; Rahman 2015, 2016).[37] Then in 1984, during the reign of the military dictator Zia ul Haq, Martial Law Ordinance XX, popularly known as the anti-Ahmadi laws, was passed amending Pakistan's Penal Code Sections 298-B and 298-C, with the latter often referred to as the 'blasphemy law' (Khan 2003). This ordinance has been used to target and persecute Ahmadis and, increasingly over time, also members of other minority faiths in Pakistan. As a consequence of this legislation, the fourth khalifa left Pakistan in April 1984 and relocated to London.

His successor, the current khalifa, was also based in London which effectively became the global centre of Ahmadiyya Islam from 1984 until 15 April 2019 when the khalifa relocated to Islamabad in Tilford, Surrey.[38]

To summarize, then, at partition in 1947 the Ahmadis went from being a minority within a minority in India to becoming a minority sect in a Muslim majority state. Despite their relocation to a new home, however, the political hostilities that had embroiled the Ahmadis in disputes in colonial India, the opposition to them led by the Ahrar and the increasingly virulent publications against Ahmadi doctrines continued to cause difficulties for Ahmadis in Pakistan, and in 1953 these culminated in riots that left many dead and led to the first imposition of martial law within just a few months of the drafting of the first constitution of the nascent state (*Report of the Court of Inquiry* 1954). The Ahmadis may have established their home in Pakistan, but they were viewed by many as an internal enemy whose loyalty to the nation could not be relied upon. They became, in other words, the source for many of what Appadurai would, some decades later with reference to globalization, theorize as the fear of small numbers (Appadurai 2006).

In this newly established country, and following the violence of partition[39] (1947 DO 142–323, *Qadian: a test case*), the refugees from India had to begin to construct a new identity as citizens of a new state. For some of those who had opposed partition, such as Jama'at-i-Islami's[40] founder, Maududi, himself born into a family with close links to the Chisti Sufi order, and the Ahrar, the new identity as loyal Pakistanis was in part created by demarcating themselves as Pakistani Muslims against both the Hindus in neighbouring India and, within Pakistan itself, in contrast to groups such as the Ahmadis whose designation as Muslims could be challenged and who, therefore, were not to be trusted as loyal to the state. For the former members of the Ahrar, a minor political party founded in Lahore in December 1929 with its base in the Punjab in colonial India, taking on the Ahmadis was a means to regain some of their former political significance by organizing crowds and orchestrating the protests against them that not infrequently turned violent. It was from the Ahrar that the organization Khatm-e-Nabuwat was to develop as a group whose sole rationale for existence was and continues to be the elimination of Ahmadi Islam (Kamran 2015).

One of the ways in which the founders of Pakistan sought to establish the new state was through its constitution. This proved to be a matter that divided those who considered Pakistan should be a Muslim majority secular state from those who considered it should be an Islamic state. As Kennedy (1992:769) notes:

> It took Pakistan nine years to adopt its first constitution. One major reason for the delay was contention over prospective Islamic provisions in the document. The first task of the Constituent Assembly was to define the basic directive principles of the new State, and in March 1949 the fruit of this exercise, the Objectives Resolution, was passed. It contained the following provisions dealing with Islam: 'The Government of Pakistan will be a state . . . Wherein the principles of democracy, freedom, equality, tolerance and social justice

as enunciated by Islam shall be fully observed; Wherein the Muslims of Pakistan shall be enabled individually and collectively to order their lives in accordance with the teachings and requirements of Islam as set out in the Holy Quran and Sunnah'.

However, the Objectives Resolution and other Islamic provisions in the 1956 constitution were ones whose manner of implementation was left ill-defined, and thus they were for all practical purposes unenforceable (Kennedy 1992:770). The same continued to be the case through the subsequent constitutions of 1962 and 1973, and this did not change until Zia ul Haq took power in a coup in July 1977. Zia set about creating a Federal Shariat Court (FSC) to examine, among other things, 'any law or provision of law' to ensure that it was not repugnant to the Qur'an and Sunnah (Kennedy 1992:772).[41] Zia also set about a process of Islamization for Pakistan, and in 1984 Article 260(3) was added to the 1973 constitution, defining for the first time what it means to be a Muslim. Such a move, the categorical definition of what a Muslim is, was one that the 1954 *Report of the Court of Inquiry* had ruled to be, on the basis of the understandings of the *'ulama* of Pakistan themselves, an impossible task. In this report, the judges Munir and Kayani, respectively president and member of the Court of Inquiry, wrote:

> The question . . . whether a person is or is not a Muslim will be of fundamental importance, and it was for this reason that we asked most of the leading *ulama*, to give their definition of a Muslim, the point being that if the *ulama* of the various sects believed the Ahmadis to be *kafirs*, they must have been quite clear in their minds not only about the grounds of such belief but also about the definition of a Muslim because the claim that a certain person or community is not within the pale of Islam implies on the part of the claimant an exact conception of what a Muslim is. The result of this part of the inquiry, however, has been anything but satisfactory, and if considerable confusion exists in the minds of our *ulema* (*sic*) on such a simple matter, one can easily imagine what the differences on more complicated matters will be.
>
> (1954:215)

There followed a list of definitions from some ten *ulama*, after which Munir and Kayani concluded:

> Keeping in view the several definitions given by the *ulama*, need we make any comment except that no two learned divines are agreed on this fundamental. If we attempt our own definition as each learned divine has done and that definition differs from that given by all others, we unanimously go out of the fold of Islam. And if we adopt the definition given by any one of the *ulama*, we remain Muslims according to the view of that *alim* but *kafirs* according to the definition of every one else.
>
> (Ibid.:218)

By 1985 the mood of the country had shifted; the more secular and liberal reasoning found in the 1954 *Report of the Court of Inquiry* was no longer in vogue, and the constitution had been further amended explicitly to classify the Ahmadis as non-Muslim (Redding 2004:769, fn. 29). The 1985 constitution also, again for the first time, incorporated the Objectives Resolution into the text of the constitution, with far-reaching implications (Kennedy 1992:774).[42]

Such constitutional reforms, however, were not unique to Pakistan. In some other nation states that became independent in the mid-twentieth century, such reforms are ones that have in recent decades been associated with an increase in violence targeted at internal minorities, some of whom may even come into existence as a consequence of constitutional reform. Geschiere, for example, notes how the 1972 Cameroon Constitution incorporated language that was inclusive and clearly intended as a nation-building exercise. By contrast the revisions in the language used in the 1996 Cameroon Constitution makes it the prerogative of the government to recognize specific groups as indigenous or as a minority, depending on the political situation. This constitutional change has had significant impact on the rights of some Cameroonians to take part in the political process and for their access to land, jobs and even protection from violence (Geschiere 2009:51). Such constitutional changes have gone hand in hand with ethnic discrimination and a rise in violence against those who now no longer belong in the nation state as they once used to. For Geschiere, the distinction that is crucial to understanding belonging and how this has changed from the 1970s to the 1990s in parts of Africa is one between autochthons and others. Autochthons are those who can claim to be the first inhabitants of the land and as such are the ones who 'really' belong in the state and should be entitled to the protections and rights of full citizens, while all others are later arrivals with lesser claims to the resources of the state. Yet, as definitions of belonging are always political, it is possible 'to go to bed as an autochthon and wake up to find that you have become an *allogène*' (Geschiere 2009:96). Geschiere further links the rise in autochthony thinking with the decentralization that has followed the era of post-colonial state-building and is associated with greater mobility and globalization. For Geschiere, the uncertainties generated by a world on the move has, rather than allowing for a positive embracing of cosmopolitan possibilities, encouraged a greater scrutiny of notions of belonging and locality-based identity formation. It has resulted in uncertainty and produced fears about who really belongs and who does not. The resulting quest for a purified and exclusive group of those who truly belong is a modern phenomenon leading to the 'constant redefinitions and shifts that inspire . . . violence in efforts to achieve an impossible purification' (Geschiere 2009:114). Where, in the Cameroons and in the parts of Europe considered by Geschiere, belonging is based on claims of autochthony, in Pakistan, a state that came into being by virtue of a refugee movement, autochthony is replaced by religion as the key to defining who really belongs (Geschiere 2009:1). In this vision of a purified Pakistan (a country whose name literally means a 'the place of the pure'), only Muslims are real Pakistanis, and even then only Muslims from particular Islamic traditions can be unquestionably loyal Pakistanis.[43] The move towards this position, one that Mohsin Hamid (2018) fears has resulted in a situation where 'in the land of the pure, no one is pure enough', and away from Jinnah's secular vision of Pakistan as outlined in his 1947 speech before the First Constituent Assembly on August 11, is one that has been facilitated by revisions of the state constitution.

In Pakistan, therefore, one consequence of the constitutional reforms has been to further legitimize the exclusion of minorities, including the Ahmadis, from public life, and to deny them access to land, education and employment. Pakistan is now a nation for Muslims, and among Muslims for those who are Sunni before all others.[44] This marks a significant change to the situation soon after partition, in 1953, when anti-Ahmadi violence broke out in the Punjab. In the year following, it was made explicit, in the *Report of the Court of Inquiry*, that the Objectives Resolution played a significant part in the demands of the *'ulama* that the Ahmadis be declared non-Muslim and that Ahmadis in high level government, military and administrative posts be dismissed. As noted above the demands of the *'ulama* were carefully scrutinized and, in the more liberal secular spirit of the times, the report concludes that they were not ones that merited assent by the government. It was this position, so resolutely taken in the 1950s, that was reversed in the mid-1980s, and while there was violence directed against the Ahmadis both in the 1950s and in the 1980s, the difference is in the extent to which the state, through institutions such as the judiciary, was prepared in the 1950s, to support the rights of minorities in the name of democracy and the international standing of the country, and in the 1980s, to facilitate and acquiesce in the discrimination against the Ahmadis in the name of Islam.

In other, more directly political, ways the Ahmadis were also politically disenfranchised when Zia, through Presidential Order No. 8 of 1984 (Clause 4A), added to Article 51 of the Constitution, gave non-Muslims their own electoral constituencies and separate representation (Malik 2002:19). As the Ahmadis did not accept that they were not Muslim, they were not prepared to stand or vote in elections as a non-Muslim minority. This constitutional amendment was not repealed until 2002, and while it meant that the Ahmadis had no electoral representation during this time, they were not the only religious minority group to be discriminated against by this constitutional amendment: Pakistan's Hindus, Christians, Parsis and Sikhs were also affected. However, while the Electoral Commission of Pakistan has allowed for Ahmadis to vote since 2002 without having to register as non-Muslim, this has not changed anything in practice. Despite the abolition of 'this discriminatory requirement and segregation between Muslims and non-Muslims. . . . Ahmadis are reportedly still forbidden to register on the general voters' list, and must still register on a separate list maintained solely for Ahmadis' (UNHCR 2017:32). Ahmadis have in recent years described being physically intimidated to prevent them from voting (USSD 2018:21), and separate lists have been maintained for those wishing to vote, as a letter from the Election Commission of Pakistan dated 17 January 2007 (with the heading 'Preparation of Separate List of Draft Electoral Rolls for Ahmadis/Qadianis') makes clear (HRC and IHRC 2015:106–107).

Rabwah: home and ghetto

The lack of political say in local matters has also impacted on the territorial rights of Ahmadis. Rabwah is home to some 70,000 Ahmadis who constitute about 95% of the population living there, but the Ahmadis have virtually no administrative control over the town. Ahmadis are not permitted to buy land to extend the territory covered by Rabwah (Tanveer 2016), and even the name of the town was changed in 1999 when, without the consent of the Ahmadis:

> the Punjab Provincial Assembly, with the backing of the Federal Shariat Court, unilaterally decided to change the name of the Ahmadi-founded and ninety-eight percent Ahmadi-populated village of Rabwah (an Arabic word meaning 'higher ground' used reverentially in the Qur'an) to Chenab Nagar (an Urdu phrase used pejoratively in Pakistan meaning 'Chenab river village') and infiltrated its housing projects with non-Ahmadi settlements in an effort to transform permanently the composition of the village itself.
>
> (Khan 2003:229)[45]

This enforced name change was, in effect, a symbolic erasure of the Ahmadi community, which was denied the right to name its town as it would choose to.

Delimiting the relation of the Ahmadis to the land, to the earth of the nation, as a way of, in effect, erasing them has also manifested itself in a different but no less profound way through the curtailment of Ahmadi burial practices. In Pakistan, prior to the declaration of Ahmadis as non-Muslims in 1974, there were cemeteries where both Ahmadis and other Muslims were buried together. Such shared graveyards are no longer possible in Pakistan. Yet even in colonial India, the Ahmadis sometimes had conflicts with the Ahrar centred on burials of the dead, as when attempts were made by Ahrar workers, in 1934 at Amritsar, to prevent the burial of Ahmadis in Muslim cemeteries. A month earlier, Ahmadis had beaten a person over a dispute in the Muslim graveyard at Qadian itself during the burial of Ahmadi children. As a consequence of this and following police intervention to end the violence, some 11 Ahmadis were later prosecuted and fined. And in 1937 in Gurdaspur district, the police had to intervene to maintain peace when an Ahmadi was buried in a Muslim cemetery. In this case the local Ahrar leader instructed workers to put up signs at the graveyards forbidding the burial of Ahmadis (Awan 2010:fn 94). These acts by the Ahrar followed resolutions in their meetings at which it was decided to forbid the burial of Ahmadis in Muslim cemeteries (Awan 2010:85). In colonial India, therefore, the Ahrar had already targeted Ahmadi burials and made this one focus for their anti-Ahmadi campaigns. The authorities at this time, however, appear to have sought primarily to maintain the peace rather than adjudicate on the rights of individuals to be buried where they and their families chose.

Post 1974 in Pakistan, the situation changed and cemeteries were divided with sections for Muslims and sections for Ahmadis. In addition, in Pakistan headstones commemorating the Ahmadi dead are now at risk of vandalism, in some cases by the police themselves who erase the *kalima* (declaration of faith) from the graves, claiming that they are doing this in the interests of preserving the peace (Hamdani 2012; Islam 2012; *Dawn* 2014). The reason given to justify such acts is that the Ahmadis, by 'posing' as Muslims, offend and insult real Muslims. In one case in 2012:

> An application was moved to the area police of Uncha Mangat claiming Kassoki villagers' demands of the removal of Quranic verses and religious text from Ahmadi graves in the graveyard on Hafizabad-Sheikhupura Road.
>
> The applicants threatened of (*sic*) religious clashes and bloodshed if this was not done.
>
> The DPO [District Police Officer] Hafizabad asked the police station in charge to take appropriate steps for averting any untoward incident or clash on religious basis.
>
> The local SHO [Station House Officer] summoned elders and notables of the Ahmadi community of the village who met him under the supervision of Nasir Javaid, acting Ameer Jamaat Ahmadiyya, Hafizabad.
>
> The SHO, according to Nasir Javaid, asked them to remove religious inscriptions, adding that if they did not do so themselves, the police would take measures for removing them in order to maintain peace and tranquillity in the area.
>
> When they disagreed, says Nasir, the police went on with the operation anyway and forcefully entered the graveyard and whitewashed all religious text from the graves late Friday.
>
> (Islam 2012)

Other reported incidents of the desecration of graveyards include that of an organized team of 12 to 15 men who in 2012 tied up a graveyard caretaker and in just 30 minutes dug up and smashed more than a 100 tombstones because they objected to the Islamic inscriptions on them (AHRC and IHRC 2015:76). And more recently in 2014, as reported in the *Dawn* newspaper, not only were the inscriptions on headstones erased but the gravestones themselves were also removed. The *Dawn* report states that this happened because 'a man submitted an application to the police for removal of the gravestones, claiming that the words written on these were hurting his religious feelings'. When the Ahmadis refused to remove the gravestones, 'the policemen themselves removed the gravestones of seven graves on March 9' (*Dawn* 2014). Perhaps even more distressing in some respects is the current practice of the Ahmadis themselves, who paint over the words Sunni Muslims consider offensive on Ahmadi tombstones in order to prevent their desecration by non-Ahmadis. This, I was told, happens in the main Rabwah cemetery where, for example, the word 'Muslim' has been painted over on the grave of Abdus Salam.[46] This is done in order to keep the police and others out of the cemetery but results in a situation in which the Ahmadis themselves carry out the work of their oppressors, thus making them complicit in their own persecution.

By these means, the self-identification of Ahmadis as Muslim is challenged not only in life but also in death. And in the process, their right to be buried as they wish to be in the state where they are citizens is brought into question. The ways in which Ahmadis belong and their claims to belonging which are made in the burial of their dead are challenged by those who find the existence of Ahmadis unacceptable. This constitutes a form of erasure which is made in other forms too, as in the refusal to allow Ahmadis to call their places of worship mosques and the official removal of the name they chose for their town just post-partition. Yet once again, while such practices, facilitated and encouraged by the state, may have targeted the Ahmadis first, they have not been confined to them. Christian cemeteries have also been vandalized in Pakistan, and in these instances it cannot be because the use of the *kalima* by those deemed to be non-Muslim is considered offensive (Craig 2015). Rather, the attack on burial sites for Ahmadis and Christians may be viewed as an attack on the rights of members of these communities to belong and to make this manifestly the case by becoming, quite literally, part of the land of Pakistan.[47]

The association of both Ahmadis and Christians as the unwanted in Pakistan is one that is made explicit in a quote from a 'prominent activist of the Khatme-Nabuwwat Lawyers Forum' who stated: 'By the grace of God, Mirzais had been reduced to the level of *chooras* (Christian sweepers) and soon they will be cleaned up altogether' (Hamdani 2012). Ahmadis are thus targeted not simply because they are Ahmadis but because, like Christians, they are a non-Sunni Muslim minority. The connection made in the quote about sweepers, Christians, and Ahmadis in a South Asian context also recalls a history of untouchability in the subcontinent, a human form of what Douglas (1984) refers to as 'dirt' or 'matter out of place'. Many low-caste South Asian Hindus converted from Hinduism to Christianity in the hope of escaping the demeaning caste position they had as *achut*, literally meaning 'untouchable',[48] because of the work they did with polluted materials, including the refuse and remains of others, human and animal (Michael 2010). In India in the 1930s, the Ahrar had feared that the minority position of the Muslims would result in them living as a 'scheduled caste', and led to accusations that the Congress Hindus practiced *chootchaat* (untouchability) against Muslims (Kamran 2013:470). Such concerns, linked to notions of purity and pollution demarcated some groups as rightfully belonging as full members of the society while others are permanently excluded.

A 2007 UK report of the Parliamentary Human Rights Group (PHRG), which looked into the claim that Rabwah was a safe haven for Ahmadis in Pakistan, informs us that Rabwah itself, which covers some 1,043 acres:

> is not a commercial/industrial centre and has no manufacturing, distribution or service industries. . . . The only jobs are low skilled work such as farming and trades. However the number of jobs in these sectors are limited by the size of the town . . . there are no Ahmadis in public office in Rabwah. The post office, telephone office, railway station, police force and magistrates office have no Ahmadi employees.
>
> (PHRG 2007:24)

It is elsewhere reported that 'most of the town's infrastructure is maintained on contributions made by the community, including . . . a community organized garbage clean-up' (Sayeed 2017). The Human Rights Commission for Pakistan (HRCP) concluded that an Ahmadi fleeing to Rabwah would find it hard to secure any employment in the town itself and also outside the town, as a Rabwah address marks a person as Ahmadi and so employers would hesitate to employ such an individual.

> [T]he HRCP summarised the situation by describing Rabwah as a place for 'hardcore Ahmadis who want to be martyred': there is a mullah there who abuses Ahmadis 'all day long'. Those Ahmadis who live in Rabwah are 'very brave'. There are families where the men live in Rabwah and the women do not. Ultimately, it is a question of how much abuse – and occasional violence – an individual can stand. 'Rabwah is a place for martyrs, cut off from their roots', the mission was told.
>
> (PHRG 2007:25)

The situation had certainly not improved by the time of the 2010 PHRG report:

> It was clear that whilst in the very short term there may be some shelter in the safety of numbers the ever present threat for Ahmadis manifests itself with greater force in Rabwah. This is because opponents of the community are fully aware that there is a concentration of Ahmadis in Rabwah and seek to focus their attention upon this city.
>
> Thus, we were informed, every year thousands of Khatme Nabuwat supporters from across the country converge on this beleaguered city and boisterous demonstrations which intimidate the local population take place three or four times in the year. Each year at least three rambunctious anti Ahmadi conferences are held in Rabwah with 'opponents of the community' bussed in from elsewhere in Pakistan. The October conferences are attended by up to 9,000 to 10,000 vociferous individuals who shout anti Ahmadi slogans via loud speakers whilst the community barricades itself in. By contrast the Ahmadi community is forbidden from holding any gatherings whatsoever, including sport tournaments and are banned from using any public address systems whatsoever. Thus 'refugees' who seek sanctuary within Rabwah hoping for safety in numbers feel no safer there than elsewhere in Pakistan.
>
> (PHRG 2010:74)[49]

It will be clear from these quotations that, despite the aims of these reports to produce objective records of the situation for Ahmadis in Pakistan, and while some of the language of 'martyrs' and 'hard core' Ahmadis is directly quoted from interviews incorporated into the reports, the report writers perhaps inevitably find themselves drawn towards charged and dramatic descriptions: a 'beleaguered city', an 'intimidated' population and 'vociferous', 'rambunctious' and 'hate-filled' opponents. The reports also draw parallels with historical conditions that paved the way for acts of genocide in Europe during the twentieth century. The visual images in the reports include barbed wire, men restrained by manacles, and photographs of desecrated cemeteries and heavily guarded or alternatively vandalized mosques and burnt out homes and businesses. Such language and visual images provide a counter point to the series of factually recounted legal provisions discriminating against the Ahmadis and of the bald enumeration of acts, including murders, committed against individuals reproduced in tables and charts in the reports.

Here it is not the content of the reports, which make for relentlessly grim reading, so much as some of the terms which seem to be increasingly used to describe the plight of Ahmadis in Pakistan which I focus on. Lord Avebury, in his preface to the 2007 PHRG report *Rabwah: A Place for Martyrs?* described Rabwah as follows:

> This place is not a safe haven for Ahmadis fleeing persecution elsewhere in Pakistan; it is a ghetto, at the mercy of hostile sectarian forces whipped up by hate-filled mullahs and most of the Urdu media. The authors of this report expose the reality of a dead-end, to which even more victims should not be exiled.
>
> (PHRG 2007:iv)

And 'ghetto' is a term which, to a man of Lord Avebury's generation, would inevitably recall the historical segregation of Jewish communities in European cities, and above all the plight of Jews during the Second World War. The term in this context cannot but lead to a consideration of what happened to many of the European Jews, who were made to live in ghettos and forcibly removed from them as the genocide proceeded during the course of the war.[50] And indeed, as recently as 24 May 2018, in a debate on the Ahmadiyya Muslim Community in the House of Commons, the Liberal Democrat MP Edward Davey, talking the day after an attack on an Ahmadi mosque in Sialkot,[51] stated:

> Given the murders, the assaults and, as we saw last night, the attacks on mosques, there is a concern that this is becoming endemic and deep-rooted, particularly due to the textbooks that children are reading. I do not want to go too far along this road, but what is happening to the Ahmadi Muslims will ring awful bells for those of us who have had the privilege to visit Auschwitz with the Holocaust Educational Trust to learn about the eight steps to genocide. Although we should not throw the word 'genocide' around too freely, the UN Office on Genocide Prevention and the Responsibility to Protect needs to do a study. This may not be something that comes and goes; it might be something that has potentially disastrous outcomes.[52]

The analogy with a ghetto is not entirely unreasonable. The 2015 AHRC and IHRC report notes that Rabwah itself is surrounded on all sides, and that the Ahmadi population of the town live in:

> an enclave where each entrance to the town is controlled by guards who vigilantly enquire into the business of all entrants to the town. Notably we learned

that 100% of the local police force and local councillors are non Ahmadi and that the city is hemmed in by the Muslim Colony where madrassas have sprouted and that neighbouring Chiniot is reportedly a hotbed of anti Ahmadi activity. The mission was informed that Mullah Ilyas Chinioti who is a known anti Ahmadi activist is based here and is thus only 8 km away from Rabwah.

(AHRC and IHRC 2015:74)

Unlike the ghettos of European cities, however, which were created by the authorities specifically to confine, dispossess and degrade their minority inhabitants through overpopulation and lack of amenities, Rabwah was chosen, bought and developed by the Ahmadis themselves as a place of refuge and hope for their community. This place of refuge has not been realized, and after reading a draft of this section of the chapter, an Ahmadi interlocutor who lives in Rabwah simply commented, 'perhaps Rabwah could be described as a self-created or self-realised ghetto'.

If Rabwah is now besieged and a place to which Ahmadis are confined, territorially segregated within an 'architecture of surveillance' (Cole 2003:7), this is a consequence of a spatial politics resulting from the acts of hostile groups and laws which have sought to make the home town of the Ahmadis what geographer W.A. Jackson calls a 'pariah landscape', a place where the 'unacceptable, the rejected, are society's pariahs, and their spatial separation from society may take the form of banishment to a colony, a camp, an institution, a ghetto or a reservation. These latter entities may be designated pariah landscapes' (Cole 2003:21). Drawing on Doreen Massey's insights on relational space, power, and inequality, space here becomes an active element in the segregation and exclusion of the Ahmadis from the wider social order (Massey 2005). In this respect, the containment of the Ahmadis in Rabwah, surveilled at every entrance and exit from the town, is the spatial equivalent of the constitutional and legislative changes enacted in the 1970s and 1980s in Pakistan to curtail the expression of Ahmadi faith, and to restrict the professional ambitions of Ahmadis considered by their detractors to be, as indeed were the Jews in mid-twentieth-century Europe, over-represented in positions of power (Cole 2003:79).[53] And as now happens every year at the annual anti-Ahmadi conference held at Rabwah, somewhat bizarrely, those organizing the conference appear to be so concerned with the possibility that Ahmadis might be in positions of power that they adopt a resolution stating that 'Qadianis should be removed from all key positions in the government departments across Pakistan', thus repeating demands that have been made since the 1950s (Ahmad, T. 2017). As with the legislation excluding the Ahmadis from the fold of Islam, an act of religious 'purification' for those who pursued this end, the confining of Ahmadis to Rabwah is, from the perspective of those who wish to rid the country of Ahmadis, a purificatory act, an act of spatial exclusion through the exercise of domination and control made possible by creating and policing a boundary around the town (Cole 2003:21–22).

In a perverse respect, the demands in the early 1950s to take Rabwah away from the Ahmadis and to redistribute the land and homes to the refugees from India[54] in order to eliminate the Ahmadi connection to the land of Pakistan has been achieved by other means. It did not happen by taking the land from the Ahmadis to give to non Ahmadis but rather by isolating the Ahmadis on land which is thus rendered distinct and separate, symbolically cut off from the rest of Pakistan. Rabwah is a space which is guarded and under constant observation, marched through by Khatm-e-Nabuwat cadres on a regular basis to demonstrate their control over the space and their ability to enter and terrorize at will (*Report of the Court of Inquiry* 1954:110, 114, 137; Ahmad 2017). The goal for those who wish to eliminate the Ahmadis is, by creating a landscape of exclusion which is also a space of domination, to terrorize Ahmadis in a manner that becomes routinized so as to force 'people to live in a chronic state of fear with a façade of normalcy, while that terror, at the same time, permeates and shreds the social fabric' (Green in Lewin 2002:17).

Nor can the Ahmadis extend their town by buying new land to accommodate increasing numbers and so lessen overcrowding, or to provide a buffer zone between themselves and others. This is because another now routinized form of violence against the inhabitants of Rabwah is enacted through a raft of bureaucratic and legal measures which makes it impossible for Ahmadis to buy properties in the vicinity of Rabwah. In 2016, the Punjab Housing and Town Planning Agency (PHTPA) auctioned lots in Chiniot, the district in which Rabwah is located. The auction was advertised in a local Urdu language newspaper and explicitly excluded Ahmadis from the proceedings. As reported in the *Express Tribune* in March of 2016, the advertisement announcing the auction read:

> "anyone related to the Qadiani/Ahmadi/Lahori/Mirzai sects cannot participate in the Area Development Scheme Muslim Colony, Chenab Nagar. Every aspirant has to file a duly certified affidavit stating that he/she has no relation to Qadianis/Ahmadis/Lahoris." It requires the participants to submit an undertaking that they will not sell the property or transfer its ownership to anyone belonging to the JA [*jama'at* Ahmadiyya]. . . . The advertisement also stipulated that anyone interested in participating in the auction had to file another affidavit certifying their unqualified belief in the finality of prophethood. It referred to a directive issued by the Department of Housing, Urban Development and Public Health Engineering Department (dated July 7, 1976) to justify the prohibition on members of the Ahmadiyya community.[55]

In this instance, an urban development office, drawing on a directive relating to a plot of land taken by the government from the Ahmadis in the 1970s, an action which the Ahmadis have been contesting through the courts, denied Ahmadis the right to participate in the auction of land which the Ahmadis claim is theirs to begin with.[56] The deputy director of the Punjab Housing and Town Planning Agency was able to distance himself for responsibility for this decision by stating that 'he was bound to prohibit the community from the auction under the 1976 directive. . . . [as] the government's policy was to not let Ahmadis participate in auction of plots in localities where land was owned by non-Ahmadis'.[57] The bureaucratic manoeuvre of a claim to be just following the rules, or what Hannah

Arendt (1967) described as the 'rule by nobody' is, just as much as the rowdy marches through Rabwah or the attacks on property and persons, an act of violence. It may not be 'the kind of occasional, spectacular acts of violence that we tend to think of first when the word is invoked, but . . ., the boring, humdrum, yet omnipresent forms of structural violence that define the very conditions of our existence' (Graeber 2012:105). Structural violence, a term Johann Galtung first used to argue that peace is more than simply the absence of physical violence, is any form of unevenly distributed resource, and perhaps more importantly unevenly distributed power to decide over the allocation of resources, that result in harm, physical or psychological, to sections of the population, or which limit their freedoms and thus also harm by this means (Galtung 1969; Graeber 2012:112).

This everyday, routine bureaucratic violence is a form of structural violence which, unlike overt physical acts of violence, seeps into the person, changes behaviours and becomes normalized without, for all that, ceasing to be violent. This was brought home to me when I heard a young Ahmadi man who now lives in Rabwah but who grew up in the UK speak about his life in Pakistan. At the All Party Parliamentary Group (APPG) inquiry into the denial of freedom of religion and human rights violations of Ahmadi Muslims and other religious communities in Pakistan, held at Portcullis House in London on 23 April 2018, he talked of the constraints placed on the lives of the Ahmadis in Rabwah, including the hostile activities of organizations such as Khatm-e-Nabuwat. He also described the enclosed and cautious life many of the young lead, most of whom socialize only with other Ahmadis to avoid harassment and discrimination. The effect, he made clear, was that the impact of segregating the Ahmadis and compelling them to remain in Rabwah had resulted in a generation whose 'ambitions have been hampered', whose lives are 'on hold' and who wish only to leave the country that affords them no future. But perhaps most notably, the young in Rabwah, because of their isolation, have become what he described as 'enablers of their own persecution'. This was, for me, a chilling statement and one that was reinforced when I met with this articulate Ahmadi representative a few days later to discuss the plight of Ahmadis in Rabwah.

During our meeting and in subsequent email exchanges, he gave examples of situations that reveal both how the wider Sunni Muslim population now views the Ahmadis, and also how Ahmadis have been made complicit in the discrimination against them through the mundane and unavoidable bureaucratic systems in place in the twenty-first century. One example of just how the anti-Ahmadi discrimination in Pakistan has resulted in self-censorship and the internalization of hostile anti-Ahmadi attitudes was recounted to me as follows:

> On my last visit to England I was speaking with a life devotee there who I knew in Rabwah. He was posted to England several years ago. He told me that he used to refer to the names of our mosques in the UK with the word '*bait*' instead of '*masjid*' (in Pakistan Ahmadis are forbidden from using the word *masjid*). So instead of saying 'Masjid Fazl' (the Fazl Mosque) he would say Baitul Fazl. Anyway he told me that he used the term Baitul Fazl in front

of our Khalifa and the Khalifa corrected him by saying 'you aren't in Pakistan anymore there is no reason why you shouldn't use the word *masjid* here'. I found the incident incredibly illustrative of how deeply oppressors are able to penetrate the minds of those they oppress and force them to see themselves through the tyrannical eyes of their master. The way I see it another overlooked aspect of Ahmadi persecution is how they have been prevented from establishing agency in the world around them.

A final example of the forms structural violence can take concerns everyday life and the administrative forms we are now all used to completing as a matter of routine in our increasingly bureaucratized lives. When Rabwah's name was changed to Chenab Nagar against the wishes of the majority inhabitants of the town, there was a determination by the population not to use the new name and in this way to resist the erasure of a name which held meaning and significance for the Ahmadis. Two decades after the name change, the reality is that using Chenab Nagar on official forms has become unavoidable. When an application for a driving licence has to be completed, Chenab Nagar is the only officially recognized place name for an inhabitant of Rabwah. When children are registered for school, Chenab Nagar is the only officially recognized address for a child living in Rabwah. And so on. By this apparently neutral and agentless means, the necessary routine of bureaucratic form-filling without which modern life becomes simply impossible, Ahmadis have been compelled to become complicit in the erasure of the name of their town and hence the erasure of an important aspect of their identity as Ahmadis.[58] Similarly, the online register for schools in Punjab makes it compulsory for the applicant to disclose her or his religion: Muslim or non-Muslim. The process directly targets Ahmadis because they consider themselves to be Muslim but risk penal sanction if they declare this to be so. In other words, Ahmadis must either deny their faith or to break the law but without a declaration a child cannot register for school (Islam 2011; HRC 2015:1).[59]

Ahmadis have, in a matter of decades, gone from being considered as a Muslim sect to a non-Muslim group, and from a group which had influence at the very centre of the state in the years leading up to partition and in Pakistan in the years following independence, with statesmen such as Zaffrulla Khan, to a non-Muslim minority whose name has been removed from their town and who are unable to bury their dead so that they rest in peace. This change did not just happen but was produced by concerted and repeated effort to make of the Ahmadis the internal enemy of Sunni Islam in Pakistan. This marks a dramatic change from the 1940s when Cantwell Smith was able to write:

> There is nothing in the Qadiyan Ahmadīya that is not in orthodox Islām, except: its novelty, and the consequent enthusiasm; its authoritarianism, with a *khalīfah* who can relieve his followers of the moral responsibility of deciding even modern questions; and finally, and most important, its cohesion – the fellowship and solidarity of a small and active community.
>
> (Cantwell Smith 1943:326)

And perhaps this evaluation of the Ahmadis as offering little new to Islam other than its newness and the cohesion of its members, provides a clue as to why the Ahmadis were focused on and have continued to be the target of relentless Sunni opprobrium in Pakistan. They are certainly not the only group to be targeted in this way but they were the first to be dealt with so systematically and perhaps served as the model to follow for those who seek to eliminate all other minorities from Pakistan.

Yet the scrutiny of insiders with the aim of delimiting and then eliminating internal minorities, and particularly those who may be able to pass as members of the majority and so call into question who really belongs and upset the certainties of a supposed fixed and immutable majority identity, does not result in a steady state of public violence against such minorities. Rather, there are peaks and troughs in levels of violence which are themselves linked to events outside the state itself and which the state is not able fully to control. In Pakistan there have been moments of particular violence against Ahmadis which have followed major and deeply traumatic events. The violence in the early 1950s against the Ahmadis came at a time following partition when the immediate violence the refugees from India had experienced had, for many, begun to be dealt with in practical terms but not yet in emotional ones. This was at a time when the shape of the future state and its constitution was in debate and loyalty to the state was something that had to be declared and made public, especially for those, like the Ahrar, who had earlier opposed the formation of Pakistan. Turning the focus onto a small internal minority, who counted among their number some high profile and very visible public figures, was all the more tempting as it was possible to rouse the masses against them by appealing to some of the latter's deeply held religious beliefs. Later, the 1974 declaration of Ahmadis as non-Muslim followed in the aftermath of the 1971 war between East and West Pakistan when loyalty to the state was again an issue. This war, which had started between members of the same nation, ended up by dividing them into two states and called into question just how committed to Pakistan the East Pakistanis had been. But the citizens of the former East Pakistan were no longer part of the state and so any remaining insecurities and anxieties were more easily directed onto an internal minority who could come to stand for the enemy within, and against whom loyal Pakistanis could unite. To this situation can also be added the increasing influence of religious groups, particularly, in Pakistan, of the Jama'at-i-Islami, that, in the wake of the 1973 Muslim/Arab-Israeli War, by drawing on external as well as internal political events, were able to capitalize on the 1974 Ahmadi riots to achieve their aim of having the Ahmadis declared non-Muslim (Belokrenitsky and Moskalenko 2013:242). And during the early 1970s, the Prime Minister Zulfiqar 'Ali Bhutto himself turned towards the Middle East and in particular to Saudi Arabia for economic resources to finance a military buildup. The price for this was increased Saudi soft power materialized in the form of new mosques and madrassas across Pakistan which further undermined Sufi groups and worked against minorities such as the Shi'a and Ahmadis (Weinbaum and Khurram 2014:21–218; Jalal[60] 2014:201ff). In the 1980s, increasing levels of sectarian violence, partly as a consequence of the turmoil in neighbouring Afghanistan, again turned the spotlight on internal minorities, the Ahmadis among them but now increasingly also on the minority Shi'a Muslims and other non-Muslim faith groups in the country.

Violence and diaspora

The relocation of the Ahmadi khalifa to the UK in the 1980s did not stem the violence against the Ahmadis in Pakistan but rather brought it more directly to the attention of Western nations, partly because of the increase in Ahmadi asylum seekers fleeing persecution who hence became a matter of policy concern to Western and generally anti-immigration nations. It has also resulted in the transnational spread of anti-Ahmadi practices as the anti-Ahmadi groups in Pakistan have continued their campaigns in the diaspora, and this too has made it necessary for Western governments to learn about the various groups and their positions and then to intervene as and when deemed necessary. This global shift is also one that has taken a primarily local and regional sectarian conflict and introduced it to Muslims on a global scale. While some 25 or so years ago, it was the case that anyone who had been educated in Pakistan knew about the Ahmadis and most had clear ideas about what they thought of them, it was still possible for Muslims from other parts of the world not to have heard of Ahmadiyya Islam. Even some of the now middle-aged converts to Ahmadiyya Islam I came to know, and who themselves came from Muslim backgrounds, North African and other, told me that until they moved to London they had never heard of the Ahmadis.

Today that position has changed, and this is in part because of the use of the internet and satellite television which are means for both the Ahmadis to present their faith using new technologies and for those who oppose them to counter them using the same means. The Ahmadi Baitul Futuh mosque in South London, for example, houses a fully functioning television studio and many programs are made and broadcast from this location on MTA (Muslim Television Ahmadiyya), which celebrated its twenty-fifth anniversary in 2017.[61] Ahmadi public functions are always recorded, edited and broadcast, and easily accessed on YouTube. So too are the many programs made by those hostile to the Ahmadis and which from time to time include materials which are considered to overstep the bounds of what is acceptable, as happened, for example, in 2008 and 2014 on Geo TV in programs broadcast from Pakistan and on Channel 44 in 2017 (Ahmad, W. 2008; *The Nation* 2014; Taylor 2008a; Tobitt 2019).[62]

And while the Ahmadis had, from early in the twentieth century, sent their missionaries west to convert Europeans and Americans to Ahmadiyyat, the current difficulties they experience in Muslim countries such as Pakistan have meant that their efforts in this regard have simply been refocused on Western nations and elsewhere, as with their campaigns in West Africa. In the UK, for example, there is a current Ahmadi plan to establish five new mosques a year for five years across the country, while in Pakistan Ahmadis are not allowed to call their places of worship mosques and their places of worship are vandalized and closed (AHRC and IHRC

2015:75; House of Commons 2013:1–2; IRB Canada 2013:2–3).[63] Paradoxically, therefore, in a West that post 9/11 has been less than welcoming to Muslims, the Ahmadis are able to build places of worship and to call them mosques which they cannot do in Pakistan. And more generally, for the majority non-Muslim population of the UK, the Ahmadis and their mosques are self-evidently Muslim and this is how they are represented in the often hostile mass media, which lumps them together with all other Muslims.

In some ways, the current location of the Ahmadis in the West is one that resembles the situation of the Ahmadis in colonial India, and this has made it necessary for non-Muslim authorities to mediate and regulate the interactions between mutually antagonistic Muslim groups. The strategies used by those opposed to the Ahmadis in colonial India and independent Pakistan, such as boycotting their shops and businesses, continue to be among those used in the UK today (Awan 2010:59; Awan, Kokab and Iqbal 2013:185; Saeed 2010:44, 212; Westminster Hall Debate 2010:7, 13, 2016:12, 20). And the hostility shown to Ahmadis who seek political office in the UK today also has a history that can be traced back to both colonial and post-colonial times. So while the level of violence against Ahmadis in the UK has certainly never equalled that faced in Pakistan, and has never led to incidents on the scale of the mass murder of over 90 men and boys as they prayed on a Friday afternoon in May 2010 in Lahore, there is continuing evidence of discrimination and harassment of Ahmadis taking place across the UK and certainly so in south London where much of my fieldwork was conducted.[64]

In the months following the 2010 attacks on Ahmadi mosques in Lahore, London Ahmadis found that they were increasingly the targets of discrimination and abuse in the diaspora. A member of Khatm-e-Nabuwat gave a speech at the Tooting Islamic Centre denouncing Ahmadis and calling on Muslims to boycott their businesses and to refuse to interact with them. Ahmadi women reported they were refused service in local restaurants as waiters informed them that they could not serve Ahmadis and Ahmadi shopkeepers lost income because of the boycott. At least one Ahmadi man in Tooting, south London, lost his job during the year because of his faith, though he later won a case for unfair dismissal at an industrial tribunal, and shops had notices in Urdu in their windows stating that they would not serve Ahmadis who were described as infidels, heretics and unbelievers. It was reported that leaflets denouncing Ahmadis and calling on Muslims to use violence against them were distributed in parts of the UK. During the UK election campaign in April 2010 a non-Ahmadi Conservative candidate was mistaken for the Ahmadi Liberal Democrat candidate when he went to speak at the Tooting Islamic Centre. He had to be locked into a room for his own protection against an angry mob which had gathered outside believing him to be Ahmadi (Oates 2010a, 2010b; Westminster Hall Debate 2010). On satellite television, a Muslim channel broadcast material which media regulators, Ofcom, described as a breach of broadcasting regulations because of its ' "abusive treatment" of the religious views and beliefs of members of the Ahmadiyya community' (Ofcom 2010:11). This abuse and calls to use violence against Ahmadis replicated patterns of harassment that are routine in Pakistan.

In October the MP for Mitcham and Morden, Siobhain McDonagh, secured a debate in Parliament on the Ahmadiyya community and announced the formation of an All Party Parliamentary Group (APPG) for the Ahmadis. Yet, despite the monitoring of the situation by Parliament, the police and local council officials, discrimination and boycotts continue. In January 2013, an Ahmadi woman told me of a conversation she overheard a few days earlier in Tooting between a shopkeeper and a man dressed in what she described as 'Islamic clothing'.[65] In Urdu, the bearded man in *shalwar kamiz* (traditional clothing of baggy trousers and loose over-shirt) asked the shopkeeper if any Ahmadis were still working in a shop across the road. The shopkeeper told him that there were no longer Ahmadis there so he could buy goods from this shop without any worries.

As the Ahmadis have migrated from South Asia, so too have those who oppose them, including a few who advocate for their eradication as a faith group. Global movements of people are matched too by the rise of global media, ensuring that no place in the world remains free from the consequences of historical clashes that originated over a century ago and continue with persecution in Pakistan today. The result of this is that in the UK today public officials, the police and members of the wider community who have to engage with a multi-faith general public have had to learn not only about an abstract and generalized Islam in order to carry out their jobs, but also about the realities of sectarian divides within Islam located in the specific histories and politics of particular nations, and to find strategies to deal with the historically rooted and entrenched positions that have been transplanted from the subcontinent to the UK (Balzani 2014:119–120).[66] In 1943, Cantwell Smith wrote that '[t]he most important fact about the Aḥmadīyah Movement in Indian Islām is that the Aḥmadīyah Movement is not important in Indian Islām' (Cantwell Smith 1943:324). Even then, just a few years before partition, this assessment was too dismissive, though one could argue that it had some basis in historical circumstances. Today, Friedmann's assertion that 'the Aḥmadī movement has been since its inception in 1889 one of the most active and controversial movements in modern Islam' (Friedmann 1989:1) seems altogether more accurate.

The Ahmadis are now viewed, in the Western countries they have made their homes and no matter what other Muslim groups believe to be the case, as just one more diasporic Muslim minority. And as with all diasporas, they have their own particular history and understanding of who they are, where they come from, and what their position in the places they now call home is. For the Ahmadis, this is not just a case of locating themselves as Muslim by contrast to the majority non-Muslim population of the UK and dealing with the often routine negative perceptions of Muslims and Islam in the country. It is for the Ahmadis, in ways perhaps more pronounced than for Muslims who identify with particular Muslim sects against others which are nonetheless accepted as Muslim, also a matter of how they deal with the negative perceptions and practices of other UK-based Muslims that merits further ethnographic scrutiny. In this regard, some of the hostilities directed against the Ahmadis in Pakistan today and in past decades are ones that have come, together with some of those who make up the Sunni

Pakistan diaspora, to the UK. Migration brings not only people with their positive differences and desires to contribute to their new countries but also past divisions, controversies and antagonisms. And if it were not for the hostilities Ahmadis face in Pakistan, the community in the UK would comprise those who arrive as missionaries, students and migrant workers but not as asylum seekers and refugees. What has taken place, and what continues to happen, in Pakistan has a very clear and direct impact not just on who is in the UK but also on some of the local and national events that take place between Ahmadis and other Muslims and which British authorities have to deal with, as the following chapters make clear.

Notes

1 For example, Muhammad Iqbal's (1877–1938) call 'for the Ahmadīyya to be excluded from the fold of Islam must be seen in the light of his belief that the survival and development of the Muslim community in a religiously diverse country like India was dependent on its solidarity' (Sevea 2012:171). Such exclusion did not lead to a call for violence against the Ahmadiyya.

2 This figure needs to be treated with some caution as the 1947 figure was for East and West Pakistan and the 2013 one is just for today's Pakistan (i.e. the former West Pakistan), which had a lower percentage of religious minority groups even in 1947 (see Davis 1949; Zaidi 1988 and Malik 2002 for details on the minority faith groups in Pakistan over the last 60+ years).

3 For example, by comparison with the Ismaili community headed by the Aga Khan, and in some respects also other non-Muslim new religious movements such as the Mormons, e.g. in Jones (1986).

4 'Hostile views of minority religions were sometimes associated with conspiracy theories. ("Ahmadis are the result of a grim conspiracy of Christians and Jews, and they are just like them; they have turned away from their religion [Islam] and are liable to be killed." Madrassa Teacher (Balochistan))' (Hussain, Salim, and Naveed 2011:68–69).

5 Responsible for managing and maintaining mosques, shrines and religious endowments, publishing religious books, etc. See www.punjab.gov.pk/a_and_ra_functions.

6 For the maternal lineage of Ghulam Ahmad, see Khan (2015:22 and 191, fn 6). And from an Ahmadi perspective, see https://ahmadianswers.com/ahmad/allegations/writings/lineage/. Archer (1946:289) states that Ghulam Ahmad claimed descent from the Mughal Emperor Babur. His title 'Mirza' is Mughal, meaning 'gentleman' or 'lord'. Dard (2008:8) reconciles the Persian heritage with the Mughal thus: 'the Promised Messiah[as] was originally Iranian by race, though he and his family were all known as Mughals in India'.

7 Ghulam Ahmad was born in 1835, according to current Ahmadi texts, but inconsistencies in dating mean that he could have been born later, and so his date of birth is probably between 1835 and 1840 with some reason for considering a later date more likely. *The Census of India*, vol. xiv. Part 1, Punjab for 1911, states he was born in 1839 (Kaul 1912:168). This would mean Ghulam Ahmad was just 17 when the Mughal empire came to an end in 1857 following what the British called the Indian Mutiny.

8 Awan (2010:xxxv, fn65) writes: 'The Ahmadiyya movement was founded in 1889, but the name Ahmadiyya was not adopted until about a decade later. In a manifesto dated 4 November 1900, the founder explained that the name referred to Ahmad, the alternative name of the Prophet Muhammad (PBUH). According to him, "Muhammad", which means "the praised one", refers to the glorious destiny of the prophet who adopted the name from about the time of the Hegira; but "Ahmad" stands for the beauty of his sermons, and for the peace that he was destined to establish in the world

through his teachings. According to Mirza Ghulam Ahmad, these names thus refer to two aspects of Islam, and in later times it was the latter aspect that commanded greater attention. In keeping with this, he believed that his objective was to establish peace in the world through the spiritual teachings of Islam'.

9 Later academic publications outlining the prophetic claims of Ghulam Ahmad are heavily indebted to the work of Friedmann, and so it seems redundant also to incorporate and cite these here.

10 'Among the literates were doctors, attorneys, landowners and businessmen. They tended to come from the district towns rather than from the few major cities, and were somewhat separated from a growing rural and less affluent membership' (Jones 2008:119). The movement continues to have a bipolar aspect in the UK today. While there is an educated professional section of the Ahmadi community, those most often elected to official positions, there are also members of the community who have come in more recent years from Pakistan (often via Germany), who lack formal educational qualifications, employment experience and sometimes fluency in English. The UK Ahmadis are rather heterogeneous, as described in Chapter 4.

11 This phrase, capturing as it does so well the attraction of the charismatic leader for his followers, is the final phrase in a paragraph which reads: 'The subjects may extend a more active or passive "recognition" to the personal mission of the charismatic master. His power rests upon this purely factual recognition and springs from faithful devotion. It is devotion to the extraordinary and unheard-of, to what is strange to all rule and tradition and which therefore is viewed as divine. It is devotion born of distress and enthusiasm' (Gerth and Mills 1946:249). For a rather more negative appraisal of the social and religious consequences of a charismatic leader who arises in times of disempowerment and distress, see Iqbal quoted in Sevea 2012:123–124. Cantwell Smith describes the context in which Ahmadi Islam began and the need it satisfied among its followers: 'The Aḥmadīyah Movement arose . . . amidst the turmoil of the downfall of the old Islamic society and the infiltration of the new culture, with its new attitudes, its Christian missionary onslaught, and the new Aligarh Islām. It arose as a protest against Christianity and the success of Christian proselytization; a protest also against Sir Sayyid's rationalism and westernization; and at the same time as a protest against the decadence of the prevailing Islām. It combined a purifying spirit of orthodox reform, a tinge of new liberalism, a mystic irrationalism, and the authoritarianism of a new revelation. It appealed, therefore, to a group who were somewhat affected by the new conditions, but did not wish to make the complete break of becoming Christians, and were not sufficiently affected by those conditions to rely upon their own new position to take responsibility themselves for Islamic modernism. The Aḥmadīyah supplied such persons with a reform of the more obvious superstitions and corruptions; with a little liberalism; with an emotional security against Christianity; and underlying all, the authoritarianism of an accepted dogmatic infallibility, plus the enthusiasm and support of a small and self-conscious group' (1943:325).

12 Friedmann (1989:69, 71ff) outlines the thought of Ibn al-Arabi (1165–1240 CE), a late Sufi thinker, on prophethood and considers his work a source of inspiration for Ahmadi prophetology. For similar Shi'a traditions, see Friedmann (1989:75ff).

13 For more on this, see Moin 2012, who connects royalty and shrine-centred Sufism as part of the imperial culture of the Mughals in India. These imperial cultures interwove politics, millennialism and Sufi expressions of faith.

14 See Moin (2012:1): 'both the Mughals and the Safavids embraced a style of sovereignty that was "saintly" and "messianic". . . . This similarity resulted from a common pattern of monarchy based upon Sufi and millennial motifs. There developed . . . an ensemble of rituals and knowledges to make the body of the king sacred and to cast it in the mold of a prophesied savior, a figure who would set right the unbearable order of things and inaugurate a new era of peace and justice – the new millennium'. Further,

'Akbar [r. 1556–1605] had claimed to be the world's greatest sovereign and spiritual guide at the turn of the Islamic millennium. He had fashioned his imperial self, in effect, in the mold of the awaited messiah. In doing so, he had embraced a powerful and pervasive myth of sovereignty. It was widely expected that the millennial moment heralded a grand change in the religious and political affairs of the world. A holy savior would manifest himself, it was thought, to usher in a new earthly order and cycle of time – perhaps the last historical era before the end of the world' (Ibid.:3–4).

15 This view is not shared by all Ahmadis, and as Ahmadiyya Islam has grown and become an increasingly formalized and institutionalized organization run on modern bureaucratic lines over the course of the twentieth century, it is possible for different subgroups within the community to understand what this requires of them and means for their faith, in distinct ways. One interlocutor who was born in Rabwah but has lived most of his life in the UK told me, in April 2018, that he thought younger people and converts were less likely to have Sufi influences but that older members of the community, particularly those from Pakistan, might still engage in what he considered to be 'cultural' rather than religious practices. He ended this part of our conversation by saying that in any case, 'only that which is permitted in Islam is acceptable'.

16 Sevea (2012:121) notes that Atta Muhammad, Iqbal's brother, was thought to be a follower of Ahmadiyya Islam. Iqbal's childhood teacher, Mir Hassan, was also closely associated with many Ahmadis (Ibid.). According to Lavan (1974:172), both Iqbal's father and brother were Ahmadis and he himself may have taken *bai'at* from Ghulam Ahmad in the 1890s. His eldest son was also sent to study in the Ahmadi high school in Qadian. This is rejected by those who would see in Iqbal a strong critic of Ahmadiyya Islam, e.g. Zafarul-Islam Khan, who makes this point in his 1995 Introduction to Iqbal's *Islam and Ahmadism*. It is also worth noting that Iqbal was born in Sialkot, Punjab, and strongly influenced by 'the "true Sufism" of his father, a mystic consciousness he felt he himself possessed' (Sevea 2012:16).

17 Sevea summarizes Iqbal's position as follows: 'the expectation of a messiah which characterized the Ahmadiyya movement served to perpetuate disempowerment. Nietzsche had argued that the doctrine of seeking redemption through Christ had been a masterstroke of the priests who sought to perpetuate a slave mentality. . . . Iqbal argued that the expectation of salvation through a messiah had only served to disempower and reconcile people to a position of decline. . . . The Ahmadiyya stress on a continued prophethood would only detract from the individual striving to achieve his own as well as society's development, as he would continue to look to the arrival of a messiah to salvage him. The Ahmadiyya were thus playing a role similar to Nietzsche's life-negating priests' (2012:122).

18 See also Muhammad Iqbal's 1995 [1936] *Islam and Ahmadism.*

19 As Raja (2010:135) states: 'while Mawdudi's Islamic government does not discriminate on the basis of race, language, culture, or colour, it will, however, in the end, include only those as equals who believe in the state ideology, and as state ideology is based on Islam, the state would, thus, automatically become an Islamic state'.

20 'The Majilis-i-Ahrar-Islam-Hind was founded in December 1929, at the time of the Congress session of 1929–1930, in Lahore. . . . Persuaded by Maulana Abul Kalam Azad, some prominent *Ulema* (Muslim religious scholars) of India, mostly hailing from Punjab and led by Maulana Syed Ataullah Bokhari, Chaudhry Afzal Haq, Maulana Zafar'Ali Khan and Maulana Mazhar Ali Azhar, established the Majilis-i-Ahrar Islam 1929. . . . All the above-named leaders of the Majlis Ahrar had been very active in the Khilafat Movement. They had previously made important contributions to the Muslim cause in India in educational, religious and political fields' (Chawla 2011:83). See also Awan 2010.

21 Muslims in British India launched the Khilafat Movement, which lasted from 1919 to 1922 to seek to prevent the British abolishing the Ottoman Caliphate. For Awan

(2010:71), 'Muslim support of the Khilafat Movement led to the emergence of a new political force, the ulema. Thus, the result was the infusion of religion into politics, and it assumed a formal role through the JUH [Jamiat-i-Ulama-i-Hind], which was formed in 1919'. For the Khilafat Movement in relation to the Ahrar, see also Kamran 2013, and for a general overview see Robinson 2005.

22 Awan states: 'Amongst . . . party objectives were: complete independence for India; better relations among different Indian communities; establishment of an Islamic system for the Muslims in the country; and the socio-economic development of India, with special emphasis on the well-being of the Muslim community. The MAI [Majlis-i-Ahrar] stood for equal distribution of wealth; eradication of untouchability; respect for every religion; and freedom to live according to Sharia (2010:15). Khatm-e-Nabuwat, which grew out of the Ahrar, has discarded many of these original reformist goals of the Ahrar.

23 Ghulam Ahmad claimed that Jesus had not died on the cross. Again, as with many of his other spiritual claims Ahmad was not the only Muslim, or even the only Muslim in colonial India, to hold such a view even if others used such views for different ends. Among Indian Muslim contemporaries of Ahmad, Sir Sayyid Ahmad Khan, the rationalist founder of Aligarh University, for example, also considered that Jesus did not die on the cross but of natural causes in later life. In fact, so 'rational' in terms of their discussions on the crucifixion and death of Jesus were both Ahmad and Sayyid Khan that Griswold, writing in 1912, concluded: 'If the Ahmadiya should break up, it will be a question whether it will be re-absorbed into orthodox Islam, or whether its members will take refuge in the rationalism of the Aligarh School' (cited in Walter 1916:66).

24 Copland (1981:254) argues that the Ahmadi's role in Kashmir cost them the goodwill of the British and supports this with the prosecution of an Ahmadi branch secretary in 1934 for publishing an inflammatory tract and the British refusal in the same year to prevent the Ahrar Tabligh Conference from taking place in close proximity to the Ahmadi headquarters.

25 Other tactics employed by the Ahrar in India included campaigns in which they asked Muslim villagers to buy goods only from Muslim shopkeepers and boycott Hindu businesses (Kamran 2013:474; Awan 2010:73). Such tactics have been continued by Khatm-e-Nabuwat in Pakistan and also in the UK in recent years though now directed at Ahmadis, where Ahmadi shops and businesses are boycotted and Ahmadis refused service in Muslim shops and restaurants.

26 The loyalty of the Ahrar to the state of Pakistan was questioned in the 1954 *Report of the Court of Inquiry*, p. 11. This is somewhat ironic given the accusations levelled by those who followed the Ahrar in their attacks on loyalty of the Ahmadis.

27 The Humanity First end of year report for 2016 to the UK Charities Commission records the Aims and Activities of the charity as providing: 'immediate relief to people in those areas of the world who have been the victims of natural or man made disasters irrespective of creed, race, colour or religion'. http://beta.charitycommission.gov.uk/charity-details/?subid=0&regid=1149693.

28 The *Census of India, Punjab* for 1911 (Kaul 1912:165) lists the numbers of Ahmadis at 18,695, stating that in 1901 the number of males over 15 years of age was 1,113, from which was extrapolated a total population of 3,450 (p. 168). The census continues: 'In the last ten years, therefore, the number of adherents of the faith has multiplied more than 5 times. One great stimulus for conversion has been the assertion of the founder that all those owing allegiance to him would escape the scourge of plague. But after a certain period of immunity, the Ahmadis began to succumb to the disease like others and the faith in the efficacy of the Prophet's declaration was somewhat shaken' (p. 168).

Official figures obtained from the Pakistan census, conducted in 1998, recorded that Ahmadis represented 0.22% (Population Census Organisation) of the total Pakistan population (at that time) of 132,325,000 (Population Census Organisation) – approximately 291,000 people. The USSD IRF Report 2009 noted that there are 'according to Jamaat-e-Ahmadiyya . . . nearly 600,000, although it is difficult to establish an accurate estimate because Ahmadis, who are legally prohibited from identifying themselves as Muslims, generally choose to not identify themselves as non-Muslims'. The USCIRF Report 2009 stated that there were between three and four million Ahmadis in Pakistan while the USSD IRF Report 2006 noted that the Ahmadi population was centred around Rabwah, which has a population, based on official government figures, of about 70,000 (PHRG Report 2007; *Pakistan Country of Origin Information Report* January 2010:104). A *Country Information and Guidance Pakistan: Ahmadis* report for the Home Office (2015:15) states: 'Figures estimating the number of Ahmadis in Pakistan varied greatly, ranging from 500,000 to three to four million'.

29 A comparison between the Ahmadi bureaucracy and charismatic leadership with the organizational structure of the Ismailis and the reverence based on descent in which the Aga Khan is held merits further exploration, as do interactions between the British Indian colonial rulers with both Ismailis and Ahmadis.

30 One Rabwah-based Ahmadi interlocutor stated that he considered that the Ahmadi response in Pakistan to increased hostility from others, which has been to withdraw from many public arenas over time as a form of self-defence, has contributed to the current plight of the community which remains in the country.

31 Among his many accomplishments, Chaudhry Sir Zafrulla Khan, a British-trained lawyer, was elected to the Punjab Legislative Council in 1926 and participated at the Round Table Conferences held in the 1930s. He was also a member of the Executive Council of the Viceroy of India from 1935 to 1941 and represented India at the League of Nations in 1939. He was Pakistan's first foreign minister from 1947 to 1954, representing Pakistan at the UN Security Council. From 1954 to 1961 he held the post of judge of the International Court of Justice at The Hague, becoming the vice president of the International Court of Justice in 1958. From 1961 to 1964 he was Pakistan's permanent representative at the UN and from 1962 to 1963 the president of the UN General Assembly. In 1970 he was elected president of the International Court of Justice, The Hague, and remained in that post until 1973 (www.alislam.org/library/articles/brief-life-sketch-chaudhry-sir-muhammad-zafrulla-khan/). See also Chester (2009:59) who writes: 'In 1931 he [Zafrulla Khan] was elected president of the Muslim League but recalled later that the League "was not a very active or effective organization in those days."' Chester (2009:64) describes the impression of 'bedlam' during the boundary discussion meetings just prior to partition and his impression that in this shambles the Ahmadiyya 'by contrast, were resourceful and efficient, and they worked closely with the larger Muslim League effort'.

32 On the Dervishes, see Salaam 2008.

33 'Migration from Qadian' (www.alislam.org/library/history/ahmadiyya/64.html). The 313 men who remained in Qadian are listed in Dard 2008. The number 313 is significant as this is the number of men who were with the Prophet Mohammad at the battle of Bad'r. For an Ahmadi account of the partition and the violence in Qadian at this time in an Ahmadi women's journal, see Salaam 2008. During the Punjab Boundary Commission meetings to decide on partition the Ahmadis argued that Qadian should be in Pakistan because of the one million Ahmadis in the world at the time, half were in the Punjab and that of 'their 745 branches as many as 547 lay in Pakistan (according to the notional division). Three fourth's [*sic*] of entire people who contributed to the Ahmadiya treasury lived in territories which belonged to Pakistan. Further, "The economic stability of the community also requires that Qadian should fall within the area of Pakistan"' (Ahmad, I. 1999:148).

34 In 1948 Rabwah comprised 1,034 acres of barren land (Ibid.:4). Brush (1955:145) states that there were just 4,000 Ahmadis in Rabwah eight years post-partition.

Rabwah, the name given to the Ahmadi new town, is an Arabic word from the Qur'an and is used in reference to a place of refuge granted by God for Mary and her son Isa (Jesus). As the 2008 issue of the US Ahmadi journal *Al-Nahl* (vol. 2/6) explains: 'The word Rabwah appears in 23:51 in the Holy Qur'an. And We made the son of Mary and his mother a Sign, and gave them shelter on an elevated land (Rabwah) of green valleys and springs of running water. Thus, this name suits very well the town established as a haven for the organization and followers of the Second Messiah. Water ran out of the arid ground and the greening of the town shows itself everywhere'. Those who object to the name Rabwah for the Ahmadi town in Pakistan use the following rationale for their objection: 'Bashiruddin Mahmood misappropriated this term to offend the religious belief of Muslims, draw a parallel between the migration of Eisa (pbuh) and his group from Qadian, India, to Rabwah, Pakistan, and deceptively lend support to his father's claim that he had been the Messiah, Eisa (pbuh), whose return was foretold by the last Messenger of Allah, Muhammad (peace be upon him)' (Idara Dawat-o-Irshad USA, inc. www.irshad.org/info_m/news/idar1125.php).

35 Jinnah's presidential address to the Constituent Assembly of Pakistan on 11 August 1947 can be read in full at www.pakistani.org/pakistan/legislation/constituent_address_11aug1947.html. While this address has long been taken as evidence for the secular Muslim state Jinnah sought to found some recent analyses of Jinnah's corpus of speeches have presented a revisionist perspective which, by considering this speech in the context of many others, suggest that Jinnah, as a politician, tailored his speeches to his audiences often using purposively ambiguous language. Given the political reality of the time and the need to unite very different groups into a coalition in support of Pakistan this is perhaps understandable. However, it also means that it is today possible to find material in support of both a secular and also an Islamic state across Jinnah's speeches and interviews (Hoodbhoy 2007).

36 The Jama'at-i-Islami was founded by Maududi in 1941 and sought to establish a distinctly Islamic political system. It has been described as 'Islamist'. In the UK, many of the Muslim Council of Britain leaders have roots in groups linked to the Jama'at-i-Islami (Mandaville et al. 2010:24).

37 The Constitution (Second Amendment) Act, 1974 added a third clause to Article 260 of the Constitution stating: 'A person who does not believe in the absolute and unqualified finality of The Prophethood of MUHAMMAD (Peace be upon him), the last of the Prophets or claims to be a Prophet, in any sense of the word or of any description whatsoever, after MUHAMMAD (Peace be upon him), or recognizes such a claimant as a Prophet or religious reformer, is not a Muslim for the purposes of the Constitution or law'. The Ahmadis, although not explicitly named here, were clearly the target of this amendment. They were, however, explicitly named in the Amendment of Article 106 of the Constitution.

38 Ahmadiyya press release www.khalifatulmasih.org/press-releases/islamabad-markaz-2019/.

39 For a small selection of the literature on partition relevant to the Punjab, see Talbot and Singh 2009; Gilmartin 1988; Chester 2009; Brass 2003; Chattha 2011.

40 The *Report of the Court of Inquiry* states: 'The ideology of the Jama'at-i-Islami . . . aims at the establishment of the sovereignty of Allah throughout the world which, in other words, means the establishment of a religio-political system which the Jama'at calls Islam. For the achievement of this ideal it believes not only in propaganda but in the acquisition of political control by constitutional means and where feasible by force. A Government which is not based on the Jama'at's conception . . . is, according to Maulana Amin Ahsan Islahi, a Satanic Government, and according to Maulana Abul Ala Maudoodi himself *kufr*, all persons taking part in such a Government, whether as administrators or otherwise, or willingly submitting to such system being sinners. The

Jama'at was, therefore, professedly opposed to the Muslim League's conception of Pakistan, and since the establishment of Pakistan, which it described as *Na Pakistan*, has been opposed to the present system of Government and those who are running it. In none of the writings of the Jama'at produced before us there is to be found the remotest reference in support of the demand for Pakistan, and, on the contrary, these writings which contain several possible hypotheses, are all opposed to the form in which Pakistan came into being and at present exists. According to the statement of the founder of the Jama'at before a Military Court, short of an armed rebellion the Jama'at believes in, and has its objective the replacement of the present form of Government by a Government of the Jama'at's conception' (1954:243).

41 There were, however, limitations placed on the jurisdiction of the FSC, on which see Kennedy 1992:772–773.

42 'Among other things the Objectives Resolution in turn mandated that in Pakistan "Muslims shall be enabled to order their lives in accordance with the teachings and requirements of Islam as set out in the Holy Quran and Sunnah". Therefore, if the courts could be convinced to adopt the doctrine that the Objectives Resolution held precedence over competing provisions of the constitution it would follow that the courts would have jurisdiction to rule accordingly. This is, the courts could employ the Objectives Resolution as a vehicle to assume a more activist role in the Islamisation process' (Kennedy 1992:774).

43 The notion of purity however is one that was questioned from the earliest years of the idea of Pakistan in Ahrar speeches in 1940 and again post-partition as when, for example, Maulvi Muhammad Ali Jallundhari, an Ahrar, in 1953 in Lahore described Pakistan as 'Palidistan' (impure) (*Report of the Court of Inquiry* 1954:11, 256).

44 This situation is ongoing as the recent attempts by the Pakistan courts to require all applicants to 'declare their religious affiliation before joining the civil service, military or judiciary' makes clear. While such declarations of faith may have had an original intent to single out Ahmadis because as one judge stated, 'it was alarming that one of the minorities was often mistaken for being Muslims' now all minority groups in Pakistan find themselves potentially targeted (Inayat 2018).

45 A Wikipedia page states: 'The Punjab Assembly passed a resolution on 17 November 1998 to change the name of Rabwah. The government of Punjab issued a notification on 12 December that Rabwah town was renamed 'Nawan Qadian' with immediate effect. On 14 February 1999, another notification was issued that in suppression of the earlier notification, the Nawan Qadian was renamed as 'Chenab Nagar' (meaning The Town of Chenab). . . . The resolution to change the name of Rabwah was passed unanimously by the Punjab Assembly on a Private Members Business Day. However, only 67 members out of a House of 275 were present. The name was changed without consulting the local populace. The Citizens Rights Committee (in Rabwah) called the resolution "Unconstitutional, unethical, malicious and against all norms of civilized society, which will trigger intolerance, narrow approach and fanaticism"' (https://en.wikipedia.org/wiki/Rabwah#Name_change). An Ahmadi web page, www.persecutionofahmadis.org/change-of-name-of-rabwah/ links the name change to senior politicians, the president of Pakistan and the Federal Minister of Religious Affairs, who it claims are members of Khatm-e-Nabuwat.

46 www.bbc.co.uk/news/av/world-asia-29415121/pakistan-s-nobel-prize-winner-s-gravestone-defaced-in-rabwah.

47 There are also more prosaic reasons for desecrating Christian cemeteries in the form of land grabbing by local non-Christian groups. As reported in the USSD (2006:21), 'In August 2004, a portion of a Christian cemetery in Basti Bohar was seized by local Muslims who refused to return it'.

48 For more on the concept of untouchability and how it was used over the twentieth century, see Charsley 1996.

49 On October 19–20, 2017, anti-Ahmadi conferences were held across Pakistan. 'As per a media report, approximately 150,000 people attended the main conference in Chenab Nagar, where more than 2,000 volunteers provided security arrangements. According to a report in the Urdu daily Roznama Express, the speakers at the main conference said that "as long as the Qadianis are occupying important positions, peace cannot be established in the country. . . . Therefore, Qadianis should be removed from all important positions [in the military and government of Pakistan]" (Ahmad 2017).

50 One of my Ahmadi interlocuteurs, on reading this chapter in draft form, commented: 'Obviously it's not to the same scale but there are real parallels between Nazi Germany and what is happening to Ahmadis in Pakistan but ironically I think the greater parallel exists with the situation of Arabs in Israel and Palestine and how they are viewed as existing in opposition to Israeli identity and hence met with exclusionary treatment. In relation to the main point, Rabwah is perhaps not a traditional ghetto but it in its current state it certainly shares some of the principle features'.

51 For more on this see Sadiq 2018. Gillani (2018), also writing on the destruction of the mosque in Sialkot, describes its historical connections to the founder of Ahmadiyyat and also to Iqbal.

52 The full debate is at www.theyworkforyou.com/debates/?id=2018-05-24a.1040.0. The IHRC (2017:14) report on the Ahmadi situation in Pakistan includes a prologue from Dr Swett which references the Holocaust and states: 'the Ahmadi community in Pakistan is facing an existential threat. Sadly, this stark conclusion is neither alarmist nor is it hyperbole. Rather it is a prudent reading of the facts and it is informed by history and its sobering lessons. I write these words as the daughter of Congressman Tom Lantos, the only Holocaust survivor ever elected to serve in the Congress of the United States and its most outspoken human rights leader. My late father famously said, "The veneer of civilization is paper thin. We are its guardians and we can never rest". In Pakistan, the veneer of civilization has dramatically weakened as it relates to protecting the fundamental rights of the Ahmadi community and it is incumbent on the civilized world to speak and act on their behalf before it is too late'.

53 Cf. Cole (2003:79), citing Patai: 'the year 1937 was memorable in that it signaled the beginning of Hungarian governmental engagement in fostering anti-Jewish sentiment by publicizing information that showed the overrepresentation of Jews in land-ownership, industry, the press and publishing, and higher-income groups in general'. Similar strategies have been used against the Ahmadis in Pakistan to arouse fears that this numerically small population has too much power over economic and political resources.

54 This was one of five demands made by Khatm-e-Nabuwat in the 1950s as described in the *Report of the Court of Inquiry* (1954:137). The demands were: '(1) removal of Hon'ble Chaudhri Muhammad Zafrullah Khan from the post of Foreign Ministership, (2) declaration of Qadianis as a minority, (3) taking away the land which has been given to the Qadianis in Rabwah and utilising it for the rehabilitation of refugees, (4) removal of Qadianis from key posts and their replacement by Musalmans, and (5) framing the constitution of Pakistan on purely Islamic lines.'

55 Tanveer (2016).

56 Sayeed (2017) states: 'on the edge of Rabwah lies a small settlement and a mosque run by a right-wing Islamist organization that openly professes hatred for Ahmadis. The organization, Khatm-e-Nubuwwat . . . ., built the mosque on land the Punjab government ordered confiscated from Ahmadis in 1975 for low-income housing'.

57 Ibid.

58 On the importance of Rabwah as an Ahmadi identity marker, see also Bajwa and Khan 2015.

59 As the 2015 HRC submission to the APPG states: 'Recently the State introduced a column in "Educational Forms" for examinations to educational boards where every

person has to declare as to whether he/she is a Muslim or a non-Muslim. This places Ahmadis in a situation where if they say they are Muslims they are liable to punishment according to the laws of Pakistan while on the other hand if they say they are non-Muslims it is specifically against their faith. Further in case of a Muslim declaration they are forced to sign a declaration that founder of Ahmadiyya Muslim Community is an imposter or a liar, which no Ahmadi can do. This effectively amounts to closing the doors of education to Ahmadi children unless they violate their religious beliefs or face prosecution'. Children who attend Ahmadi-run schools do not face these issues.

60 On the relationship between the Saudis and Bhutto in the early 1970s Jalal (2014:203) writes: 'Protecting their Wahabi ideology with a newfound confidence, the Saudis called for the excommunication of the Ahmadis and began denying them Haj visas'. Zaidi (2017), however, in a review of Jalal's book states that she provides no evidence for this assertion and that other scholars have considered domestic reasons were more significant in the decision to declare the Ahmadis non-Muslim.

61 For the Ahmadi press release marking the 25-year celebration of MTA see: www.khalifaofislam.com/press-releases/mta-dinner-2017/.

62 'The Ahmadis have made effective use of modern media technologies from the very start of the movement. Ghulam Ahmad's use of the newspaper as a medium to call for people to offer him *ba'ya* is significant. The centrality of printing to Ghulam Ahmad's mission is reflected in the fact that he wrote more than 88 books in Urdu, Arabic and Persian and founded a number of journals, such as the Urdu weekly journal *al-Hakam* (*Wisdom*) in 1897 and the *al-Bard* (*Cold*) in 1902. The initial *ishtihar* was followed shortly later by a formal initiation ceremony held in Ludhiana' (Sevea 2012:6). The use of print media was one Ghulam Ahmad had learnt from the Christian missionaries and used to good effect but which could also be viewed as a means to facilitate 'the fragmentation of religious authority: modern intellectuals challenged the position of the traditional religious authorities by publishing works on Islam' (Sevea 2012:32). See also Robinson 2003 for a general overview of the impact of print on Muslim India. The Ahmadi position on the use of printing presses is that Allah had made print media available in the late nineteenth century in India as part of the divine plan to spread the message of Ahmadiyyat across the globe. So, rather than printing presses being utilized by Ahmadis who recognised their potential, the presses were made available by Allah when it was time for Ghulam Ahmad's message to be broadcast (*Barahin-e-Ahmadiyya* vol 5:xxiii, 148–149).

63 Such attacks on Ahmadi mosques are no longer confined to Pakistan but have, in recent years, also been recorded in countries such as Indonesia while in Europe and America the attacks on Ahmadi mosques have been the result of a more general rise in anti-Muslim rather than specifically anti-Ahmadi sentiments (Langer 2010; Ahmadiyya Muslim Jamaat International 2012; Cornwall 2017; Coates 2016; *Rabwah Times* 2017).

64 Freedman 2010. For an overview of the attacks from an international organization, see Human Rights Watch, May 2010.

65 This woman does not veil in the traditional Ahmadi way or wear traditional clothes on a routine basis and so would not have looked 'typically Ahmadi' to the shopkeeper and his conversation partner as in Tooting there are many Hindu and Sikh South Asians as well as more secular Muslims who do not follow the dress codes of more conservative Muslims.

66 From 2008–2010 I worked, with Dr Nicholas Swann, as an independent consultant providing faith literacy training for Wandsworth Council. This work engaged with front line staff including librarians, police officers, and social workers to equip them with sufficient knowledge of the main faiths in the borough to be able to manage faith-related situations which might arise during the course of their work. I was impressed

by how much many of those who attended our sessions already knew about the differ-ent faith groups in the borough and just how much detailed and practical knowledge they drew upon to negotiate often tense local situations such as where to place copies of the Qu'ran in libraries (on the top shelf as Muslims wished or in alphabetical order as some Christian groups wanted) and whether or not to put Ahmadi Qu'rans next to those of other Muslim sects.

2   Ceremonial occasions

Repetition and time

Introduction

The early part of the twenty-first century was for the Ahmadis marked by two commemorations that were of great historic and symbolic significance for the community, both globally and nationally. In 2008 Ahmadis all over the world celebrated the centenary of the Ahmadi khilafat, the institution of the chosen successor to Ghulam Ahmad, the Ahmadi promised messiah.[1] More locally, British Ahmadis just a few years later in 2013 celebrated the centenary of the arrival of the first Ahmadi missionary in the UK. The events of both commemorations forged relations across time and inserted the Ahmadi present into a historical trajectory which not only looked back into the past to find legitimacy and authority for its institutions in the present but also looked forward to the continuation of the Ahmadi khilafat into the future. For example, a special issue of *Tariq*, a UK Ahmadi magazine, published on the occasion of the centenary of the khalifat, explained that 2008 represented 'a most significant milestone in the history of Islam and Ahmadiyyat, the true renaissance of Islam', because 'it is the Ahmadiyya community that today stands unique amongst all Muslims to have at its helm a spiritual leadership which reflects the very essence of the divinely inspired leadership of Khalifat', a khalifat that follows in a direct line from 'the advent of the Holy Prophet Mohammed' (Ahmad, T. 2008:7). It is by such means, by creating particular relationships to the past, that individuals and groups can imagine, and hence fashion, possible futures for themselves: as Munn puts it, in this process 'temporalizations of past time create modes of apprehending certain futures' (1992:112).

The Ahmadiyya Muslim Association (AMA) UK set about commemorating the centenary of the khilafat within the community but also with special events that were 'outward facing' and aimed, as I was told by one of the committee members who has helped organize some of the larger national celebration events in recent years, to fulfil the Ahmadi mission of 'spreading the word'. These outward facing events included the first-ever visit of an Ahmadi khalifa to the Houses of Parliament in London to address parliamentarians, ambassadors and invited guests on 22 October. And four months earlier, on 10 June, there was a VIP reception and dinner to mark the centenary, held not at the Baitul Futuh Mosque but at the

Queen Elizabeth II Conference Centre, close to the Houses of Parliament. This was another important event for the Ahmadis to showcase their faith and celebrate the centenary in the presence of high-ranking British politicians, including Jack Straw, Lord Avebury and Baroness Warsi, who all spoke at the event.[2]

But alongside such high-profile events there were many other more modest local events which allow us to see no less clearly how in 2008 contemporary Ahmadis situated themselves in relation to their own history and to the non-Ahmadi communities around them. And all these events, it should be noted, were planned, organized and funded by the AMA UK in addition to the many regular religious and community events held, as usual, throughout the year. These events included innovations on past charity fund raising events such as when three separate charity walks organized annually by three sub-groups within the AMA, the women's organization (*Lajna Imaillah*), the senior men's organization (*Majlis Ansarullah*) and the junior men's organization (*Majlis Khuddam ul Ahmadiyya*), joined together for the centenary year in a united single walk from the Baitul Futuh Mosque in Merton to the Fazl Mosque in Southfields. The start and end points of the walk linked the two Ahmadi mosques, each built in a different century, and so also marked a walk across not just space but time in Ahmadi London history. To commemorate this special event, a pre-walk dinner was held at the Baitul Futuh Mosque on 18 June 2008 at which the deputy mayor of Merton spoke. Representatives from the charities to which the funds raised in the walk were to be donated were also present to explain how the donations would help them carry out their work. For this dinner, organizers of the event had set up an exhibition to celebrate the khilafat centenary with large print colour photographs of missionaries and newly built mosques. To mark the centenary, the halls and corridors of the mosque were decorated with fresh flowers and the windows of the ground floor festooned with strings of white and green lights. All events in 2008 were thus also venues for the presentation and display of the khilafat centenary to visitors, not simply as the survival of Ahmadi Islam but its growth, spread and continued vitality.

On the occasion of the pre-walk charity dinner, I sat in the large Tahir Hall with the Ahmadi women, separated by a screen from the men and non-Ahmadi women who had also been invited to attend the dinner. After the speeches and prayer, as food was served, the women I sat with talked about how they too, as Ahmadi women, wanted to organize their own celebration of the khilafat centenary. While there was swift and broad agreement on a women-only khilafat celebration dinner, the focus of the discussion centred on precisely when to hold the event. A suggestion to have the dinner event around Christmas time when women were likely to be free from work commitments was quickly ruled out because so many families in 2008 had already booked trips to visit Qadian during their winter break as they planned to celebrate the khilafat centenary in the birthplace of Ahmadiyya Islam itself. The year 2008 was so important that a return to the site where Ahmadiyya Islam began, a place of origins and a significant place to visit at any time, was all the more meaningful for those who were able to travel to India to spend this time in the birthplace and hometown of the promised messiah.

The first women's dinner event was eventually set for 22 November at Baitul Futuh Mosque. The arrangements for the ladies-only dinner included an exhibition displaying Ahmadi mosques around the world, and one in particular was pointed out to me as only recently completed in Berlin. The woman who showed me around this display had attended the opening of the Berlin mosque a month earlier and announced that it was Ahmadi women who had raised the funds to build the mosque in the khilafat centenary year. This was another significant event for the Ahmadis as they had first set out to build a mosque in Berlin in the 1920s and had even purchased land for this purpose but were prevented from completing their goal for various reasons, including the state of the German economy in the 1920s, anti-Ahmadi Muslim groups in the country who campaigned against the building of the mosque and, to some extent also, by the German authorities who, at the time, were inclined to consider that the Ahmadis were too pro-British to be trusted (Majoka 2017). The money which had been raised by Ahmadi women in India in the early twentieth century and initially intended for the Berlin mosque was used to build the Fazl Mosque in Southfields in London instead, thus altering the future course of Ahmadi history. Almost a century later, another generation of Ahmadi women had succeeded in getting their Berlin mosque built and on this occasion an Ahmadi woman architect was commissioned to design the mosque (Majoka 2017:38, fn 39). That all this should have been achieved in the year of the centenary of the khilafat was somehow all the more fitting, and the important role of Ahmadi women from the past, and in the present, was highlighted demonstrating that Ahmadi women too make and record their own history. The first Ahmadi women's dinner event was a well attended and successful occasion and the Ahmadi women have since gone on to institute regular women's dinners and use the organizational expertise they have developed over recent years also to host their annual Ladies Peace Symposia. So while the UK Ahmadi women used the 2008 centenary to reaffirm their faith through travel to Qadian and to commemorate communally accepted narratives of collective Ahmadi history, they also used the occasion to re-position themselves as women within the community by founding a new calendar of events independent of the male Ahmadi administration.

However, rather than simply enumerate the very many events that are organized by the different groups that make up the AMA UK each year and the additional events in years which have particular significance for the Ahmadis, this chapter focuses on just two events to develop from these an Ahmadi perspective on time, place and events. The decision to hold an event, the audience the particular event is aimed at, the precise narratives and messages about the Ahmadiyya Muslim community the event seeks to transmit, and the location and recording of the event all serve to place the Ahmadis in a context they manage and control that proclaims not only the truth of their message but the inevitability of their presence and establishment in the UK. This is achieved by drawing on verifiable historical events, a chronicle of undisputed occurrences, in other words, the 'historicity' of historians, as well as on prophecies, a form of historicity that is culturally coherent if not one that traditional historians would consider strictly 'factual', and by locating the Ahmadis of today in a space that is self-evidently British but now also equally an Ahmadi space, in part at least as a consequence of the fulfilment of past prophecies.

The first event I consider was of particular importance to the UK Ahmadi diaspora as it celebrated the arrival of the first Ahmadi missionary to London. This was in many respects, therefore, a local rather than a global Ahmadi event and drew on a local history and on Ahmadi prophecies which are well known to UK Ahmadis precisely because they refer to the development of the Ahmadi community in Britain. While there were many celebrations designed specifically for Ahmadis on this occasion, I focus my discussion here on just one of the outward facing 1913–2013 centenary events, the Conference of World Religions: God in the 21st Century. This was a one-off event, but one which drew for its inspiration on a history of Ahmadi participation in previous conferences, and referenced these across a range of media to establish the significance of the message of Ahmadiyyat for the people of Britain. It also served to place the Ahmadis themselves at the heart of long-established British institutions and so into a British history that extends into the distant past. In effect, Ahmadi faith was inserted into a history of Britain that long preceded not only the arrival of Ahmadis in Britain but even the advent of Ahmadi Islam itself.

The second event I consider in this chapter is a repeated annual event, the *jalsa salana*, a community-wide gathering which today takes place in some 25 countries where the Ahmadis have sufficient numbers, and where they are permitted to hold the event. For Ahmadis the *jalsa salana* is an opportunity to come together to repeat the first Ahmadi *jalsa* that took place in Qadian from 27 to 29 December in 1891 with just 75 invited male participants.[3] Over a century later, the UK *jalsa* in 2018 catered for an estimated 35,000 participants, including women and children, per day on each of its three days.[4]

These two events, the centenary conference marking the arrival of the first Ahmadi missionary to the UK and the *jalsa salana*, are clearly very different in terms of frequency and scale. Where the latter welcomes some 35,000 people a day over three days, the former had an invitation list of some 500 guests. The centenary conference was a singular event, even if it was, in fact, a modified repetition of a conference that took place in London 90 years earlier, and the *jalsa* an annual event recalling and reprising the original *jalsa* first held in Qadian. Both events re-enact earlier events and so actualize Ahmadi faith and practice in relation to time, as both repetition and continuation of earlier precedents. The conference was in the style of an academic gathering while the *jalsa*, which also incorporates lectures and exhibitions, is a gathering more centred on the development of the spiritual and religious aspects of the faith. The *jalsa* has elements of what may, by some, be thought of as a distinctive Ahmadi form of pilgrimage, a repeated ritual event that brings the community together to celebrate and take stock of their faith in a liminal place. Both events were also similar insofar as they were organized by the Ahmadi *jama'at* and so the histories presented and messages shared about Ahmadiyyat were those the Ahmadis chose to make known. Both events thus incorporated time 'as a dimension of the exercise of power'. Temporality, as Hodges reminds us, 'is a hinge that connects subjects to wider social horizons', to 'control over pasts and futures that are temporalized' and that 'also influence action in the present' (Hodges 2008:406). It is the case with both the events that I examine that Ahmadi engagements with Christian belief and Biblical narratives, elements that seem at first to be at best peripheral to the events themselves, prove upon reflection to be especially helpful for understanding the ways in which each event helped Ahmadis pursue self-fashioning and self-positioning in relation to their conception of time and the sacred.

The Conference of World Religions: God in the 21st Century

The Ahmadi 1913–2013 centenary marking the arrival of the first Ahmadi missionary to London was a distinctly UK Ahmadi affair of particular importance to the British Ahmadi diaspora. For this centenary celebration, the connections between the history of Britain, the prophecies of the promised messiah and a visit to London by the second khalifa in 1924 were brought together to create a coherent narrative of the Ahmadi presence in the UK.

When I received an invitation to attend the conference, I wondered why the Ahmadis had decided to hold a conference on God in the 21st Century in the Guildhall in London rather than in the Baitul Futuh Mosque, a spacious and flagship Ahmadi mosque, as part of their centenary celebrations. After the conference I also wondered why, in particular, the Ahmadis chose to highlight, across a range of publications, in sermons and speeches, the connections between this conference and one held in London some 90 years earlier which the Ahmadi khalifa of the day had attended in person. Given that from 2003 the Ahmadis have hosted well-attended Peace Symposia at their Baitul Futuh Mosque in Merton, inviting prominent politicians and dignitaries to take part in an evening at which, from 2009, they have also awarded an Ahmadiyya Muslim Prize for the Advancement of Peace, why was the additional effort of organizing the 2014 God in the 21st Century conference even considered and where did the idea for this event come from?

One possible answer, I thought, might be found in a khilafat centenary celebration issue of the February 2008 *Review of Religions*, an Ahmadi journal established in India in 1902.[5] On page 39 of the February 2008 issue are to be found two photographs of the khalifa. This raised for me the question of whether the publication of these photographs in 2008 and the reminder of the event which they commemorated, 'The Conference of Religions within the Empire', also known as the Wembley Conference, in London in 1924, had not planted the idea of a future conference along similar lines. The 2014 conference, unlike its 1924 precedent, was planned and executed by the Ahmadis themselves to foreground the role of the Ahmadi khalifa in the propagation of knowledge about Ahmadiyya Islam as a means to bring about peace in a troubled world. In a sequence of conferences held 90 years apart, the second and fifth khalifas, the son and great-grandson respectively of Ghulam Ahmad, would have in addition reprised an even earlier conference presentation written by Ghulam Ahmad himself for the Conference of Great Religions held in India in 1896. Three men, across three centuries, each

Figure 2.1 Khalifa Bashir ud-Din Ahmad (seated in the centre wearing a white turban) at the Conference of Religions within the Empire, 1924, with 11 fellow travellers

Figure 2.2 Khalifa Bashir ud-Din Ahmad (standing at the podium wearing a white turban) at the Conference of Religions within the Empire, 1924

with the same message for their followers and for humankind. Each later conference recalled the earlier one, the past in the present, and repeated an unchanging message, in some respects, erasing the passage of time as the past is not past at all but relived and re-experienced with the necessary variations and inflections to accommodate contemporary conditions both for and across the generations.

When I asked one of the men on the centenary events committee about the choice of the Guildhall for the conference, I was told that the committee members, who had been brought together to form the committee some 12 to 18 months before the centenary year began, had decided that they wanted what he described as a 'neutral' venue for the conference but one that had sufficient significance for such a momentous event in the history of Ahmadiyyat in Britain. The decision not to use the Baitul Futuh Mosque for the conference, therefore, was a choice explicitly discussed by the committee members. The committee had considered and, mostly for practical reasons, rejected several other possible venues including Inigo Jones's Banqueting House. So while the Guildhall was the place eventually chosen for the event and hence the one that has entered into Ahmadi history as the site of the centenary conference, this was not an inevitable outcome at the initial planning stage itself.

And as for the idea of a conference in 2014 replaying, this time under Ahmadi auspices, the 1924 conference which the second Ahmadi khalifa himself attended and spoke at, spurred by the reawakened memory of this event from the photographs reproduced in the 2008 *Review of Religions*, well this, it seems, was a concoction of the anthropologist's imagination. It was made clear to me that the Wembley Conference and the presence of the khalifa in London in 1924 were, in fact, matters of general knowledge to UK Ahmadis as this was also the year in which he laid the foundation stone for the Fazl Mosque, the first Ahmadi mosque in the country, in Southfields, London.

When it came to the guest speakers for the conference, the British politicians and human rights activists one might expect to attend such an event were duly invited. In addition, and unusually for such events, the centenary committee also took the decision to invite and host speakers from Jerusalem. The significance of the centenary justified the additional expense of hiring the Guildhall and meeting the costs of inviting international speakers to the conference. And the choice of Jerusalem is clearly one that has religious significance as a place of origin for the Abrahamic faiths, but also links to another Ahmadi diaspora: the Haifa Ahmadi community, which now numbers about 2,000 people who descend from those who settled in there in the 1920s in what was at the time the British Mandate of Palestine (Del Re 2014; Farhat 2013; Rudee 2018). The Haifa Ahmadis maintain good contacts with their neighbours, including the 40,000-strong Druze community and the Baha'i community, who have established their World Center in Haifa (Del Re 2014:117). Long-term relationships already in place in Haifa between the Ahmadis and other faith groups meant that invitations from the Ahmadis to, for example, the spiritual head of the Druze community in Israel to attend a conference in London would be more readily received and positively responded to.

The 1913–2013 centenary conference to mark the arrival of the first Ahmadi missionary to the UK was, in fact, held in early 2014. I was told this was because the Ahmadi missionary had arrived part way through 1913, so strictly speaking, the centenary year also began part way through 2013 and therefore extended, quite legitimately, into 2014. After more than a year of planning, on 11 February 2014 the Ahmadiyya Muslim community held the evening-long conference in the medieval Great Hall at the Guildhall in London. The setting for the conference, with its sixteenth-century 'soaring high-arched ceiling . . . Gothic stained glass windows'[6] and statues of Gog and Magog (a detail that became unexpectedly relevant to some Ahmadis subsequently, as we will see) in the heart of the city of London, evokes permanence, gravitas, grandeur and spectacle. I attended this event as one of the 500 guests from some 26 countries invited to listen to a keynote speech by the Ahmadi khalifa. The khalifa's speech was preceded by brief comments on the role of religion today in promoting world peace from dignitaries, including Rabbi Jackie Tabick, joint president of the World Congress of Faiths;[7] Umesh Sharma, the chairman of the Hindu Council UK; the Rt Hon Dominic Grieve QC MP, attorney general; Geshe Tashi Tsering representing His Holiness the Dalai Lama; Prof Kwaku Danso-Boafo, high commissioner of Ghana; Sheikh Moafaq Tarif, spiritual head of the Druze Community of Israel; Dr Katrina Lantos-Swett, vice chair of the United States Commission on International Religious Freedom; Baroness Berridge, chair of the UK Parliamentary Group on International Religious Freedom; Archbishop Kevin McDonald, representing the Roman Catholic Church; the Rt Hon Baroness Warsi, Senior Minister of State at the Foreign Office; and Rabbi Professor Daniel Sperber, representing the chief rabbi of Israel. This was clearly a distinguished set of conference speakers and testament to the Ahmadi community's ability to organize a major event and attract such participants. The evening also included messages of support from 'Her Majesty, Queen Elizabeth II, His Holiness the Dalai Lama, Prime Minister David Cameron and several other dignitaries'.[8]

Figure 2.3 Guildhall, Great Hall with Khalifa Masroor Ahmad addressing the invited guests at the Conference of World Religions, 11 February 2014

While representatives of Hindu, Christian, Druze, Buddhist and Jewish faiths spoke at this event, the absence of Muslim speakers was noted by some of those sitting at my table. Rather, and to be more precise, while Baroness Warsi, a Muslim, did speak, she did so not do so as a faith representative but as a British politician who highlighted the Ahmadi Guildhall event as one that 'celebrated all faiths'. And from an Ahmadi perspective, the Muslim speakers at the event were, of course, the Ahmadis themselves. Other speakers represented organizations that monitor religious freedom around the globe – a matter of obvious concern to the Ahmadis – or were representatives of governments in countries such as Ghana, where the Ahmadis have long-term educational and social projects and established communities.

The Conference of World Religions in 2014 was significant in many respects. For the Ahmadi community it was one highlight of their centenary celebrations commemorating the initially tentative spread of the faith in the diaspora with the first Ahmadi missionary to come to the UK, Chaudhry Fateh Muhammad Sayal Sahib.[9] His arrival marked the start of the Ahmadi presence in what was at the time the heart of the British empire.[10] In 2014 this event also, for Ahmadis, served to symbolize their continued success and survival in spite of hostility and persecution from other Muslim sects and states. Whatever the event may have meant to non-Ahmadi attendees, this conference was eagerly anticipated with places at the event limited and keenly sought after by Ahmadis themselves. In fact, one senior Ahmadi woman I had hoped to meet during the evening (who did not, as it turned out, attend) later told me that she thought the scramble for invitations among the Ahmadi ladies was so unseemly that she had decided to withdraw from any attempt to secure herself a place at the conference.

The Ahmadi Conference of World Religions was not, however, only an Ahmadi centenary event. It also marked, as the Ahmadis themselves recognized, the ninetieth anniversary of the 1924 Conference on Living Religions within the British Empire held in London, a conference which itself took explicit inspiration from the Chicago Parliament of World's Religions in 1893 (Howard 2017; Hare 1924).[11] The 1924 Conference on Living Religions within the British Empire, held in conjunction with the British Empire Exhibition of 1924, was widely reported in the British national media at the time, with the Ahmadi Khalifa, Bashir-ud Din, regularly featured in the reports as a conference speaker of particular interest to the British public. The Ahmadi khalifa's paper on 'The Ahmadiyya Movement' was delivered during the second day of the conference which was reserved for Islam (Hare 1925:xxx). Despite representing a religious movement that was at the time just in its thirty-fourth year of existence and had an estimated half million followers,[12] the khalifa did not speak in the section of the conference reserved for 'modern movements' in religion which covered the 'Baha'i Cause' and the Brahmo and Arya Samaj, and took place later in the course of the ten-day conference (Hare 1924:735–739). Perhaps even more surprisingly from a twenty-first-century perspective, the *Yorkshire Observer* on 30 August 1924 gave advance notice of the Islam day of the conference by declaring: 'The three great branches of the Islamic faith – the

Sunnis, Shiahs and the Ahmadia – will have representatives, and so will the Sufist sect' (in Howard 2017:9).

It appears that an Ahmadi, Hadrat Maulwi Abdul Raheem Nayyer Sahib, who had taken *bai'at* in 1901[13] and had arrived in the UK in 1923, came to hear of the conference as it was being organized. He took it upon himself to meet with the conference secretary, Miss Mabel Sharples, and seems to have managed to persuade the conference organizers to discuss the inclusion of an Ahmadi representative at the conference. All this, according to a Friday sermon given by the current khalifa on 28 February 2014, happened after speakers for the conference had already been chosen. However, the success of Hadrat Maulwi Abdul Raheem Nayyer Sahib in securing a place for the Ahmadi khalifa to speak at the 1924 conference may also have had to do with Sir Thomas Arnold, a key member of the Executive Committee for the Conference on Living Religions within the British Empire (Howard 2017:7). One of Arnold's offices was as a member of the Trust for Guardianship of the Woking Mosque in Surrey, which had appointed Khwaja Kamaluddin, a Lahori Ahmadi, as imam of the mosque (Germain 2008:95).[14] Khwaja Kamaluddin himself wrote a paper on 'The Basic Principles of Islam' for the conference in 1924 which was, in his absence, read by Mr Yusuf Ali as the first paper given by a faith representative on the day of the conference reserved for Islam (Hare 1924:719, 1925:65–85).[15] This in effect, meant that two of the papers on the Islam day were written by Ahmadis, one a member of the Lahore Ahmadiyya Movement, which had split from the Qadian branch in 1914 over a succession dispute (Friedmann 1989:147ff; for the Ahmadi position on this, see Ahmad 2008:10–46), and the other, the khalifa of the Qadian branch who represented the great majority of Ahmadis on the subcontinent. A third Ahmadi, Dr Muhammad Din, read, with the khalifa's permission, the paper prepared by Hafiz Raushan Ali on Sufism which was also presented on the same day (Howard 2017:15).

Arnold had himself had a distinguished career which included a position teaching in the Mohammedan Anglo-Oriental College, Aligarh and a post, from 1898, as professor of philosophy at Government College, Lahore.[16] In 1896 he published the first edition of *The Preaching of Islam: A History of the Propagation of the Muslim Faith*, which focused on the missionizing of Islam with a chapter devoted to the spread of Islam in India and, although he does not explicitly mention the Ahmadi Muslims in this text, it is very likely that he was aware of them during his time in India and certainly so by the time of the 1924 conference.[17] Arnold was clearly familiar with the Lahori Ahmadis and had spent time in India lecturing in Lahore where Muhammad Iqbal, who had close associations with Ahmadis in India, was one of his students.[18] The invitation to the khalifa of the Qadian branch of Ahmadiyya Islam was, therefore, one that Arnold, as a member of the Executive Committee, may have agreed to when the opportunity presented itself, in full knowledge of how such missionizing Muslim groups were organized in India and increasingly also abroad.[19] In other words, Arnold's experiences in India and his pre-existing knowledge of proselytizing Muslim movements may well have worked to the advantage of Hadrat Maulwi Abdul Raheem Nayyer Sahib when he came to make the case for inviting the Ahmadi khalifa to the conference.

In due course, the khalifa was invited to travel to England to speak at the conference and, 'after prayer and Istikhara and consultation with the Jama'at the journey was made with special Divine succor'.[20] While the Friday sermon of 28 February 2014 given by the current Ahmadi khalifa makes clear that the journey of Bashir-ud Din to the UK with an entourage of 11 represented a significant financial burden for the community, Howard and Hare both note that of the three official receptions given during the conference, one was hosted by the khalifa at the Ritz hotel (Howard 2017:16; Hare 1924:53).[21]

In what follows I consider what the Guildhall Conference of World Religions: God in the 21st Century means for Ahmadis today and why it was important for the khalifa to make the connections to the 1924 Conference on Living Religions explicit in his Friday sermon on 28 February 2014. The importance of the 1924 and 2014 conferences is also made clear by the lengthy coverage of the events in the April–June 2014 issue of *Maryam*, a journal for the women and girls of the *jama'at*, and in texts designed to educate children about the history and significance of their faith. Here, I also discuss the relation to time, prophecy and historicity in the Ahmadi re-presentations of past events as well as consider some of the implications and outcomes of the repeated conference attendance and speeches over time and in different venues by Ahmadi leaders. Additionally, I consider how the Ahmadi recounting and remembrance of each conference, noting both comparisons and differences, of past events discussed in the present is a means of making Ahmadi historicity, understood as a social relation with time. In other words, what difference did it make that the 1924 conference to which the Ahmadis were invited was, in significant ways, reprised in the 2014 Ahmadi centenary conference which they took the lead in organizing and to which they invited speakers? What kind of ceremonial event was the 2014 conference and what did it say about Ahmadiyya Islam in the diaspora in the twenty-first century?

At one level the conference of 2014 served to create collective memories for Ahmadis in the present at a point when, in Pierre Nora's terms, the memory of the 1924 event has become history: no longer part of experience, living and present but an artefact, 'the reconstruction, always problematic and incomplete, of what is no longer' while 'memory, insofar as it is affective and magical, only accommodates those facts that suit it; it nourishes recollections that may be out of focus or telescopic, global or detached, particular or symbolic . . . memory installs remembrance within the sacred' (Nora 1989:8–9). Those who attended the conference in 2014 now have this event both as embodied experience and as a memory forged during the evening itself, while those who watched the filmed event on MTA, heard about it in sermons, or read about it in journals, experienced the event in mediated form. Even though only 500 or so persons participated directly in the evening conference, many hundreds more have seen, read or heard of this event and it has become part of their knowledge, and mediated memory, of Ahmadi achievements. Those who read about the conference of 2014, or who listened to the khalifa's sermon about the 1924 conference, given less than two weeks after the 2014 event, were encouraged to link the two conferences and to see them in terms of historical continuity. The early twentieth-century conference was one in which the khalifa of the day made a memorable impression on all those who were present, but it was an occasion which no one in 2014 could claim, heeding Berliner's warnings about the '"danger of overextension" of the [memory] concept', to have as an actual memory, whether collective, vicarious or otherwise.[22] The linking of the two conferences, both ceremonial events, made them become, for Ahmadis, part of a single historical trajectory, something which was not in any sense a necessary outcome of the first conference. In Kapferer's (2010:16) terms, events such as these conferences, are creative and generative of possibilities when the 'connection, as it were, is made by events in the future that do not flow as a necessity from specific preceding events'. To understand why, and in what ways, the 2014 conference became, in Ahmadi understandings, the necessary historical successor of the 1924 conference, some of the features that were kept from the 1924 conference as well as the differences in the organization and form of the 2014 conference can be explored.

One key feature of both the 1924 and the 2014 conferences was the decision to have representatives of faiths, 'native expositors' as Hare (1924:711) described them, rather than academics and experts, talk about their faiths and for there to be no opportunity for discussion or questions after the presentations. The papers presented at both conferences were also not to include material that might challenge or cause offence to any of the faith groups present. For the organizers of the 1924 conference this was an explicit break with the World's Parliament of Religions held in Chicago in 1893, and designed to avert any possible religious controversy (Hare 1924:707–709; Howard 2017:3). As the *Times of India* (30 June 1924) had noted for the Conference on Living Religions within the British Empire:

> This important gathering is not to be regarded as a sort of re-establishment of the Congresses of Religions held in pre-War years at Chicago, Paris and Oxford. At these assemblies there were animated, if not indeed controversial, discussions of the respective claims of different religions. The present purpose is to present a conspectus, made as authoritative as circumstances will permit, of the religions followed within the dominions of the King. . . . Apart from such remarks as the various chairmen may make in opening or closing each day's proceedings, there will be no discussion. The papers read by adherents of the faiths brought under review one by one are not to contain hostile criticisms of other systems, encomia of persons, or historical narratives, except so far as these may be necessary for understanding the system.

Key differences between the two conferences, however, included the fact that in 1924 Christianity and Judaism were not represented on the grounds that the conference organizers did not wish to be in the invidious position of having to choose among the many Christian groups which few were to be represented, and also because they did not want to find themselves 'instructing the already instructed' (Hare 1924:712). In 2014, by contrast, both Christian and Jewish faith representatives gave short talks. The 1924 conference was a ten-day affair and included, on its final days, papers by academics presenting their work on the 'Psychology and Sociology of Religion' (Howard 2017:8; Hare 1925:401ff), while the 2014 conference was a single-evening event concluded by a three-course dinner for all the participants. Both conferences were focused on the role religions have to play in the contemporary world, and in this respect there were some clear continuities between the two conferences. As Sir Francis Younghusband stated in his 1924 opening address on the intended outcomes of the conference:

> We hope . . . that the conference will testify to our faith that religion is no waning force in human affairs, but that more than ever before it should be the vital and determining factor in human progress, the inspiring motive of all morality and all art as well as of science and philosophy, and should compact that solidarity which welds men into nations and binds nations to mankind as a whole and mankind to that great world from which mankind arose.
>
> (Hare 1924:716)

This, with the explicit addition of a focus on the role that religion can play in securing world peace, something that perhaps did not need to be spelled out just six years after the end of the First World War, was very close to the sentiments expressed by the speakers at the Ahmadi conference 90 years after Younghusband first gave his speech. It was also close to the sentiments expressed in the June 2014 issue of *Review of Religions* article, which presented the Ahmadi account of the two conferences (Hayat 2014:18–23) and further linked them to the Annual Peace Symposium held from 2003 onwards by the UK Ahmadis to promote 'tolerance and respect' (Hayat 2014:20). In this article Hayat goes on explicitly to describe the 1924 conference as one in which the Ahmadis continued the promised messiah's somewhat anachronistically expressed 'vision for interfaith conferences to be held around the world to unite all religions on a common platform', and notes that 'such conferences hosted by the Ahmadiyya Community continue to be one of its hallmarks' (Hayat 2014:20–21).

One significant difference between the two conferences of 1924 and 2014, however, was the fact that the 2014 conference was organized not by a committee comprised of academics including Sir E. Denison Ross, the director of the School of Oriental Studies (later to become the School of Oriental and African Studies [SOAS]) and experts in comparative religion but by the Ahmadis themselves who invited all the other speakers and participants to attend and who gave pride of place, and the longest talk, to their own khalifa. The conference of 1924 to which the Ahmadi khalifa had been invited to speak on the same terms as all other speakers, was repeated in 2014 but this time as a vehicle for the Ahmadis as hosts, inviting others to speak and listen to a well-orchestrated and orderly presentation, the focus of which was the Ahmadi khalifa and the Ahmadi perspective on the need for faith in the twenty-first century as a guarantor of world peace.

By taking the initiative to organize this conference, to invite others to participate and to link it in a historical trajectory from the 1924 conference, the Ahmadis were locating themselves in the present in a form that made the past tangible to produce a distinctive Ahmadi history, or what Stewart describes as one form of 'historicity' – that is to say, 'the culturally patterned way or ways of experiencing and understanding history' (Ohnuki-Tierney 1990 in Stewart 2016:82) which 'calls attention to the techniques such as rituals that people use to learn about the past, the principles that guide them, and the performances and genres in which information about the past can be presented' (Stewart 2016:79). In this sense, the 2014 conference was a means not only to showcase Ahmadi success and longevity to themselves and to their invited guests but also a performative event in which this history could be presented and experienced.

The very building in which the 2014 conference was held became part of Ahmadi history, as a location which itself mattered because of its own particular history as was made clear in the April–June 2014 issue of *Maryam*. This issue of *Maryam* devoted some 22 pages, a third of the entire issue, to the conferences of 1924, 2014 and additionally also to the second Conference of Great Religions held in Lahore from 26 to 29 December 1896, at which a paper written by Ghulam Ahmad was read. The historical importance of the Guildhall is noted in one article in *Maryam* that begins with the Roman and Saxon origins of the Guildhall site and then quickly moves through history to link the Guildhall's statues of Gog and Magog to 'Ahmadiyyat and . . . the writings of the Promised Messiah[as]' who connected the pair, Gog and Magog, to Western nations and to the end times. As Khokhar (2014:16) explains:

> According to Islam, Gog and Magog were two nations that made use of fire. The Promised Messiah[as] wrote that there were nations who used fire; so that their 'ships, trains and machines will run on fire' and who 'will fight their battles with fire'. He went on to suggest that these are the countries of Europe, Russia in particular. This can now be interpreted as the Western superpowers including America. In the Holy Qu'ran, Surah Al-Kahf makes reference to these nations of Gog and Magog as 'creating disorder in the earth', as well as being a sign of the 'latter days'. Later in the same Surah it states:
>
>> And on that day We shall leave some of them to surge against others, and the trumpet will be blown Then shall We gather them all together.

The prophecy from the Qu'ran which ends this quote is explained as relating to Ahmadiyyat with the trumpet as a symbol referring to the promised messiah and the Guildhall 'statues of Gog and Magog linked to the Surah Al-Kahf' making possible this 'reflection of the Qu'ranic interpretations of the figures' (Khokhar 2014:17). By this means the Qu'ran is connected, via the statues of Gog and Magog, to the Guildhall, and this centre for government in England from the fifteenth century, one where the Lord Mayor of London continues to takes office,[23] is further explicitly linked to Ahmadiyya Islam in particular. In essence, the Guildhall by this historicizing process is transformed into an always already Ahmadi site, and so becomes one that was a clearly suitable location for the conference held there in 2014.[24]

Railton (2003:25) notes that Gog and Magog 'play an important role in Muslim eschatology, in particular with regard to the re-appearance of Isa (Jesus)'. Further, he adds, Muslim commentators divide into two groups:

> those who seek an historical interpretation, either in the past or in the future, and those who see these eschatological personages as purely allegorical, applying not to any specific tribes or beings but to a series of social catastrophes which would cause a complete destruction of man's civilization before the coming of the Last Hour.
>
> (Ibid.:26)

For the Ahmadis, Gog and Magog symbolize the Christian nations where materialism is rife and spirituality wanting,[25] and even more precisely as the Ahmadi commentary on the Qu'ran (2016:849) states: 'The Book of Ezekiel mentions Gog as "Prince of Rosh, Meshech and Tubal", evidently Rosh standing for Russia, Meshech for Moscow and Tubal for Tobolsk'. And, after explaining that the modern Western countries of Europe are those of Biblical prophecy, the Ahmadi Qur'anic commentary informs the reader of the existence of the statues of Gog and Magog in the Guildhall in London, and then continues with reference to the Bible, stating:

> Again from Ezekiel and Revelation it appears that Gog and Magog were to make their appearance in the Latter Days, i.e. in the time just before the Second Coming of the Messiah: 'After many years thou shalt be visited in the latter years, thou shalt come into the land that is brought back from the sword' (Ezekiel, 38:16. See also Rev., 20:7–10). These verses show that this prophecy refers to a people who were to appear in the distant future. The age in which Gog and Magog were to make their appearance was to be marked by wars, earthquakes, pestilences and terrible catastrophes.
>
> (2016:849)

Gog and Magog are memorialized in sculptural form in the Guildhall and hence refer to past events as those described in ancient texts, yet they also look to the present as a time of war and catastrophe and the near future when history will end. Writing on Islamic apocalyptic eschatology, Railton (2003:27) concludes:

> The Anglo-American 'democratic' Christian block and the Soviet-led 'Communist' block . . . (as in the Ahmadiyyah Koran), are the Yajuj [Gog] and Majuj [Magog] in the Islamic end-times scenario. They represent, metaphorically, the forces of materialism and falsehood. Together they will wage war and no earthly power will be able to resist their military might. God himself will bring about the circumstances which will usher in their annihilation. The material glory of Christendom, in its Western democratic and Comminist [*sic*] expressions, both camps showing in different ways an utter disregard for God and religion, will be destroyed by Allah at the end of history.

The Ahmadi strand of Muslim apocalyptic thought linked to Gog and Magog views the pair as symbols of materialist Western nations which the promised messiah has come to vanquish. For the:

> Promised Messiah, Hadrat Mirza Ghulam Ahmad, will succeed in delivering the Muslim world from this great danger. The cross will be broken as this was one of his missions. With the prayers of the Promised Messiah and frightful heavenly signs, . . . the power of Gog and Magog will be shattered. The Promised Messiah said that all nations will be united under the banner of Islam.
>
> (Chaudhary 1996:231–232)

The 'breaking of the cross' in this quotation is a reference to Christianity, and to the Ahmadi belief that when the message of Ahmadiyyat is understood Christianity will give way to Ahmadiyya Islam. This is also when Ahmadis believe the sun will rise from the west, signaling the acceptance of Islam by the West.

The process of inserting Ahmadi Islam into what might be called by historians 'the verifiable past' or 'factuality' serving to produce a coherent and inevitable historical narrative, is further shown by additional articles in the April–June 2014 issue of *Maryam*, which draw on visions and prophecies to explain how and why the conference of 1924 and that of 2014 not only happened and were linked, but had to happen. Visions, dreams and prophecies are all means by which the past can be drawn upon to make sense of the present and of events that take place between the time of the prophecy and today. This is shown most clearly in two sections of *Maryam* where the same vision or prophecy is recounted, the first time in a question and answer section in the 'Kid's Spread' of the magazine, where girls are asked what was the vision that 'the Promised Messiah[as] saw . . . during his lifetime that was fulfilled through Hazrat Musleh Maud's[ra] [the second Khalifa, Bashir-ud Din] attendance at the Wembley Conference [?]' The answer which immediately follows the question reads:

> The Promised Messiah[as] described the vision as follows: 'I saw in a vision that I was standing on a pulpit in the city of London and was setting forth the truth of Islam in the English language, in a very well reasoned address. Thereafter I caught several birds who were sitting upon small trees and were of white colour and their bodies resembled the bodies of partridges. I interpreted this vision as meaning that though I would not be able to travel to that country but that my writings will be published there and many righteous English people will accept the truth' (Tadhkirah 2009:239). Hazrat Musleh Maud's[ra] treatise being read out at the Wembley Conference was the fulfillment of this vision about the propagation of Islam and Ahmadiyyat in London.
>
> (*Maryam* 2014:31)

Thus, the vision was seen to foretell the conference paper given in 1924 by the khalifa in London, some 16 years after the death of Ghulam Ahmad himself. This same vision, however, was also used to show the inevitable spread of Ahmadi

Islam during the lifetime of the promised messiah and once again in the context of a conference presentation, this time in Lahore, India, in 1896. This makes the Ahmadi historical chronology of conferences linked to visions and a proselytizing mission that spread from India to the UK, and from there to the rest of the world, a mission that begins with an invitation to a conference in colonial India in 1896, continues in British colonial London in 1924 and then is organized and directed by the Ahmadis themselves in post-colonial London in 2014. At each, the Ahmadi khalifa of the day sets out the tenets of the faith for an awestruck audience of primarily non-Muslims.

The same April–June 2014 issue of *Maryam* includes a four-page article outlining the Conference of Great Religions held in Lahore in 1896, for which the promised messiah wrote a paper that itself was the subject of the same vision from God: 'God the All-Knowing, has revealed to me that my paper will be declared supreme over all other papers', and further that 'it was thus disclosed to me that the wide publication of this paper would expose the untruth of false religions and the truth of the Qur'an will spread progressively around the earth till arrives its climax' (Rehman 2014:33). This paper, which was translated into English and published as *Grand Piece of News for Seekers after Truth*, was also considered to be the fulfillment of the prophecy cited here in which the promised messiah saw himself in a vision preaching from a pulpit in London. This point is reinforced by Rehman (2014:36), who adds:

This vision of the Promised Messiah[as] clearly shows Islam Ahmadiyyat spreading through London and Britain. Ahmadiyyat has shown the truth to the people of the West through the hand of Khilafat; London has become the centre for the community and hundreds of Englishmen and women have already embraced Ahmadiyyat to be the truth and accepted Islam Ahmadiyyat as a result.

Here the contemporary situation of the Ahmadis, many of whom migrated to London because of the difficulties they face in modern Pakistan, is incorporated into the fulfilment of a divine vision and precursor of the necessary spread of Ahmadiyya Islam rather than the capricious outcome of political and religious persecution resulting in the formation of a diasporic community now settled in the UK. Historicity as factuality, verifiable actual events and occurrences, becomes historicity as the selective remembering and reshaping of particular events to produce a coherent and compelling historical narrative for members of the Ahmadi community in the present (Stewart 2016:80).

The historical import of the Ahmadi conference presentations, however, does not rest simply on a community-focused and divinely ordained narrative of events; it is one that also includes and reaches out to Ahmadi involvement in national, international and global affairs of historical significance. This was made explicit in the 2014 conference itself and also in the Ahmadi texts about the conference with reference to the participation, in 1924, of Zafrulla Khan as the person chosen to read the khalifa's paper at the Conference on Living Religions within the British Empire which was discussed in *Maryam* (2014 April–June, issue 10), as well as in the February 2008 issue of the *Review of Religions* (Khan 2008:76–79). In these Ahmadi publications the high-profile political career of Zafrulla Khan does not need to be spelled out. But in 2014, for example, one of the speakers at the conference, Dr Swett, the vice chair of the United States Commission on International Religious Freedom, noted 'the role of the late Sir Chaudhry Zafrullah Khan Sahib in negotiating the United Nations Declaration of Human Rights and the fact that he signed it on behalf of the State of Pakistan' (in *Maryam* 2014:22). Zafrulla Khan's political position in Pakistan would have been well-known to all Ahmadis present but not to many of the invited conference participants. Zafrulla Khan's career extended beyond more parochial Ahmadi limits and connects him – and through him also Ahmadiyyat – to events of global historical significance. And while Zafrulla Khan's later political career was the focus of much religiously inspired political strife in the newly formed Pakistan, 1924, as the Friday sermon of 28 February 2014 noted, was a time before the Ahmadis were known, as they are today, to human rights organizations because of the state-sanctioned discrimination and persecution they experience. The irony of the fact that the high-ranking Pakistani politician who signed the United Nations Declaration of Human Rights on behalf of the State of Pakistan should be himself an Ahmadi and personally the subject of much anti-Ahmadi rhetoric was not lost on the Ahmadis present at the conference in 2014. And while the 1924 conference resulted in positive national newspaper coverage for the Ahmadis and for their khalifa, the current khalifa lamented in his Friday sermon of 7 March 2014 that the *jama'at* had not done enough to promote the event beyond the community itself. Before going on to describe the conference in some detail, he stated:

> the administration of UK Jama'at which organised such a big event did not promote it ahead of time as they should have and were satisfied by simply organising it and anticipating a large number of guests. This was a chance to introduce the Jama'at on a wide scale and disseminate the beautiful teaching of Islam to as many people as possible. If the media had been contacted properly it would have produced better results than what we have as a result of efforts Ameer Sahib and his team is making now. These days press is a huge source of promoting one's message. In this regard most Jama'ats around the world do not perform as required and show failings. USA is now improving somewhat in this regard and good work is being carried out in this regard in Ghana, Sierra Leone and francophone Africa [*sic*] countries. We should have access to the media on every level so that the world gets to know the beautiful teaching of Islam. This is great source of Tabligh and Jama'ats need to pay attention to this.[26]

An opportunity to disseminate, using modern media, the Ahmadi message appeared to have been missed, and this failing is one that other *jama'ats* were quite bluntly warned not to emulate.

Conferences such as the ones described earlier matter for who they bring together, what they say and for what might become of them as they are remembered, reinterpreted and perhaps repeated in the future, in ways that participants in the present cannot foresee. For the Ahmadis, invitations to conferences organized by authoritative others, such as the committee that came together for the 1924 conference, is testament to their important message and the desire of non-Ahmadis to hear it. The willingness of those invited to the 2014 conference organized by the Ahmadis to celebrate their centenary in the UK, along with the good wishes read out from highly placed politicians and dignitaries, including the Queen, is further evidence of their legitimacy and a public recognition of their place in the UK. Ahmadi accounts of the reception of the conference papers written by the khalifas in both 1924 and 2014 stress how well received they were and indeed, for 1924 there are statements in the British press to support this. The reporter for the *Manchester Guardian* of 24 September 1924, for example, noted (under a heading that read 'The New Messiah'):

> The sensation of the conference so far was the appearance this afternoon of a new sect of Islam (a convenient description, however, which is not admitted as accurate by the new sect), which claims to have been founded 34 years ago by the Messiah of Biblical and other prophecy and to have an express divine command to lead mankind to God through Islam. A white-turbaned, black-bearded Indian of a radiant, pleasing countenance, who described himself as his Holiness the Khilafat Al Massiah Alhaj, the Hirza Bashir-ud-Din Mahmud Ahmad - or for short his Holiness Khalifatul-Masih - presented this bold claim in a paper entitled 'the Ahmadiyya Movement in Islam'. . . . The paper, it must be added, was followed with much more applause than any of its predecessors.

And yet, despite the success of the Ahmadi contribution to the 1924 conference together with the media coverage of this at the time and the opening of the Fazl Mosque in Southfields in 1926, it is clear from British National Archive records for 1935 about the annual convention (*jalsa salana*) the Ahmadis were planning that the Ahmadis were not yet very well-known and had not yet made a strong impression on the British authorities in the UK itself.

On 4 February 1935, Dr Y. H. Sullaiman, the foreign secretary to the imam of the London Mosque, called on the Colonial Office to request the attendance of a representative at the annual festival which was held by the community in March each year. This event, the *jalsa*, was going to be held on 19 March at the Fazl Mosque, and the community was hoping 'the Secretary of State, or failing him someone else from the Colonial Office, could attend the festival representing the Ahmadiya Community in the Colonies' (CO 1935 323 1346/4). Following this meeting, on 5 February, a note was sent by a member of the Colonial Office asking for information about the Ahmadiyya community and advice on 'how much importance should be attached to Dr. Sullaiman's request'. A handwritten note was added to the bottom of this note on 12 February which states:

'The importance of the movement is hardly sufficient to justify the presence of the S. of S. [Secretary of State], but it seems to me that it would be an easy piece of courtesy, which would probably be much appreciated for someone to go from the C.O. [Colonial Office]'. On the same day a further handwritten response in reply to this one adds: 'We appear to have very little information of the importance of the sect and it seems to me rather difficult for the C.O. to send a representative'. The following day a curt message was added to the file: 'The Ahmadiyya are one of many Mohamedan sects in the Empire and I don't think the S. of S. could be expected to attend their function any more than those of any other sect'. Other contributors note that they have not heard of this group and one suggests asking the I.O. (India Office) about it, but somewhat peevishly adds: '(If we are to be represented at the festivals of all the sects which have adherents in the Colonial Empire, I hope that Personnel Division will accept the responsibility.)' The exchanges which followed seem to focus on the relative lack of knowledge in the Colonial Office about the Ahmadiyya sect, even though it is acknowledged that they appear to be a 'reasonable and moderate body'. A particular concern raised is that by sending a representative to one event the Colonial Office might be starting a 'practice of which [they] cannot see the end'. The decision is eventually, and by general consensus, taken to send a letter declining to attend the *jalsa* but seeking also to ensure that it is 'wrapped up': as one note puts it, 'the "wrapping up" might take the form of an expression of interest in the special features of the movement'. The matter was in essence sealed by a typed letter from the India Office to the Colonial Office in which it was made clear that the India Office saw:

> no harm in some lesser personage [i.e. not the Colonial Secretary] attending one of their functions, but at the moment we ourselves should be inclined . . . to keep aloof from them for the following reason. There is a feud going on between two different sects of Moslems in the Punjab, and the people at the London Mosque keep bothering us with representations in favour of one of the parties and protesting against the line which is being taken by the Government of the Punjab. This is embarrassing to us, and, in the circumstances, we should prefer not to show them any particular favour at the moment so far as the India Office is concerned.

The party against which the UK Ahmadis in the 1930s were 'bothering' the India Office about were the Majlis-i-Ahrar, a Muslim political party founded in 1929 in Lahore, which campaigned in the 1934 elections for the Indian legislature in the Punjab and appealed to the Muslim masses with their calls for the 'explusion of the *farangis* [i.e. English rulers] from India, and the Ahmadis from Islam' (Awan 2010:109; and Chapter 1). In the post-partition period the Ahrars would go on to re-invent themselves as Khatm-e-Nabuwat and in this guise continue to agitate for the expulsion of Ahmadis from Islam and latterly also from Pakistan. As Khatm-e-Nabuwat, members of this organization continue to pursue anti-Ahmadi objectives in the diaspora and in the UK from its base in Forest Gate, London (Balzani 2015:58–59; Qureshi 2016:29ff; Mortimer 2016).[27] But in 1935, what the

Ahrar-Ahmadi conflict in the Punjab meant for the London Mosque was that no official representative of the Colonial Office would attend the annual *jalsa*.

Yet, despite the Colonial Office's concerns about how sending a high-ranking representative to one Muslim group would be interpreted by other Muslim groups already based in the UK, in 1936 Prime Minister Lloyd George saw fit to give a speech titled 'Islam and the British Empire' in front of dignitaries comprised of 'ambassadors and ministers, chargés d'affaires, London mayors, ex-governors of Indian provinces and famous Oriental scholars' at the Woking Mosque in Surrey (Germain 2008:95–96). In 1935, therefore, some 11 years after the khalifa's well-received and successful first European visit, the delivery of his paper at the Wembley Conference and nine years after the opening of the Fazl Mosque in Southfields, London, the Ahmadi community was not yet well-known to the Colonial Office and did not have the visibility of the Woking Mosque, where 'its first imam, Khwaja Kamaluddin could present himself as the paramount Muslim authority for London and the whole kingdom' and claim as he did in 1924, the year of the Wembley Conference, to have 'spiritual leadership' over 'the thousand British Muslims scattered about the country and the 10,000 Muslims from overseas' (Germain 2008:95).

Jalsa salana in the twenty-first century

By contrast with the situation in the early decades of the twentieth century, the UK Ahmadi *jalsa* today is well-known to MPs, local officials and representatives of many organizations and charities. Politicians and dignitaries attend, give speeches or send messages of support if they are unable to take part in person. The event has grown from a small gathering in Southfields in the 1930s to one that now takes up a large area on a Hampshire farm, bought when the Ahmadi site known as Islamabad in Surrey was no longer large enough to cope with the year-on-year growth of participants who came from across the country and beyond to hear the khalifa speak.[28] So onerous is the organization required to manage and cater for the shelter, dietary, sanitary and other needs of 35,000 people each day over three days that the committee which plans and prepares for the *jalsa* now meets all year round. As soon as one *jalsa* ends, the *jalsa* committee gathers to debrief and then immediately begins to plan for the next one.

A leaflet from the first *jalsa* I attended, in 2003 in Islamabad in Surrey, explains the meaning and purpose of *jalsa* as holding:

> deep spiritual importance for members of the Ahmadiyya Muslim Community.
> Jalsa Salana is the focal point of the year for the Ahmadiyya Muslim Community and provides members . . . with the opportunity to:
>
> - reflect on . . . progress . . . made during the year
> - remind themselves of the key messages of Islam . . .
> - be inspired to become better Muslims . . .
> - listen first hand to Hazrat Khalifatul Masih V in setting the agenda for the future . . .

Jalsa also provides an opportunity for the UK community to reflect on . . . its contribution . . . in developing and enhancing . . . multi-cultural society . . .

- the Ahmadiyya Muslim Community UK is committed to being a force for good in promoting the UK as a centre for freedom, morality, integrity and prosperity
- through our work and the way we live our lives . . ., we aim to become the role model for how Muslims can be true to their faith and to the ideals and principles that the United Kingdom holds dear and which differentiates it from so many other countries in the world
- as such, the presence of guests . . . adds [an] important dimension to this occasion . . . which is highly valued by the Community.

Not only are the religious expectations of *jalsa* highlighted in this leaflet, but so too is the commitment to place and to the national links established between UK Ahmadis and the country in which they live. The leaflet also allowed the Ahmadi national president the opportunity to focus on what he considered to be distinctive about Ahmadis, in a then still palpably recent post 9/11 context, when he wrote:

The Annual UK Convention event is indeed a blessed occasion and unique experience. Ahmadi Muslims from . . . around the world meet at the Jalsa Salana in a spirit of fraternity. It enables individuals to strengthen their faith and establish friendships with people of all races, colour and nationalities. In the wake of September 11th when Muslims are portrayed in a negative light, we feel it is important to demonstrate the true spirit of Islam – of love, tolerance and goodwill for all. This peaceful message would be a welcome relief from the noise one hears from the fanatical Muslim clergy.

We welcome you with warm greetings and to come and experience for yourself the true Islam through the Ahmadiyya Community whose simple motto is 'Love for All, Hatred for None'.

The three day *jalsa* is one of the few events in the ritual calendar that all Ahmadis, including those who are not otherwise particularly active in the *jama'at*, will make an effort to attend, even if they can only manage partial attendance on just one day out of the three. While the *jalsa* is particularly important for Ahmadis themselves it is an event that also has an outward facing aspect as important guests, including national and international politicians, are invited to speak at *jalsa* or simply to attend to have the opportunity to visit the displays and exhibitions and to listen to the many speeches and prayers over the course of the three days.

And yet despite the scale, regularity and media coverage of the *jalsa*, there continues to be, in certain quarters at least, some debate about the nature, purpose and meaning of the event. After noting that the second-ever *jalsa* in Qadian in 1892 catered for some 500 participants who had travelled from as far as Mecca, Delhi and Aligarh to attend, Lavan (1974:92) adds: '[f]or Ahmadiyah the annual *jalsah* became a kind of *hajj* for the supporters of Ahmad's claims' and, as Arjana (2017:33) more recently elaborates:

> [t]he annual gathering in Rabwah, known as *jalsa salana*, functions for some Ahmadiyyah as a replacement for *hajj*, in part because Ahmadis are banned from entering the holy city of Mecca. This is one of many instances where Muslims have a substitution pilgrimage for *hajj* that is seen as being as meritorious as visiting Mecca, or as a reasonable alternative due to political or financial circumstances.

These statements are problematic for various reasons, not least because Ahmadis have not been permitted to hold their annual *jalsa* in Rabwah since 1983 and also because Ahmadis who have the necessary means have never stopped going, and continue today to go, on *hajj*.[29] For British passport holders, this is facilitated by the fact that the passports do not include details of the passport bearer's faith. I have myself seen the photo albums of UK Ahmadis who have been on *hajj*, in some cases more than once, and it was only in 1973 that the Saudi authorities stopped issuing *hajj* visas to Ahmadis. Prior to this time Ahmadis who were able to go to Mecca for *hajj* did so quite openly. Included among prominent Ahmadis who undertook the pilgrimage prior to 1973 were the second khalifa who went on *hajj* in 1913 and again in 1924, and Zaffrulla Khan who even wrote a book-length account of his 1967 pilgrimage to Mecca (Metcalf 1990:170).[30] Given this, it is difficult to understand *jalsa* as a replacement for *hajj*. And even if any Ahmadi were wont to consider *jalsa* as a 'a substitution pilgrimage for *hajj* that is seen as being as meritorious as visiting Mecca' (Arjana 2017:33), the current khalifa has made very clear that this is not the case. In a sermon given at the 2016 *jalsa* in Germany he categorically stated: 'We do not say, God forbid, that the status of the convention [Jalsa] is that of Hajj as some of our adversaries blame us that we go to Qadian and give it the status of Hajj. This is incorrect'.[31] The need to make this point at all to an Ahmadi audience, however, suggests that the idea that *jalsa* is the Ahmadi *hajj* is one that is widespread and one the Ahmadi leadership considers it important to address. I have attended several *jalsas* over the years since I was first invited to attend in 2003, and have talked about *jalsa* with many Ahmadis including some of those on the *jalsa* organizing committee, yet I have never once heard any Ahmadi describe this event as a pilgrimage. Indeed, when I asked one Ahmadi woman I know well if she had ever thought of *jalsa* as a kind of pilgrimage, her response was one of surprise that I would even think such a thing before discounting this notion as simply 'bizarre'. The Ahmadi literature on *jalsa* describes the event as a 'convention' or 'gathering', never as a pilgrimage. If *jalsa* was indeed a substitute pilgrimage or had the features of such for Ahmadis it is difficult to understand why no one would have simply described it as such.

Nonetheless, while the *jalsa* is not, for Ahmadis, a pilgrimage or in any sense a replacement for *hajj*, there are aspects of the three-day convention which align rather closely with much of the anthropological literature on pilgrimage. Taking part in *jalsa* requires participants to journey from the everyday world of routine and work to a place that is outside of the quotidian and the profane to a place where the spiritual and sacred are foregrounded. This is similar to the journey of the pilgrim and to 'the temporal structure of the pilgrimage process, beginning in a Familiar Place, going to a Far Place, and returning, ideally "changed", to a Familiar Place', a process which 'can be . . . related to van Gennep's concept of the rite of passage, with its stages of separation, margin or limen, and reaggregation'. Further, as Turner notes, 'the liminal stage, when the subject is in spatial separation from the familiar and habitual, constitutes a cultural domain that is extremely rich in cosmological meaning' (Turner 1973:213). Attendance at *jalsa* requires participants to leave behind profane concerns, to journey to the *jalsa* site and ideally spend three days there, during which one is exhorted:

> to make an effort to be attracted towards God, to advance in knowledge and understanding, to bring about positive changes making them part of one's life, to save oneself from the desires and futilities of the world, to make a pledge and a promise to spread the message of Islam in the world, and to fulfill it with all of one's abilities and capabilities, and to enhance the relationship of love, affection and of brotherhood (khalifa's sermon, 2 September 2016).[32]

Jalsa attendees are expected to cut themselves off from the world for three days and to benefit from this time outside profane time to absorb 'the blessings of Allah despite living in this [profane] world' (ibid.). As with traditional pilgrimage, the *jalsa* is viewed as a time away from mundane distractions to renew and strengthen faith and from which to return to the quotidian realm spiritually reformed. The 'relationship of love, affection and of brotherhood' the khalifa considers should be cultivated during the *jalsa* is perhaps best encapsulated in the moment on the last day of the *jalsa* when Ahmadis collectively reconfirm their faith and commitment to Ahmadiyyat through a pledge of allegiance, the *bai'at*. This moment unites everyone at *jalsa* and exemplifies, perhaps, what Victor Turner called 'communitas' – a feeling made possible in the liminal space of *jalsa* in which the 'direct, immediate, and total confrontation of human identities' (Turner 1969:131) is experienced and made visible. The pledge results in a 'feeling of unity and comradeship that bonds the group of initiates, irrespective of their previous social status, political or economic power, or class affiliation; a recognition that despite social differences, all are the same' as they share together in a moment of 'Durkheimian collective effervescence: a fleeting, rejuvenating feeling that occurs outside of quotidian experience' (Di Giovine 2011:251). Certainly, this is a very powerful moment during *jalsa*, when men place their right hand on the shoulder of the man in front and in this way reach out to touch the khalifa himself. This symbolically charged moment reveals that:

> the passion which is seen through the tears which are shed is proof enough to the fact that bai'at is not a physical but is an emotional and spiritual thing. . . .

This is a chain, a strong and sturdy chain, almost like a spider web. It has the ability to expand unlimitedly. Each bond is just as important and vital as the other. If one bond breaks, the whole chain will fall apart. This is brotherhood. This is Ahmadiyyat. This is Islam.

(Tahir 2018)

Men who are not sitting in the hall where the khalifa is present at the time of the renewal of the *bai'at* pledge stop whatever they are doing, turn to face the nearest television screen on which the khalifa is being broadcast and place their right hands on those of the men in front of them while the *bai'at* pledge is renewed.[33] There is a strong sense that this moment of collective pledge unites not only the Ahmadis who are present but connects them also to those from earlier years and ultimately back to the first 40 men who took *bai'at* at the hand of the promised messiah on 23 March 1889. Yet this international *bai'at* ritual first took place only in 1993. It is now repeated each year in the UK and watched by Ahmadis around the globe as described in a text for Ahmadi children.

The Baiat is performed in the following manner. Huzoor stretches out his right hand; persons sitting immediately close to him put their hands on his sacred hands while others put their hands on the shoulders of these persons to make a continuous link with Huzoor. Everyone in the assembly puts his/her hands on the backs of others, thereby the entire gathering is connected with each other leading up to Huzoor. Huzoor recites a portion of the words of Baiat in English, he then pauses so the portion is translated into various languages. When the whole text of the Baiat is completed, Huzoor recites the Istighfar [act of seeking forgiveness from Allah]. At the end everybody prostrates along with Huzoor.[34]

Figure 2.4 Bai'at at a UK Jalsa

Women, despite the use of the pronoun 'her' in this quote, for their part, do not place their right hands on the shoulders of those in front of them but quietly watch the large screen in the women's hall which shows what the men are doing and, from my observation, some will quietly repeat the *bai'at* pledge to themselves. While this is indeed a key moment during the *jalsa* and a powerful, emotionally charged, collective symbol of unity and strength, the *bai'at* pledge is just one, albeit very important, part of the *jalsa* as a whole and it would be difficult to maintain that communitas, at least as Turner understood it, pervades the *jalsa*. Rather, as Sallnow (1981) and other pilgrimage scholars have repeatedly found, most pilgrims do not understand their pilgrimage in terms that exemplify communitas. It might perhaps be said that the repeated exhortations to the faithful to turn their thoughts to spiritual affairs and to share in brotherly feelings with their fellow Ahmadis is evidence that this does not come easily to many, and that while some enduring communitas-like experience may be desired by those who organize and plan the *jalsas*, the mass of the faithful may, for the most part, fall short of such high expectations.

Another feature common to pilgrimages around the world is the connection made to a particular place, often one that is held to be sacred because of where the place is or because of some apparition, miracle or event that took place there.[35] In this respect also Ahmadi *jalsas* do not fit the pilgrimage model. If a pilgrimage entails a journey to a place made sacred because of what is said to have transpired there at some point in the past, then the Ahmadi *jalsa* which can take place anywhere a sufficiently large and suitable space can be found is not a pilgrimage. *Jalsas* take place in countries where there are sufficient numbers for a convention to be held and in these countries the location for the *jalsa* depends on the size of the gathering and other practical matters such as links to transportation. In the UK, the location of the Ahmadi *jalsa salana* has changed over the years as existing sites became too small and larger ones were required. Nor do the *jalsas* in every country take place at the same time as each other. In fact, they are spread across the year in part to fit with local conditions with regards to practical matters such as weather conditions and times that the largest possible number can be absent from work to attend. The khalifa spends a good deal of his time traveling from country to country, going from one *jalsa* to another around the world. If there is a focus and centre which holds the *jalsas* together and helps to unite the global Ahmadi diaspora, it may well be the presence of the khalifa himself at many of the *jalsas* that take place each year. And certainly, for those Ahmadis who make the effort to attend the UK *jalsa*, beyond the opportunity to visit family and friends in the country, the key reason is to be in the presence of the khalifa and to hear him speak in person at *jalsa*.[36] For Pakistani Ahmadis, attending *jalsa* in India, the UK or some other Western nation is the only way to take part in this important annual event as *jalsa* in Pakistan is no longer permitted by the Pakistani authorities or, to be more precise, while the Ahmadi *jalsa* has not been officially banned, each year when the Ahmadis apply for the licence to hold the event their request is turned down.

A 2018 *jalsa* blog describes the loss felt by Pakistani Ahmadis after the exile of the khalifa to London. For those millennials who never had the opportunity to attend *jalsa*, we are told of childhoods spent:

> in a constant state of interval. Jalsas will happen when Huzoor comes, or Huzoor will come when Jalsas happen. . . . By the late eighties and early nineties, the waiting became burdensome. It was nearly a decade that Jalsas were banned in Pakistan, Khalifa was in some far off land and soon they started to realize that they are missing out big time. Now they were old enough to do Jalsa duties, but there was no sign of Jalsas to take place in Pakistan anytime soon.[37]

While this is still the case it is now possible for those who cannot attend in person to watch *jalsa* live on MTA. This is the culmination of a long process of media development which has made the separation between the khalifa and the Ahmadis in Pakistan one that can now be bridged, to some extent at least, through technology:

> gradually . . . Video tapes replaced audio cassettes and brought 4th Khalifa's Jalsa speeches to his people. It seems trivial now, but back then it was a giant step especially for the kids. Now they could actually see their beloved Huzoor and could establish a connection with him. As they were getting used to this model of waiting for the Jalsa UK guests to return to Pakistan and watch those video tapes upon their arrival, something amazing happened. In the summer of 1992, out of the blue, they were able to watch the live transmission of Jalsa UK. . . . Little did they know that a new era was dawning upon them. From then on, Jalsas became late night events for them during their summer break. It couldn't have gotten any better. The sheer fact that they could listen to Huzoor as he was speaking was surreal. . . . Dish antennas mushroomed on Ahmadi rooftops across Pakistan. As teenagers, with the blessing of MTA, millennials developed such a strong relationship with Khilafat that left older generations startled. They were deprived of Khalifa's presence in Pakistan, and now because of MTA the Khalifa was personally mentoring each single one of them.[38]

Counter intuitively perhaps the relationship between the khalifa based in the UK and young Ahmadis in Pakistan is here presented as one of individualized mentoring mediated by television. Geographical distance is erased through the intimacy young Ahmadis experience when viewing the khalifa on television and, perhaps a little paradoxically, some Ahmadis who have never met the khalifa in person even told me that they felt they knew the khalifa personally because they see him so regularly on MTA. Yet, other Ahmadis did not express this shared feeling of co-presence with, and assumed knowledge of, the khalifa and so, as must be obvious for any large cohort, there are different ways of experiencing and being Ahmadi whether or not this is (partially) achieved through mediated experiences such as MTA.[39]

The immediate, repeated and sensory experience of hearing and seeing the khalifa (and also in particular the fourth khalifa whose programs are popular and regularly repeated on MTA), and keeping up with his sermons and travels allows those Ahmadis who desire it to be with their spiritual leader and to have him in their homes with them at all times. The complex and expansive Ahmadi technological machinery which records in film, in photographs and in writing all public events and Ahmadi gatherings produces an archive so large and continually added to such that no individual could possibly hope ever to gain a comprehensive overview of it. For *jalsa* this means that any given convention happens once in real time during which it is live streamed across the globe but also continues to be re-experienced in edited versions broadcast on MTA, on YouTube and in Ahmadi publications and other media.[40] Here Ahmadis can witness their own participation in *jalsa* and view the success of the *jama'at* as evidenced in the large-scale, disciplined and orderly unfolding of the *jalsa* programme.

The preservation in digital media and the reproduction of *jalsa* events and talks, not only those of the khalifa, but also of the invited guest speakers additionally allows those who cannot, for whatever reason, attend *jalsa* or who experience *jalsa* only partially because they cannot attend all three days, or because, as women, the male *jalsa* space is not one they can move about in at will, to take part in events that they might otherwise miss altogether. For while *jalsa* is now open to all it is not experienced in the same way by all attendees.

The first *jalsa* was held in Qadian in 1891 with 75 invited male participants, and it was not until 1914, under the leadership of the second Khalifa, Bashir ud-Din Ahmad, that women were invited to attend. This was one element of the second khalifa's organizational changes to institutionalize and modernize the Ahmadiyya community, in effect, providing it with a viable and long-term bureaucratic structure that has enabled the growth and development of the community for over a century. In 1914, the first 400 women to attend *jalsa* were provided with instruction in the form of religious lectures scheduled over three consecutive days. And it was the wife of the promised messiah herself, Hazrat Ummul Momineen, who is said to have overseen arrangements for the accommodation and meals of the female attendees. From 1917, separate *jalsas* were held for Ahmadi women which included the partial attendance of the khalifa who gave speeches to the women.

While records from the National Archives make clear that the *jalsa* as an annual event was held in the London Mosque in the 1930s, it appears that the practice fell into abeyance and was revived from the late 1960s in the UK when five *jalsas* were held over consecutive years. These, however, did not include the participation of women. Since 1971, women have held their own *jalsas* and have made their own arrangements to ensure that the event runs smoothly for women and children. From the very first women's *jalsa*, female journalists have been invited to attend and publish articles on their experiences.[41] In the women's *jalsa*, Ahmadi women volunteers act as security personnel and direct attendees through the airport-style security scanners that are now one of the unfortunate requirements to ensure the safety of those at the convention. Once through security each attendee is given a badge that denotes her particular status at the event. The badges are colour-coded and, depending on the colour grant different privileges including access to particular areas of the *jalsa* grounds to the bearer.

In 2017 I attended the *jalsa* with some women friends: two sisters and the adult daughter of one of the women. During the course of the day at *jalsa* we also met the mother of the two sisters, a sister-in-law with her three children and some other female members of the extended family who had travelled from Europe primarily to take part in *jalsa* but also to meet with family and friends. Not every woman at *jalsa*, however, was fortunate enough to be able to meet her family members and one woman we met lamented the fact that she had come to *jalsa*, in part at least, to meet cousins who had travelled from Australia to be there but had not been able to find them. This woman had not managed to locate her relatives and said that she remembered *jalsa* in the 1980s at the Fazl Mosque when the community gathered from across the country was still small enough for everyone to fit in the mosque and for everyone to know each other. Even when the *jalsa* later moved to Islamabad in Surrey, she said, the community was larger but still small enough for her to know just about everyone attending, if not personally, then at least she knew the families and recognized people as familiar faces that reappeared at *jalsa* from one year to the next. Nowadays, she said, the *jalsa* is so 'massive' that it is difficult to meet up and see people.

During the journey to the convention by car from London, it transpired that the woman driving us had not gone online to pre-register her car licence plate and receive a designated parking pass for *jalsa*. For some years now this has also been a requirement, partly because of the sheer number of attendees and the advance planning needed to work out where each car should be parked to avoid chaos, as tens of thousands of people arrive almost simultaneously at the *jalsa* site, and partly, again, for security reasons.[42] Undaunted by this news we continued to drive towards the *jalsa* entrance when a volunteer in a stab vest, another unfortunate sign of the times, told us we had to turn around and leave because we did not have a pass for the car park we were heading towards. Not willing to be turned away so easily, one of the women in our group asked everyone to look round to see if we could spot anyone we recognized. As we reached what looked like the literal end of the road to *jalsa*, the daughter with us saw one of her uncles ahead directing cars to their parking spots at the convention. He was called over by one of the older women, his cousin, and our plight quickly explained to him. The man who was, as are all those who actually make the *jalsa* run smoothly, a volunteer, shook his head in disbelief that we had managed to get as far as we had without the right paperwork and then, discretely, directed us to a parking space that was available and remarkably well positioned, close to the *jalsa* entrance. This was one of those fortuitous situations when bonds of kinship can make all the difference.

We made our way to the women's registration section to enter the women's *jalsa*, only to find that while my friends went through the security screening and picked up their *jalsa* badges without any problems, I was a cause of some consternation for the women volunteers on security duty. One of the women, who as it happened turned out to be someone I knew and had often spoken with in the past, explained that the problem was that if I was given a badge of a particular colour, such as silver that granted me privileges, then I would not be able to stay with my friends in the women's section for the *jalsa* but would be ushered off to another section of the convention. However, if I was given the same badge as my friends, I would not easily be able to access all sections of the *jalsa* grounds and might miss out on some of the events and exhibitions. There were in fact not just two but several categories of badges, each colour coded and granting the wearer access to different parts of the *jalsa* grounds and different privileges. Reassured that I was more than happy to just have whatever badge my friends did, I was, after a short delay and a discussion about whether I should have a purple or a blue badge, able to rejoin my *jalsa* companions and share in their experience of the convention. And the women's *jalsa* is a very different experience to the VIP ones I had previously enjoyed in the men's *jalsa*. As might be expected, there were more facilities for women with young children and also more reminders about modest dress that applied to women only, along with a notice about the *Rishta Nata* (marriage) office meet and greet to find spouses for community members who wish to marry.

In the marquee which live-screened the sermons and speeches from the men's *jalsa*, women had brought their own picnic blankets, cushions, low foldout seats and baskets with provisions to demarcate the space on which they and their family members sat. Women volunteers, wearing armbands to distinguish them

Figure 2.5 Notices at the UK Women's *jalsa* 2017

from ordinary *jalsa* attendees, patrolled the marquee urging women to be silent, pay attention to the proceedings on the screen and to adjust their veils in accord with Ahmadi notions of modesty. Despite this, most of the speeches by non-Ahmadis, including a pre-recorded message from Prime Minister Theresa May were, for the most part, ignored as women dealt with children, met relatives and discussed matters that were of more pressing concern to them. The *jalsa* is, for some women, a good time to look for suitable spouses for their sons and for mothers of daughters of marriageable age to make discreet inquiries about suitable boys from respectable families. It was only at prayer time, during recitations from the Qur'an and when the khalifa himself spoke, that the atmosphere in the marquee markedly changed. At prayer time, the mood became one of quiet concentration, as women prayed and young children were kept as quiet as possible while older ones were encouraged to follow along as best they could. When the khalifa spoke, women who did not understand Urdu would wear headphones providing simultaneous translation into whichever of the many languages available they required. When prayer was over, and if the khalifa himself was not speaking, women would also visit the stalls at the *jalsa* to buy religious books, visit the bazaar, look at the exhibitions or get tea. Yet, while all these facilities were available for women, the *jalsa* program for 2017 offered women the following advice:

> Ladies are advised that they should take care not to roam around aimlessly. However, those ladies who are not Ahmadis and do not observe Purdah, should only be requested to do so politely. There is no need for force or coercion. If there is an Ahmadi who has difficulty to cover her face, she should not wear make-up and remain simple. Spread the habit of keeping your head covered. It should be remembered that we are spending our time in a spiritual environment during these days. We should not try to find excuses not to observe Purdah.

As with the khalifa's reminder that the *jalsa* is a call to brotherhood, to focus on the spiritual and a rejection of the profane, the advice for women from the *jalsa* organizers is repeated each year in the knowledge that for a proportion of those who attend *jalsa* this is more likely to be honoured in the breach than in the observance.

The women's *jalsa* included a range of talks and presentations by women, including the UK *Lajna Ima'illah* women's president who in 2017 spoke on '*Istighfar*[43] – the True Key to Bringing One's Soul to Peace'. Earlier in the day, other talks by and for Ahmadi women included one on 'Maintaining Your Muslim Identity in the West' and another, in Urdu, on 'Avoiding Bad Rituals and Innovations'. A highlight of the women's *jalsa*, however, was the arrival of the khalifa to give his address to the women and to distribute academic awards to girls and women who had performed particularly well in national examinations or at degree level. This part of the women's *jalsa* was transmitted live from the women's section to the rest of the *jalsa* and to the rest of the world.

There were also in the women's *jalsa* some small tents with exhibitions of the charity work and history of the *jama'at*. One such tent in 2017 celebrated the *lajna* diamond jubilee and included a display of the history of the UK *lajna*. To celebrate this and to help fund future *lajna* initiatives, postcards had been designed by the Ahmadi women and were available for purchase.

Other *lajnas*, both local and international, had prepared displays and art works to commemorate the 60 years of the *lajna* and these included lavishly decorated cakes made of papier mâché and 3D models of Ahmadi mosques. Another display showcased the books used for religious study by Ahmadi women and girls. Ahmadi women and girls are encouraged to take part in programs of study which lead to examinations as part of the ongoing education programmes in place for the *lajna* and *nasirat*. The professionalization of such courses of study is relatively recent, and the textbooks which are now produced by the *lajna* for girls of different ages, for example, were not available just a generation ago. Yet while the women's tents were informative and welcoming, they were relatively small in scale by comparison with the exhibitions, lectures and presentations in the men's *jalsa*.

In these ways, the women's *jalsa* is distinctive and has, as one would expect, a stronger focus on matters that are more directly relevant to the lives of women. It also provides a space to meet friends and family and to share news and information. As I had always been told that women were given allocated times to visit the exhibitions or could sign up to hear lectures, in the men's *jalsa* I was somewhat surprised to find that the women I travelled to *jalsa* with in 2017 – all lifelong Ahmadis from an established UK-based family – were unaware of the events and exhibitions at the men's *jalsa*. So with the youngest member of the group I was with, I set off to see if we could cross from the women's *jalsa* over to the men's *jalsa* to view, among other things, the *Review of Religions* exhibition of Islamic calligraphy, writing implements, Islamic pottery and Qur'ans, which has been a feature of the *jalsa* for the last few years.[44] Access from the women's *jalsa* to the men's *jalsa* where these exhibitions were located required that we first get the appropriate stickers to be able to cross from the women's to the men's *jalsa*. My outsider status facilitated this, and we were each given two stickers while being told that we should only be allowed to have one but that an exception was being made 'just for us'. Each sticker allowed us entrance to one of the exhibitions in the men's *jalsa*. Once in the men's *jalsa*, we queued outside the Islamic calligraphy exhibition tent until there was room in this popular exhibition for us to enter. The exhibition was made up of Islamic material objects, some centuries old, many of them very fine, belonging to a single Ahmadi collector.

Another exhibition in another large tent was based on Ahmadi archives and included laminated reproductions of newspaper articles, several of which dated from the 1924 visit of the khalifa to the Wembley Conference. There were also photographs of the promised messiah and the khalifas, covering in particular the visits of the latter to the UK. Architectural plans for the Fazl Mosque as well as material artefacts such as wedding rings and turbans from the family of Ghulam Ahmad were also on display. One of the exhibitions I did not manage to visit on this occasion celebrated the first 25 years of MTA. Some of the exhibitions that are now a feature of the *jalsa* are curated to what appeared to be a professional or near professional standard, with display cases that would not be out of place in a museum, and reflect the increasing confidence and expertise of the Ahmadis to set up and present such exhibitions. The exhibitions also incorporate presentations by knowledgeable individuals including university academics and independent researchers who discuss aspects of the objects on display. One of the messages a visitor to the *jalsa* comes away with is that the Ahmadis, contrary to the views of their detractors, are self-evidently Muslim. The display of Islamic calligraphy, Qur'ans, textiles, Seljuk pottery, thirteenth-century Mamluk period ink pots and so forth makes this tangible. Another message is that the Ahmadis have a long history in the UK and are an established and well-regarded community. The Ahmadi archives exhibition make this point clear. Additionally, the organization of material objects on display and the academic talks for attendees and visitors also strongly suggest a rational, scientific and modern approach to religious knowledge. At the far end of the calligraphy exhibition tent, we caught the end of a talk on the Shroud of Turin, and as we had missed most of it, we were advised to watch a YouTube film called 'A Grave Injustice' to find out what had been said.[45] This was just one of several talks about the Shroud of Turin, Jesus and related matters that have become recent fixtures at the *jalsa*. It is to these I now turn to present the Ahmadi perspective on Jesus, the crucifixion and the implications of these for non-Ahmadis and for Christians in particular.

Just as the account of Gog and Magog became an important aspect of the centenary celebrations of the Ahmadi Khalifat at the Guildhall, so too at the *jalsa* one could argue that the Ahmadi engagement with the biography and fate of Christ (rather than a debate about the relationship of Ahmadiyyat to other Islamic traditions) allows us to see Ahmadi self-fashioning clearly from the periphery of the event.

Since 2015 the *Review of Religions* team has organized talks and exhibitions at the UK *jalsa* on the Shroud of Turin, the *Orviedo sudarium* and the science relating to these objects. The speakers invited to talk about their work on the Shroud of Turin are not Ahmadis, and this continues a long history of Ahmadi willingness to incorporate others who have expertise which speaks to Ahmadi matters of long-standing concern. While interesting, informative and always crowded with listeners, these talks seem at first glance out of place at a Muslim religious convention. Yet the Ahmadi conception of Jesus is one that is at the very core of what it means to be Ahmadi and one that goes back to the revelations of the Ahmadi promised messiah. Ahmadis do not believe that Jesus died by crucifixion; rather they believe that he swooned and was then taken down from the cross, unconscious but alive. His injuries were tended to and, once revived, he went on to live for many more decades in order to complete the mission Allah had set for his prophet.[46] After recovering from his ordeal, Jesus, unable to remain in safety in Palestine as a prophet and a mortal man, set off towards India and made his way to Kashmir where he lived out his days in exemplary piety, dying at the age of 120. A tomb, which still exists, located in Srinagar on Khanyar Street, was declared by Ghulam

Ahmad to be the final resting place of the prophet Jesus (Lavan 1974:50). Some of the speakers who attend the *jalsa* to describe their research and ideas about the Shroud of Turin serve the purpose of casting doubt on the death of Jesus on the cross and hence provide support for Ahmadi convictions on this matter. On this point Arif Khan (2015:50–51) states:

> several scholars have argued it proves Jesus[as] survived the crucifixion, thus validating the belief and teaching of Hazrat Mirza Ghulam Ahmad[as]. There are Shroud researchers who have reached this exact same conclusion based upon their study of the Shroud of Turin. Those that have argued this view-point draw attention to the large amounts of blood on the Shroud, and high-light that it would take an active heart to produce this. Others have stated that for an even formation of the image, the body would need to have been at a constant temperature, again requiring a living body.

Yet, other Ahmadi authors also note that the *sudarium* has 'blood stains and blood mixed with pleural edema fluid – that is, the fluid that collects in the lung during asphyxiation, suggesting that the person whose blood was on the cloth died of asphyxiation' (Ahmad 2018:35). If both the shroud and *sudarium* belonged to the same man, and if that man was Jesus, the presence of post-mortem blood on the *sudarium* might suggest, to someone listening closely to the lectures at the *jalsa* or carefully reading the articles in the Ahmadi journals, that the crucified man did not survive his ordeal. The strategy here, whether or not consciously pursued by individual authors, is to present information which suggests that the Turin shroud was placed on a still living man and to also include possible evidence that might disprove this. By doing so, the impression of comprehensiveness of the data presented and the transparency and neutrality of the writer is maintained while still guiding the reader towards the conclusion that it is possible to survive crucifixion and that in time science and reason will prove the Ahmadi position on the matter to have been the truth all along. One way in which this is achieved is by describing how past science has been shown to be wrong when assessing the shroud, for example, with the carbon-14 dating of the shroud in 1988 (Khan 2010). Science itself is thus upheld as rational and as leading to understanding but particular scientific discoveries can always be disputed and discarded when better answers from better science come along. From an Ahmadi perspective, science will eventually prove the revelations of Ghulam Ahmad on Jesus to have been right all along.

During his lifetime, the Ahmadi promised messiah held debates to promote his views on Jesus with both Muslims and Christians (Friedmann 1989:6, 108). To put the matter succinctly, as far as most Muslims were concerned, if Jesus had been raised bodily to heaven and was awaiting the time set for his return to earth in his physical form, then Ghulam Ahmad's claim to be the messiah, that is his claim that he was Jesus in spiritual likeness, was not credible and amounted to heresy (Lavan 1974:38). For their part, the Christian missionaries in nineteenth-century Punjab wielded the belief, shared by Muslims, in a living Jesus as evidence when proselytizing of the superiority of Christianity over Islam with its deceased Prophet Muhammad (Friedmann 1989:111–121). In response to the missionaries, to assert the superiority of Islam over Christianity and the superiority of Ahmadiyyat above all, Ghulam Ahmad sought to prove both that Jesus was not divine as Christians asserted but a man, and that he had died not on the cross but in old age. The death of a human Jesus on earth was necessary for Ahmad's claim that he himself was the messiah of the latter days and bore an 'absolute affinity with Jesus' to be accepted by his followers (Friedmann 1989:117). That Ahmad was to perform the expected role of Jesus in the latter days was based in part on divine revelation and in part on his study and reinterpretation of *hadith* concerning Jesus (Ibid.). Ghulam Ahmad's study of the life of Jesus, his revelations concerning his own status and his conclusions on these matters are to be found collected in his 1899 book *Jesus in India: Jesus' Deliverance from the Cross & Journey to India.*[47] In this book Ahmad sums his position up by stating:

> The truth is that Jesus, having escaped from those accursed people, graced the land of the Punjab with his presence, where he met the ten lost tribes of Israel and God blessed him with great honour and eminence. It seems that most of them had adopted Buddhism and some had degenerated into idolatry of a very low kind. But with the coming here of Jesus, most of them returned to the right path, and since the teaching of Jesus contained the exhortation to believe in the coming of another prophet, all the ten tribes who came to be known in this land as Afghans and Kashmiris ultimately became Muslims. Jesus was accorded great esteem and respect in this land.
>
> (Ahmad 2016 [1899]:59–60)

Throughout the book, evidence from religious textual sources, both Christian and Muslim, is cited as evidence that Jesus survived his ordeal on the cross, and further evidence, including some of a somewhat dubious comparative etymological nature, is used to shore up the argument about his final resting place. So for example, we are told that the name of the city where Ahmadis believe the tomb of Jesus to be, Srinagar, is composed of two Hindi words, *śri* meaning 'skull' and *nagar* meaning 'place' and that the place of the crucifixion, Golgotha, similarly means 'place of the skull' (Ibid.:61–62). More plausible etymologies for Srinagar, however, derive the name from terms that refer to radiance, wealth or the sun, hence Srinagar is, rather, the city of radiance or sun.[48]

In addition to the theological and the etymological arguments, Ahmad recounts evidence from medical science which purportedly disclosed knowledge of an ointment known as the *marham-i-Isa*, or ointment of Jesus, said to have been recorded in 'hundreds of medical books', some of which are listed (Ibid.:65–68). This ointment was prepared to treat Jesus's crucifixion wounds and so render him fit for his journey from Jerusalem through what is now Iran and Afghanistan to his final destination in Kashmir. These travels themselves are described, and evidence to prove them in the work of Ahmad is given from historical sources divided by faith group, Muslim historical sources, Buddhist historical sources and so forth. The range of sources, ancient and modern, Muslim and other, scholarly and popular, give the work the appearance of wide-ranging research which allows for the incorporation of references to the serious academics of Ahmad's day such as Monier Monier-Williams, a professor of Sanskrit, and Max Müller, a philologist, both based at Oxford University. It also permits, however, the incorporation of some rather less scholarly sources which are mined for material to support the case Ahmad is making or used to show how flawed the reasoning of others writers is.

The Buddhist materials cited in *Jesus in India* for their part serve to highlight assumed similarities between the lives and religious teachings of the Buddha and Jesus, the alleged congruities of which have had a considerable, contested and still continuing history (Ahmad 2016 [1899]:83–106; Hanson 2005; O'Collins[49] 2008; Joseph 2012).[50] In some of this literature, Jesus's lost years are said to have been spent in India learning about Buddhism, and this is what shaped Jesus's ministry after he returned to Jerusalem, thus accounting for the apparent similarities between Christianity and Buddhism. Alternatively, Jesus is said to have learnt about Buddhism from his exposure to the teachings brought by Buddhist missionaries and others who travelled along established trade routes. As Joseph (2012:177–178) notes:

> There are many ways in which Buddhist traditions could have traveled as far west as Palestine. As a missionary religion, Buddhism had been expanding westward for several centuries by the time of Jesus. The East-West trade route commonly known as the 'Silk Road' connected Palestine, India, and China. . . . A number of cities along this route had significant Buddhist populations in the first century CE. Moreover, there was a sea route connecting India and Egypt. Roman coins have also been found in Indian cities. By the first century CE, 'the people of the Roman Empire traveled more extensively and more easily than anyone before them did or would again until the nineteenth century' (Meeks 1983:17). This appears to have been the culmination of a centuries-long, diffusion-based relationship between the Greek West and the East.

The position on the life of Jesus taken by Ghulam Ahmad after much reflection, study and revelation was that Jesus had not made his way to India in his youth, from the age of 13 to 29, before returning to Jerusalem and to his final years of preaching prior to his crucifixion. This meant, for Ahmad, that as Jesus did not travel to India before the crucifixion he could not be accused of 'plagiarising the moral teaching of the Buddha' which some claimed he had learnt in his youth in India (Ahmad 2016 [1899]:86). Nor did Ahmad consider the possibility, as some later writers have, that Jesus may have learnt about Buddhism in Palestine from missionaries, migrants and travellers along the Silk Road. Rather, Ahmad concluded that as some of the lost tribes of Israel[51] had earlier migrated towards India, where some had become Buddhist, this was where the post-crucifixion Jesus headed to fulfil his mission on earth (Ahmad 2016 [1899]:86). It was after Jesus had made his way to the now Buddhist lost tribes of Israel, who accepted him as the messiah, that Ahmad states the facts of Jesus's life were written down and incorporated, anachronistically, into the life story of the Buddha, even though the Buddha had lived centuries before Jesus himself (Ibid.:86–87). In this account, it is the life of Jesus which is assimilated into the life of the Buddha and the notion that Jesus himself was a follower of the Buddha, hence accounting for a life history and teachings that had striking similarities with that of his predecessor, rejected. Much is also made by Ahmad in his *Jesus in India* of the supposed similarities of terms such as 'Metteyya', referring to the Buddha and 'Messiah' for Jesus (Ahmad 2016 [1899]:95). For Ahmad, rather than Buddhism finding it way to Palestine via travellers and hence into the teachings of Jesus, it was Jesus who made his way to 'the rocky soil of Nepal, Tibet, and Kashmir' (Ibid.:99).

In these ways Ahmad reverses the account found in Notovitch's 1890 book of the unknown life of Jesus, which Ahmad certainly knew about as a short outline of Notovitch's work is referenced in an appendix to Ahmad's work on *Jesus in India* (Ahmad 2016 [1899]:129–130).[52] While for Ahmad, Jesus first travelled to India after his crucifixion, for Notovitch, whose work is now generally considered to be a hoax (Hanson 2005:79), the missing years in the life of Jesus were ones he spent in the study of Buddhism in South Asia (Hanson 2005:79; Joseph 2012:162–163).[53]

The details of the journey of a post-crucifixion Jesus, the evidence derived from etymology, the alleged parallels in the life of Jesus and the Buddha and so forth, all served, for Ahmad, one ultimate purpose and goal, to show that Jesus was not divine, that he did not die on the cross and that thus the very foundation on which Christianity was based was untrue. This, together with the revelation Ahmad had received that he himself was the messiah of the age, the servant of God in the spirit of Jesus on earth, allowed him to reveal to his followers that God had:

> watched from on high that man-worship was running rampant the world over, and worship of the cross and the supposed sacrifice of a human being had alienated the hearts of millions of people from the true God. In His indignation, He sent to the world his servant in the spirit of Jesus of Nazareth, to demolish the creed of the cross. And he did come as the Promised Messiah in accordance with the old prophecies. Then at long last came the time for the breaking of the cross, the time when the error of the creed of the cross was to be exposed beyond any doubt quite like a piece of wood torn asunder. Heaven has now thrown open the way for the demolition of the cross, so that the seeker after truth may look around and investigate.
>
> (Ahmad, G. 2016 [1899]:99)

Ghulam Ahmad believed that he was the promised messiah who had come to break the cross of Christianity and so clear the way for the seeker of truth to find the true religion. The breaking of the cross for Ahmad could only happen:

> in the time of the Promised Messiah, [when] God would create conditions which would lay bare the truth about the crucifixion. The creed of the cross

would come to an end and complete its life span, not through war or violence, but exclusively through heavenly causes, in the form of scientific reason and argument.

(Ahmad, G. 2016 [1899]:73–74)

And it is the connection made in Ahmadi thought between revelation and prophecy and 'scientific reason and argument' that explains the presence of exhibitions on the Shroud of Turin which have become a regular and popular feature of recent UK *jalsas*. Science and rational argument are marshalled in the service of a faith Ahmadis consider to be both rational and based on reason.

Notes

1 To celebrate and explain the importance of the khilafat there were many publications, lectures and commemorations around the world, e.g. Ahmad, M. 2008; *Review of Religions* 2008 (February) Khilafat Centenary special edition; *Tariq 2008*. Souvenir Centenary Khilafat – e – Ahmadiyya 1908–2008 issue. This last magazine published in the UK, however, recognizes the particular favour and honour bestowed upon the UK Ahmadis as the khalifa in now based in the UK and thus affords British-based Ahmadis a close and personal connection with the khalifa. The event even made it to the British national press (Taylor 2008).

2 See the Ahmadi press release: 'Khilafat Centenary celebrations continue as UK Member of Parliament hosts celebratory event at Westminster', https://alislam.org/press-release/UK_Parliament_Khilafat_Event.pdf. A recording of the event can be found at www.alislam.org/v/494.html.

  For some YouTube clips of the speeches, see Jack Straw at: www.youtube.com/watch?v=ZGRkKdK037Q and Baroness Warsi at www.youtube.com/watch?v=0oT1w3fiSic&pbjreload=10.

3 A few months earlier, Ghulam Ahmad had announced that he was the *mahdi* awaited by Muslims.

4 Estimates ranged from 30,000 in *The Express*, to 35,000 on an Ahmadi website and 38,000 in a BBC report.

5 The first issue of the *Review of Religions*, in January 1902, aimed to propagate Islam in the West. The second issue was published 'In the Name of His Most Gracious Majesty the King-Emperor of India' and in 'the memory of the auspicious occasion of his majesty's coronation'. It began with 'A proposal for the utter extinction of Jehad' written by Ghulam Ahmad who signed himself 'Chief of Qadian, the Promised Messiah'.

6 www.guildhall.cityoflondon.gov.uk/great-hall.

7 It was fitting that the president of the World Congress of Faiths be invited on this occasion as Sir Francis Younghusband, who played a leading role in establishing the World Congress of Faiths in 1936, had given the opening speech at the 1924 Conference on Living Religions which the Ahmadi khalifa spoke at and which the 2014 Ahmadi Conference of World Religions referred back to (Howard 2017:12, 14). The World Congress of Faiths is the 'oldest international body dedicated to interreligious dialogue' (Howard 2017:24).

8 www.alislam.org/egazette/press-release/historic-conference-of-world-religions-held-at-guildhall-london/.

9 Another significant centenary event was the speech given by the Ahmadi khalifa in the Houses of Parliament on 11 June 2013 and which I also attended. See www.alislam.org/library/updates/address-by-head-of-ahmadiyya-muslim-community-at-houses-of-parliament-london-on-11th-june-2013/ for more details. For one such centenary

celebration at the Morden Mosque itself, see www.alislam.org/press-release/PR-Peace-Symposium-2013.pdf.

10 He arrived in the UK in the summer of 1913 to establish the London Mission on the eve of the First World War (*Maryam* July–September 2013:31). However, the mission itself does not appear to have opened until 1919 (Germain 2008:102).

11 The 1924 conference was referred to in the Conference brochure for attendees and was repeatedly addressed in the weeks that followed for an Ahmadi audience in a Friday sermon (28 February 2014) as well as in the Ahmadi women's online journal, *Maryam* for July–September 2013 and in more detail in the issue of *Maryam* for April–June 2014. It was also discussed in the June 2014 issue of the *Review of Religions*, which included a link to Hare's 1924 article on the conference. The 1924 conference is also covered in the February 2008 khilafat centenary issue of the *Review of Religions*.

12 This was an Ahmadi estimate, is difficult to verify and contested by non-Ahmadis. The report in the *Manchester Guardian* for 24 September 1924, however, notes that the khalifa, when introducing himself before his paper was read, had stated that he had 'a million followers all over the world'. The *Times of India* (6 September 1924) for its part simply states: 'Numerically at least the cult has a small place among the millions of Islam'. The quote on Ahmadi numbers from the khalifa's talk published in Hare (1925:107) reads: 'The members of the Movement number about a million, and comprise men from all nations and all religions. Christians, Sikhs, Hindus, Jews, Zoroastrians, and men belonging to different sects of Islam have joined and continue to join the Movement'.

13 According to the khalifa's Friday sermon on 8 February 2013 on the Companions of the Promised Messiah at www.alislam.org/friday-sermon/2013-02-08.html.

14 However, Shearmur notes that despite being a leading figure of the Lahore Ahmadiyya Movement, Khwaja Kamaluddin had been given a specific brief at the Woking Mosque not to spread Lahori Ahmadi doctrines (2014:165, 170).

15 Howard notes that 'The paper on Shi'ah was read by Sir Thomas Arnold and the one on Sufism was read by Dr. Muhammad Din, a member of the Ahmadiyya delegation' (2017:15, fn19). The Friday sermon given by the Ahmadi khalifa on 28 February 2014 however, states: '[Nayyar Sahib] suggested the name of Hazrat Sufi Roshan Ali Sahib for Sufism but also informed the committee that Sufi Sahib could only attend with the approval of Hazrat Mirza Bashir ud din Mahmood Ahmad, Khalifatul Masih II (may Allah be pleased with him). When these names were presented before the committee, Dr Arnold and others most warmly decided that Hazrat Khalifatul Masih II should be invited to the conference with a request to bring Sufi Sahib with him. Thus an invite was sent to Hazrat Musleh Maud (may Allah be pleased with him) from the leading Orientalists of Britain' (www.alislam.org/friday-sermon/printer-friendly-summary-2014-02-28.html). This strongly implies that the decision over the Sufi paper author for the conference was made once the khalifa had given his permission.

16 Encyclopaedia Iranica, 'Arnold, Sir Thomas Walker, British Orientalist 1864–1930', www.iranicaonline.org/articles/arnold-sir-thomas-walker-british-orientalist-1864-1930.

17 Arnold writes: 'Many Muhammadan preachers have adopted the methods of Christian missionaries, such as street preaching, tract distribution and other agencies. In many . . . cities of India, Muslim preachers may be found daily expounding the teachings of Islam in some principal thoroughfare' (1913:285), and 'much of the missionary zeal of the Indian Musalmans is directed towards counteracting the anti-Islamic tendencies of the instruction given by Christian missionaries and the preachers of the Arya Samāj, and the efforts made are thus defensive rather than directly proselytizing' (1913:286). In Appendix III, Arnold writes of the Muslim missionary societies that have 'formed in conscious imitation of similar organisations in the Christian world' (1913:438) and which first came into existence in the second half of the nineteenth century. None of this relates directly to the Ahmadiyya movement, but it does illustrate

Arnold's understanding of the activities of Muslim proselytizing groups in India in the late nineteenth century, and his descriptions of their activities also cover the practices of the Ahmadis at the time.

18 Iqbal wrote a poem on Arnold and also included a dedication to him in his *Development of Metaphysics in Persia*. The two men were in contact when Iqbal went to study in England. http://aligarhmovement.com/karwaan_e_aligarh/Sir_Thomas_Walker_ Arnold. See also Durrani 1991.

19 The *Manchester Guardian* (24 September 1924), in an article titled 'Prophet of a New Sect at London Conference', states the khalifa's paper ended 'with a perfervid appeal to his audience to accept the new Messiah and the new teaching'.

20 Friday sermon summary, 28 February 2014, www.alislam.org/friday-sermon/2014-02-28.html.

21 During their stay in London, the khalifa and his entourage were based at 6 Chesham Place, Belgravia. Zafrulla Khan arranged the accommodation and also lodged there: 'we were crowded, all arrangements were reduced to the minimum and simplest, but we were a happy and cheerful company' (Khan, Z. 2008:76).

22 Berliner (2005:208, fn 5), for example, asks how anyone can remember something that has 'not been personally experienced by her/him'.

23 www.guildhall.cityoflondon.gov.uk/great-hall.

24 Railton (2003:24–25) provides a brief history 'of how Gog and Magog became the tutelary deities of the city of London' from their appearance in the form of statues in 1415 welcoming Henry V on his return from Agincourt to their connection with the 'myth that London was founded by Greek invaders from Troy'. Statues of Gog and Magog were placed in the Guildhall from 1593. Those carved by Saunders in 1708 were destroyed by bombs during WWII and replaced by new statues carved by David Evans in 1953.

25 Ali (1992:48–49), a Lahori Ahmadi, writes on the identity of Gog and Magog as understood by Mirza Ghulam Ahmad as follows: 'the discovery that . . . Gog and Magog are no other than these nations of Europe, was made by the dweller of a village, a recluse, who had scarcely any knowledge of the world at large. More than half a century ago . . . God enlightened the Mujaddid [Ghulam Ahmad] of this century and granted him the knowledge that . . . Gog and Magog were no other than these very people who were in complete control of the world, and whose worldly eye was extremely sharp and whose spiritual eye equally blind . . . the solitary recluse of Qādiān, the Mujaddid of the 14th century of Hijrah, proclaimed it to the world with a fearlessness all his own'.

26 https://www.alislam.org/friday-sermon/2014-03-07.html

27 Their homepage states: 'Qadianism (Ahmadism) is a pseudo religion whose leadership exploits its members socially, psychologically and financially. The leaders of this group have been able to maintain their hegemony over their ordinary members through treachery, plagiarism, cruel and inhuman discipline. This group aims to steal the identity of Islam by misinterpreting the original sources of Islam. The purpose of this site is to expose the tactics and logical fallacies of this group'. www.khatm-e-nubuwwat.org. Further they describe themselves as:

> an international, religious, preaching and reform organization of Islamic Millat [Millat means a global Islamic nationality irrespective of geographical boundaries]. Its sole aim has been and is to unite all the Muslims of the world to safeguard the sanctity of Prophet hood and the finality of Prophet hood and to refute the repudiators of the belief in the finality of Prophet hood of the Holy Prophet Hazrat Muhammad.
>
> (P-B-U-H)

> By the grace of almighty Allah and under the benefices [*sic*] patronage of Shaikhul Mashaikh Hazrat Moulana Aalmi Majlis Tahaffuz Khatm-e-Nubuwwat's positive

and reformative mode of preaching and service, Qadianees and Lahories quit their previous repudiators and heretic beliefs and embraced Islam both inside Pakistan and aboard [*sic*]. www.khatm-e-nubuwwat.com.

28 The *jalsa salana* in the UK has developed significantly since the arrival of the khalifa in 1984. I was told that the well-run and well-organized *jalsas* I have attended were the outcome of years of gradual improvement and the development of organizational skills within the community. The *jalsa* was held in the small mosque in Southfields in the 1930s but from the mid-1980s the community had outgrown this venue and so the convention was held in Tilford, Surrey, where the Ahmadis have a farm known as 'Islamabad'. By 2006 even this site was too small to accommodate the increasing numbers of attendees and so a larger site in Hampshire was purchased.

29 Arjana (2017:33) acknowledges this latter point.

30 Metcalf cites the book published in 1967 as *Pilgrimage to the House of Allah*, London: London Mosque. I have been unable to locate a copy.

31 Sermon, 2 September 2016. For a transcript see www.alislam.org/friday-sermon/ printer-friendly-summary-2016-09-02.html.

32 Ibid.

33 As I witnessed from inside the VIP tent at *jalsa* in the UK in 2010 when the Ahmadi men present excused themselves to watch the television which was live-streaming the events from the men's *jalsa*.

34 Ahmad, K., n.d.

35 For Marian apparitions alone, see Harris 1999 on the pilgrimage at Lourdes in France which developed following the apparition of the Virgin in 1858 and, for a more recent apparition in 1981 of the Virgin at Medjugorje in Bosnia and Herzegovina, see Bax 1995. Such apparitions are not limited to Western nations as in 1968 the Virgin Mary appeared on the dome of a church in the Cairo neighbourhood of Zaytoun (Hoffman 1997) and more recently in 2009 in Giza Egypt (Heo 2012). Such apparitions are often the impetus for the development of pilgrimages.

36 One newspaper report (Holmes 2018) of the khalifa's arrival in Philadelphia describes him as the Muslim 'pope' to underscore not only his significance as leader of a large religious community but also to make the comparison with the pope's global tours to visit the faithful around the world. http://www2.philly.com/philly/news/ahmadiyya-muslim-philadelphia-mirza-masroor-ahmad-20181018.html.

37 www.mta.tv/jalsaconnect/jalsa-pakistani-millennials.

38 Ibid.

39 This blog, which expresses the self-presentation and idealized views of the connection between the khalifa and the Ahmadi faithful, which some individuals say they experience while others do not, is in accord with Evans's own research on the connection felt between Qadian Ahmadis and the khalifa today when he writes: 'Many people, however, privately told me that the spiritual connection of Qadian's people to the caliph was far weaker than their public displays might have suggested' (2017:495).

40 For a different understanding of how Ahmadi media is used to counter hostility from outsiders as well as to present an 'ideal' of themselves to as exemplary Muslims for themselves, including a discussion of how this is achieved at *jalsa* by stage managing the *jalsa* 'performance' to be recorded; see Evans 2017. The creative use of media to fashion religious 'publics' has been the subject of much research in recent years. Among those who have focused on media and how it has shaped modern Muslim sensibilities, morality, religion, politics and notions of belonging are Hirschkind (2006, 2012); for consideration of media and religion in Islam and other faiths see, for example, Meyer and Moors (2005); and Blank's 2001 study of the Daudi Bohra community from its centre in Mumbai to the Bohra global diaspora provides interesting parallels with the Ahmadis on how modern information technology is used for both organizational and religious ends.

41 In 'Lajna Imaillah's Jalsa History' blog: www.mta.tv/jalsaconnect/lajna-imaillahs-jalsa-history.

42 Nowadays the *jalsa* is such a large-scale event that all attendees are required to register online before the event and to present ID on arrival. The ID for British-based Ahmadis is the AIMS (Ahmaddiya Information Management System) card, and for visitors a duly completed invitation signed by the member of the *jama'at* who invited the visitor. For Ahmadi's from Pakistan where AIMs cards are not issued to members of the *jama'at* the relevant ID *jalsa* entry document is issued in Pakistan only after they have obtained a visa to enter the UK. After obtaining a British visa, Pakistani Ahmadis are 'issued an introductory letter from Wakalat Tabshir [religious department] Rabwah, Pakistan. This will enable them to obtain entry into the premises of Jalsa Salana UK' (Jalsa Salana UK Programme 2018:7). In 2018 the Jalsa programme specified that as well as the introductory letter from the Wakalat Tabshir Rabwah members would also need to bring along their passports.

43 The act of seeking forgiveness from Allah.

44 See January 2018 *Review of Religions*, which includes photographs of some objects on display at the UK *Jalsa* in 2017 in the article 'Islamic Calligraphy: The Art of Devotion'. This collection, or at least a part of it, has been a feature of the *Review of Religions* exhibition at *jalsa* since 2015. A selection of photographs of the *jalsa* exhibition can be found at www.rorexhibition.org/the-art-of-devotion.html. The collection also formed the contribution on Islamic calligraphy at the London book fair in April 2018 (*Review of Religions*, July 2018:50–61).

45 The 27-minute talk 'A Grave Injustice' from the Shroud of Turin Research Project group about the carbon-14 test on the Shroud of Turin was uploaded on 19 March 2016: www.youtube.com/watch?v=DwY74QcWaOM. Just beyond 23 minutes into the film, Barry Schwortz is described as the 'official recognized chronicler of the Turin Shroud' as he is introduced by the Ahmadi national president at the 2015 Ahmadi UK *jalsa*. The voiceover at this point announces that the Ahmadi Shroud of Turin event at *jalsa* was the biggest Shroud of Turin event ever held outside Turin.

46 Many Muslims believe that Jesus did not die on the cross but rather was lifted to heaven bodily and is awaiting his return to earth before the end of time. To account for the historical narratives of crucifixion, some Muslims believe that Jesus was raised to heaven by God and a being made to look like Jesus was crucified in his place. Some modern Muslim scholars share with the Ahmadis the 'swoon' theory but do not then also consider that Jesus walked to India to live out the rest of his days there. The one point on which most Muslims agree is that death by crucifixion was an ignoble way to die and that as Jesus is a prophet of God he could not have died in such a fashion. As Friedmann notes (1989:111–112):

The idea that Jesus was raised alive to heaven – after an attempt to kill him on the cross was foiled by Allah – had existed in the Islamic tradition since the earliest period…

The idea that Jesus has been alive in heaven since his mission on earth came to a close is consistent with the role he is expected to perform at the end of days. According to the classical *ḥadīth*, he will then descend to earth. Some traditions say that he will participate in the eschatological struggle against the anti-Christ (*al-dajjāl*), and by killing him will pave the way for the establishment of the kingdom of justice on earth. One saying maintains that he himself will be the messiah: "The *mahdī* is none else than 'Isā" (lā al-mahdī illā 'Isa).

47 This was first published posthumously in Urdu as *Masīh Hindustān Mein* in 1908 but had been previously partly serialized in the *Review of Religions* in 1902 and 1903 (*Jesus in India* 2016: publisher's note v).

48 In fact, the Hindi for 'head' is the word *sīr* (सरि in devanagri), and śri is an honorific term used as a polite form of address (or part of such) for women, men and deities (often translated as Ms/Mrs, Mr etc.). Monier-Williams Sanskrit-English Dictionary,

1899 notes that śri in Sanskrit (शरी) has roots that link it to terms that include spreading or diffusing light, radiance or beauty as well as to honour or worship. Another possible root for Srinagar is derived from Sanskrit, *Sūrya-nagar*, meaning 'city of the sun'.

49 O'Collins, a Jesuit priest and professor in theology (2008:711) writes: 'Back in 1894 Nicolas Notovitch through *The Unknown Life of Jesus Christ* created the first part of Jesus' "Indian connection": he alleged that Jesus spent some pre-ministry years in India. The second half of the legend was added by Mirza Ghulam Ahmad in an 1899 book in Urdu. According to him Jesus was saved from the cross, went to Kashmir and eventually died there at the age of 120 years in Srinagar. The entire Indian connection was created, without a shred of evidence, by these two authors'. This is in response to and as a critique of a television programme, the *Hidden Story of Jesus* by Robert Beckford, shown on Channel 4 on Christmas Day in the UK in 2007 and which O'Collins dismisses as based on a lack of evidence and poor scholarship.

50 There has been a recent resurgence of the New Age movement's interest in the possibility that Jesus spent time in India. Such interest has also been championed by leaders of new religious movements such as Elizabeth Clare Prophet, founder of the Church Universal and Triumphant (Joseph 2012:180–183).

51 Ahmad then provides what he deems to be evidence 'so strong and incontrovertible that even a dullard will not deny it' that 'people like the Afghans and the old inhabitants of Kashmir are in fact of Israelite origin' (107–108). In addition to references taken from travellers' tales, gazetteers, histories ranging from those of Josephus to St. Jerome to some of Ahmad's contemporaries and from encyclopedias, much of the evidence rests on names which bear a resemblance to terms which might suggest a Jewish origin or the physical features and dress of the people or apparent kinship practices shared between Afghans and Jews, such as the levirate.

52 Piovanelli (2005:35–36) also claims that there is evidence that the 'Ahmadiya' made use of the apocryphal *Aquarian Gospel* by the nineteenth-century American Presbyterian pastor, Levi H. Dowling, who transcribed in his work 'the "authentic" memoirs of Christ', which he received from 'Visel, the goddess of Wisdom', who appeared to him four times during his life. This gospel includes material on 'the initiatory journey that Jesus made in India, Tibet, Persia, Greece, and Egypt' but, as it was published in 1908, the year of Ghulam Ahmad's death, it is unlikely that Ahmad himself could have made use of this. It does, however, suggest that the idea of Jesus's journeying to South Asia was one that had a certain vogue at the time and was due, in part, to the popularity of Madame Blavatsky's theosophy.

53 Joseph (2012:163) states: 'Notovitch was not the first European to claim that Jesus had lived in India'. Earlier claims along these lines had been proposed by Louis Jacollist, a judge, in 1868, and by Joannes Maria Laouenan, a church official in Pondicherry, in 1884. As with Blavatsky, who 'promoted the study of comparative religion in an effort to undermine Christianity' (ibid.:180), so Notovitch promoted a clearly anti-Catholic stance when he has the Lama in the monastery he visited state: 'Buddha, indeed, has incarnated himself, with his divine nature, in the person of the sacred Issa, who, without employing fire or iron, has gone forth to propagate our true and great religion among all the world. Him whom I meant was your terrestrial Dalai-Lama; he to whom you have given the title of "Father of the Church." That is a great sin. May he be brought back, with the flock, who are now in a bad road, piously added the lama', to which Notovitch adds, 'I understood now that he alluded to the Pope' (1887:15).

3 Enchantment and the ethic of brotherhood

Dreams and the charismatic organization

Rationalization in the service of enchantment

The enchantment of the world which Max Weber's work in the early years of the twentieth century depicted as receding before an ever more rationalized and bureaucratized public life has, in fact, never quite disappeared, and in many parts of the world today it maintains an often respected and respectable place in the public domain (Jenkins 2000; Pierucci 2000; Weber 2011). Over recent decades, public religiosities have emerged across the globe, demonstrating clearly, if such were necessary, that religion and modernity are quite compatible (Deeb 2006:4; Pierucci 2000:131), and that modern manifestations of public piety enable believers to express their faith in ways that may seem, at first glance, to be at odds with the values of the modern, the secular and the rational (Luhrmann 2012; Mahmood 2005). This chapter draws on the insights from this literature to consider experiences and understandings of enchantment, and how it may be contained and ordered within modern institutional structures, by detailing the case of Ahmadiyya Islam over the last century.

Weber understood the idea of disenchantment both as an internal process within religion and also as a way of describing the fate of religion in the modern world. *Entzauberung*, the German word translated as 'disenchantment', literally means 'de-magification', and refers in the former context to the move away from magical and ritual engagement with the given world to a focus on the transcendent and otherworldly, a process Weber sees as starting as early as the time of the prophets of ancient Judaism and finding its clearest Western articulation in Calvinism (Kalberg 1980:1146, fn2; Pierucci 2000:136).[1] This description could be applied to Ahmadiyya Islam, though given its debt to Sufi traditions, it is perhaps as close to 'Catholic' Islam as to its more 'Protestant' forms. But for this chapter I use enchantment in its broader meaning as the:

> understandings and experiences of the world in which there is more to life than the material, the visible or the explainable; in which the philosophies and principles of reason or rationality cannot by definition dream the totality of life; in which the quotidian norms and routines of linear time and space are only part of the story; and in which the collective sum of sociability and belonging is elusively greater than its individual parts.
>
> (Jenkins 2000:29)

The Ahmadiyya case in particular is interesting as one where the drive to institutionalize and develop rational bureaucratic systems along lines most commonly found in secular organizations was already taking shape in the first decades of the twentieth century in colonial India. These systems were thus examples of modern rational bureaucracies – albeit at this stage small scale and often more aspirational than actualized – in the service of enchantment. This was, moreover, happening at the very time Weber (2011:120) was writing of the *Entzauberung der Welt* (disenchantment of the world), which he theorized would result as a consequence, among other things, of the drive to efficiency and rationalization manifested most clearly in the modern professional bureaucracies which trained and employed rule-following administrators to become proficient in the ordering, organization and systematic recording of myriad and ever-increasing aspects of daily life (Weber in Kalberg 2005:194ff). However, the institutional systems of recording membership, collecting dues, filling offices and so on was not, for the Ahmadis, a means by which to resign themselves to a new disenchanted modern world but rather the way through which the knowledge and experiences of enchantment could be shared, harnessed and brought to bear on the wider international and ultimately global community. In short, the organizational structure of Ahmadiyyat established within just a few years of the death of its founder became a modern, replicable, standardized container for, and transmitter of, forms of legitimate enchantment. As part of this the Ahmadi faithful were required regularly to attend meetings and events organized by their duly elected and appointed presidents and committee leaders. Here they would learn about Islam, the history of Ahmadiyyat, the correct ways to pray, how to interpret religious texts, and be expected to pass examinations set by the *jama'at* to test religious knowledge and understanding. In other words, members of the *jama'at* would learn how to become Ahmadi through an organizational structure which was modern, literate and bureaucratic and in which religious progress was, in part at least, assessed by examination results.

One part of the religious instruction for Ahmadis included the study of prophecy, the place of dreams in Islam and how to recognize and interpret the true dreams granted to the faithful. Through study, prayer and shared practices and experiences of true dreams, for example, the institutional structures of the Ahmadi *jama'at* nurtured and prepared the faithful to recognize occurrences of the divine and the transcendent in the everyday lives of believers. It is almost as though the Ahmadis had taken Weber's ideas on disenchantment to heart and, while accepting the rational calculability of the world that this resulted in, had refused the conclusion that the world was therefore meaningless and that henceforth, in a disenchanted world, the need for a divine creator was no longer necessary to explain the order of things. The enchanted world that Weber's sociology had consigned to history was one in which:

People used to see themselves as part of a larger order. In some cases, this was a cosmic order, a 'great chain of Being', in which humans figured in their proper place along with angels, heavenly bodies, and our fellow earthly creatures. This hierarchical order in the universe was reflected in the hierarchies of human society. . . . But at the same time as they restricted us, these orders gave meaning to the world and to the activities of social life.

(Taylor in Bennett 2001:59)

This was the world the Ahmadis wished to preserve and thus it was precisely Weber's vision of a disenchanted future which they rejected by, paradoxically, harnessing the structures and forms of modern organizations. This process was started by the promised messiah and consolidated by the second Ahmadi khalifa who was responsible for setting the Ahmadi *jama'at* on modern institutional lines and thus of understanding that his father's legacy could best be secured by the 'routinization of charisma' (Weber in Kalberg 2005:217ff).[2] Such routinization was necessary, as the charisma of the Ahmadi founder, which followers are able to recognize but which like all charisma is ephemeral and 'inherently transitional', rarely survives beyond the death of the charismatic leader unless it is routinized in institutional form. The paradox of charisma is that it has to change in order to survive but that in this process some of its charismatic force is necessarily diminished (Toth 1972:1). Toth notes that for the 'successful transition of collective behavior into institutionalized or quasi-institutionalized social movements', not one but two leaders, for example, Jesus and Peter, or Joseph Smith and Brigham Young, are often required (Toth 1972:1).

These two leadership roles seem to appear in both conjunction and succession, the first demonstrating 'charisma of the outer call', the second 'charisma of an inner consolidation'. It is this second leader who is able to turn the corner from charisma to routine, accomplishing it under the aegis of the more unearthly charisma of the first leader.

(Toth 1972:1)

Although Ghulam Ahmad himself created the Ahmadi *anjuman* (council) and set some of the administrative organization up, for the Ahmadis it was their second khalifa, who can be said to have taken the 'enthusiasm' of his father and complemented it with the skills of the bureaucrat to build an institution that could ensure the long-term survival of his father's vision and legacy. In other words:

what distinguishes the two leaders is not so much a difference of charisma as the direction in which their leadership efforts express their thrust and focus; the first leader is strange, fascinating, unusual, unearthly, the second is more conventional, mundane, practical; the first leader brings the elect together, the second creates an organization to contain them; the first leader is inspired by a vision, the second elaborates that vision into a plan.

(Toth 1972:2)

The routinization of charisma serves the purpose of enabling the vision of the founder charismatic leader to perdure, it is the means by which charisma:

is captured in the form of a promise unfulfilled, a gesture uncompleted, a journey of destination without arrival; it is in this way that what is yet unfinished is frozen in time, the atemporal temporalized, the sacred and exclusive transformed into something to be shared by all.

(Toth 1972:3)

For the Ahmadis, this routinization of charisma was established through an organizational framework that included constitutions, elected and nominated offices, and a clear hierarchy with directives issued by, and oversight of, the organization by higher levels of the Ahmadiyya *jama'at*. At the apex was the khalifa who retained the power to overturn decisions, including the results of elections which may thus be viewed more as recommendations for his consideration, at any level in the organization. Bureaucratic restrictions and rules which had to be followed by members of the *jama'at* did not apply to the charismatic leader himself.

I begin this chapter by examining the ways in which some Ahmadis today may use dreams as one means for maintaining a sense of enchantment in their daily lives.[3] Dreams provide these Ahmadis with the experience of divine care and guidance as a continuous presence and resource in the midst of their everyday routines. Oneiric interpretation has a very long tradition in Islam, but it has been given renewed vitality in Ahmadiyya Islam because of the central role played by prophetic dreams in the life of Ghulam Ahmad and his claims to be the *mahdi* and messiah. These prophetic dreams are, however, very different to the quotidian dreams of ordinary Ahmadis: they arise out of and also confirm the charisma of the singular spiritual leader and founder. By contrast, one dream of the fourth khalifa was, in this respect, somewhat differently interpreted and situated. He interpreted his dream as being outwardly directed towards the community of the faithful, towards in fact the channeling of the enchantment of faith into the safe repository of institutional organization in the form of an expanding bureaucracy and the establishment of a new Ahmadi institution, the *waqf-e-nau*, or new endowment/devotion, when children are pledged at birth to the *jama'at* to devote their lives to the service of Ahmadiyya Islam.

Weber proposed that 'the need for "salvation" responds to [the] devaluation' that is a consequence of the disenchantment of the world 'by becoming more other-worldly, more alienated from all structural forms of life and, in exact parallel, by confining itself to the specific religious essence'. Weber adds that 'the very attempt of religious ethics practically and ethically to rationalize the world', and 'not only theoretical thought, which disenchanted the world', leads to 'this course' (Weber in Kalberg ed. 2005:343).

> The specific intellectual and mystical attempts at salvation in the face of these tensions succumb in the end to the world dominion of unbrotherliness. On the one hand, the charisma of these attempts is not accessible to everybody. Hence, in intent, mystical salvation definitely means aristocracy; it is an aristocratic religiosity of redemption. And, in the midst of a culture that is rationally organized for a vocational workaday life, there is hardly any room for the cultivation of a cosmic brotherliness, unless it is among strata that are economically carefree. Under the technical and social conditions of [modern]

rational culture, an imitation of the life of Buddha, Jesus, or Francis seems condemned to failure for purely external reasons.

(Kalberg 2005:343)

In the ethnographic material that follows I suggest that the continued vitality of the Ahmadis as a community of faith puts into question Weber's broad conclusions about the fate of religion in the modern world (though Weber did not, of course, deny the existence of exceptions to the general development he proposed). The aristocracy of the khalifat may not be in doubt, especially of its first charismatic leader, but for the Ahmadis it is, perhaps paradoxically, precisely 'a culture that is rationally organized for a vocational workaday life' that allows for room for the 'cultivation of a cosmic brotherhood' that stretches across both nation and the global diaspora. The ethic of brotherhood, along with compassion, charity and a unified sense of self, was one of the major casualties for Weber of the process of rationalization. These values had retreated at best into the private realm 'owing to a weakening of the salvation doctrines of religious world views and their carrier strata and organizations' (Kalberg 2005:29; see also Weber in Kalberg 2005:321–327). But these are the very values that the Ahmadis strive to sustain through the creation of efficient bureaucratic organizations that in fact connect their 'workaday lives' to the prophetic charisma of Ghulam Ahmad and so to the renewal of faith he promised and initiated.

Ahmadi Muslims and the dream in Islam

For many Muslims today, and certainly for Ahmadi Muslims, access to the divine is one that those who are sufficiently devout and pious can directly experience in this life. Such experiences come in the form of true dreams which allow Muslims to be granted knowledge to help them make important decisions for themselves and for family members or alternatively, to prepare for events that are destined to happen and which cannot be altered (Amanullah 2009; Aydar 2009). In what follows, I consider some of the dreams of London-based Ahmadis which were recounted to me, supplemented with printed material from Ahmadi sources, both historical and contemporary on dreams and also the ready availability of material on Ahmadi websites. However, before outlining the importance of dreams for Ahmadi Muslims, it is necessary to provide a brief overview of the theological understanding of dreams in Islam.

Dream revelation can be said to be at the very origins of Islam, as it is said that the Prophet's first knowledge of the Qur'an came in dreams, and he himself is reported to have been a competent dream interpreter for his companions. The text of the Qur'an itself includes dream material, much of which is also found in the Old Testament, and the Prophet is said to have reassured his followers that after his death an attenuated form of prophecy would remain in the form of 'good dreams'. This is most frequently stated in a *hadith* which reads 'the good dream is 1/46 of prophecy'.[4] The interpretation of true dreams is a form of divination and offers a 'form of access to God that was unmediated, thus circumventing the vaunted institutions of Koran and Sunnah' (Lamoreaux 2002:4).[5] In the centuries that followed the death of the Prophet, the science of dream interpretation became well-established across the Muslim world, with more or less congruent classifications for categories of dreams, only some of which are worthy of interpretation and of divine origin.[6] The classification of dreams in Islam falls into three categories: true dreams which come from God; false ones from the devil; and confused ones that arise from the physiology and psychology of the individual. The latter two are not worthy of interpretation and indeed, dreams from the devil should be dealt with through apotropaic means, including prayer and the refusal to recount such a dream, lest the telling of it should make it come into being (Bausani 1985; Hoffman 1997:47).

Many manuals of dream interpretation were produced by Muslims and many of these bore the name of Ibn Sirin, although it is highly unlikely that Ibn Sirin ever actually wrote a dream interpretation manual himself (Lamoreaux 2002: 23–24). The central place of dreams and dream interpretation in Islam is revealed by Lamoreaux:

> The large number of early dream manuals should not be lightly glossed over. It offers a superficial if telling indication of the importance of dream interpretation to Muslims of the early Middle Ages. Indeed, to judge from number alone, one would have to conclude that the interpretation of dreams was as important to these Muslims as the interpretation of the Koran. Some sixty dream manuals were composed during the first four and a half centuries of the Muslim era. During that same period, very nearly exactly the same number of Koranic commentaries were composed. In short, early Muslims composed as many commentaries on their dreams as they did on their Koran.
>
> (Lamoreaux 2002:3–4)

The importance of dreams is reinforced, for example, in the work of Kinberg (1993), who outlines the parallels between the good dreams of Muslims and the prophetic *hadiths* as forms of legitimation with functionally equivalent authority to judge between different law schools, decide on courses of action to follow at both personal and community levels and so forth.[7] The significance of dreams continues in the modern era with a profusion of dream interpretation manuals in Muslim countries, and even, in Pakistan, the publication of a text in 1979 with the title *Biography of the Prophet after the Death of the Prophet*, which covers 'the continuous and important sighting of the Prophet in dreams as reported in Islamic religious and biographical literature until the present time' (M. 'Abd al-Majid Siddiqi 1979 in Hermansen 2001:87). It is a widespread belief reported to me by several Ahmadis and also found in the literature (Heijnen and Edgar 2010:222; Amanullah 2009:104), that if the Prophet appears whole (i.e. you can see him from head to toe) in your dream and the message of the dream is in accord with the teachings of Islam, then it is a true dream and this is a means by which the Prophet, who is no longer among the living, can still offer guidance to the pious and devout.

Contemporary social scientists continue to explore the relevance and place of dreams and visions in Muslim life across the world,[8] and it is clear from these studies that while the scientific rational world of modernity exists, so too, for some Muslims, does another realm, which may be reached through religious practice[9] and through *istikhara* (lit. 'seeking the best'), a dream incubation ritual. By accessing this other realm, individuals can gain spiritual guidance in their lives. *Istikhara* rituals are known throughout the Muslim world and are practiced by individuals who seek divine guidance on important matters, such as whether or not to accept a marriage proposal (Rahimian 2009; Aydar 2009; Edgar 2010; Mittermaier 2010:96–100). For some Ahmadis, I was told, such prayers are about peace of mind when making an important life decision. Even children are taught how to perform *istikhara* prayers, as an Ahmadi children's religious curriculum textbook makes clear:

> When a serious and important matter is pending, it is recommended that after the *Ishaa'* Prayer [evening prayer] and just before retiring, two *raka'aat* [series of postures which starts from standing and ends with prostration] of voluntary Prayer should be said, to seek guidance and blessings from Allah. The following supplication should be made during these two *raka'aat*:

> O Allah! I seek good from You out of Your knowledge and seek power from You out of Your power, and beg of You out of your boundless Grace, for You have power and I have no power; and You have knowledge and I have no Knowledge; and you have the best knowledge of all Unseen.
>
> O Allah! If it be within Your knowledge that this project is to my good in the matter of spiritual affairs, and in respect of my ultimate end, then make it possible for me and grant me facility concerning it; and bless it for me, but if it be within Your knowledge that this project is harmful in my spiritual and worldly affairs, and in respect of my ultimate end, then cause it to move away from me and cause me to move away from it, and designate for me good, wherever [*sic*] it may be, and then make me pleased with it.
>
> (Hadi 1997:185; cf. Aydar 2009:126–127)

In addition to having a shared understanding of how to perform *istikhara* prayers and the circumstances in which prayers seeking divine guidance are justified, my interlocutors also explained that dreams received at different points during the night were to be evaluated differently. Those that a dreamer had early in the night were considered less significant than those received just before dawn.[10] And for the *istikhara* prayers to work, the person hoping to receive divine guidance had to sleep on her or his right side. One interlocutor told me that after reciting the *istikhara* prayers in a ritually pure condition, a person could expect to receive a true dream, or perhaps even signs in waking life in the days after the *istikhara* prayer, or within 10 days and within 40 days at most. For Ahmadis, it was best if the *istikhara* prayers could be said by the person seeking guidance, or alternatively the person could ask a trusted and devout member of the community to pray on her or his behalf. It is also generally accepted among Ahmadis that the more pious a person is, the more likely the person is to receive a true dream. However, one interlocutor told me that if a person has something on their mind and might be leaning towards one particular resolution to the matter in question, it might be better for them to get another person to do the *istikhara* prayers and receive a dream with guidance. This was to avoid any possible bias in the outcome, though it was not clear to me if the bias was in the dream itself or in how it might be narrated and then interpreted.

It should be apparent that while dreams are experienced by particular individuals, their narration and the interpretation of the dreams is a culturally shared practice. We cannot share or see the dream a person has, but we can interpret dream narratives and may do so according to a long Muslim tradition of dream interpretation that is legitimated by the Prophet Muhammad's own dream interpretation practices.

Given the outline of the dream and its central place in Islam, it is not surprising to note the significance of dreams and their interpretation in the life and work of the founder of Ahmadi Islam. Indeed, a key source for the study of dreams in Ahmadi Islam is to be found in the *Tadhkirah* (Memoirs) of Ghulam Ahmad published in English in 1976 with the subtitle *English rendering of the dreams, visions and verbal revelations vouchsafed to Hazrat Mirza Ghulam Ahmad, the promised messiah and mahdi (on whom be peace)*. This text, which is found in many Ahmadi homes, is a chronological listing of all the dreams, visions and revelations of Ghulam Ahmad gathered from his published writings. The material covered spans a period of over 30 years in his life, starting with accounts of his dreams in early youth and then more systematically from the dreams, visions and revelations dating from 1870 to 1908 (the year of his death). Although the dreams are ordered chronologically, they are drawn from books, pamphlets, journals and newspapers that often recount dreams experienced sometimes years prior to their initial publication.

The dreams are of several different kinds. There are some that are closely linked to the politics and religious battles of the time in which Ghulam Ahmad lived and recount his dreams and prophecies of victories over his enemies or of the kindness of God in ensuring that his troubles, legal, financial and otherwise, would soon be resolved in his favour. Some dreams are of a more personal nature and provide Ghulam Ahmad with foreknowledge of the death of a person, or of the means by which someone may be cured of a disease that doctors have been unable to treat, or of the turning against him of a follower. Other dreams attest to the spiritual authority and special purpose Ghulam Ahmad has in this life, his duty to revive Islam and reveal to the world the true path to salvation.

In terms of narrative strategy and authentication, a common approach of Ghulam Ahmad's is to state that he had a dream or vision that something was soon to happen and that he announced this to a local 'Arya'[11] who, as a Hindu revivalist and an opponent of Islam, would have no reason to vouch for the truth of the dream if it were not so. For example, Ghulam Ahmad writes:

> Pandit Shiv Narayan, a distinguished Brahmo Samaj scholar, wrote to me from Lahore that he intended to write a refutation of part III of *Braheen Ahmadiyya* [a book by Ghulam Ahmad]. The letter had not yet reached me when God Almighty disclosed its purport to me in a vision. I related this to several Hindus and at the time of the delivery of the mail a Hindu Arya was sent to the post office so that he might serve as a witness. He brought the letter from the post office. I wrote to Pandit Shiv Narayan in reply: You desire to refute the possibility of revelation, yet God Almighty informed me through revelation of your letter and its content. If you doubt this you can come to Qadian and verify it, for your Hindu brethren are its witnesses.
>
> (Ahmad, G. 1976:40)

In other dreams, Ghulam Ahmad refers to his foreknowledge that some of his followers will desert him and in his discussion of such revelations, he appears to make reference to cultural practices which can be understood in relation to both Sufi practices and those of the majority Hindu population among which he lived in colonial India. For example:

> There was a gentleman in Ludhiana of the name of Mir Abbas Ali who had entered into the covenant of *Bai'ah* [initiation] with me. He made such good progress within a few years that his then condition was disclosed to me in a revelation (Arabic): Its roots are firm and its branches spread into heaven; which meant that at that time he was a sincere believer and all the indications supported this. . . . If he discovered a dry piece of bread as my left over he would eat it as something full of blessings. . . . At one time it was disclosed to me in a vision that Abbas Ali would stumble and draw away from me. . . . When the time came that I put forward my claim of being the Promised Messiah he took it ill and for some time did not disclose his uneasiness. Thereafter during the debate with Maulvi Muhammad Husain in Ludhiana concerning my claim he had the opportunity of associating with my opponents and then my vision concerning him became manifest and he turned against me openly.
>
> (Ahmad, G. 1976:38)

Events are recounted to show how over time dreams, visions and revelations are manifested. They are sent by God in order to prepare Ghulam Ahmad for what is to come. One interesting point in this description of the relationship between Mir Abbas Ali and Ghulam Ahmad is in the eating of the leftover bread by Mir Abbas Ali as matter full of blessings. Such a practice resonates with Sufi customs and the consumption of *tabarruk* (blessed food),[12] as well as being a commonly understood and respectful practice among Hindus for whom the *prasad* offered in temples to worshippers is explicitly understood as the leavings of the gods and is filled with their blessings. It may be that in some respects the actions of Mir Abbas

Ali always hinted at his future disavowal of Ahmadiyya Islam and that even in his most devoted period, his behaviour was such as to raise the suspicions of those who might have the capacity to understand what it truly meant. It may, however, simply be a way of recording the honour in which Ghulam Ahmad was held by paralleling the behaviour of Mir Abbas Ali with that of Umar, the close companion of the Prophet who later became the second successor (*khalifa*) to Muhammad. Umar's preservation of knowledge and religion is sometimes symbolized in the Prophet's dreams when Umar drinks the milk left by the Prophet (Hermansen 2001:75). Here the analogy would be the Prophet Muhammad and Umar with Ghulam Ahmad and Mir Abbas Ali, though this is not a perfect analogy, as Umar remained faithful while Mir Abbas Ali did not.

Throughout the *Tadhkirah*, there are many examples of dreams, visions and revelations which directly associate Ghulam Ahmad with the prophets of Islam. This is a motif that serves to legitimate the position of Ghulam Ahmad and to authorize his claims to be the promised messiah and all of this within acceptable bounds, as it is generally acknowledged and accepted within Islam that true dreams are sent by God and that if the prophet Muhammad appears in such dreams it is as if he were present in actual form, for the devil cannot take the form of the Prophet (Krenkow 1912:77).

Nonetheless, a true dream is not something that can be taken for granted and not all people receive such dreams. Only the deserving and the pious are rewarded with the divine gift of such a dream and the more one becomes spiritually developed, the more likely one is to receive such dreams as a blessing from the divine. Lamoreaux (2002:57), referring to the work of Qayrawani (fl. early fifth century AH) cites the Qur'anic verse generally taken to refer to the granting of prophetic dreams as follows: 'Those who believe and are pious have glad tidings (*al-bushra*) in this world and the next' (Q 10.63–10.64).

In this respect, the dream that opens the *Tadhkirah* is telling, as this dream vision is recounted as one that Ghulam Ahmad received in his 'early youth', and it is one in which he is led into the presence of the Holy Prophet and is given fruit dripping with honey, which is used to revive a corpse. This corpse is interpreted by Ghulam Ahmad as symbolizing Islam and he goes on to say:

> Allah, the Exalted, would revive it [Islam] at my hands through the spiritual power of the Holy Prophet (on whom be peace). . . . In this dream the Holy Prophet (on whom be peace) nurtured me with his blessed hands through his holy words and his light and the gift of fruit from his blessed garden.
>
> (Ahmad 1976:1–2)

Here Ghulam Ahmad is given, in his youth, a dream vision of his destiny. The very fact of receiving such a dream when young is significant and the mission with which he is entrusted even more so.

While not all Ahmadis can expect to receive true dreams of the import and quantity of the founder of Ahmadi Islam, and not all expect them, certainly not while still young, many Ahmadis do take their dreams seriously, and many homes

I have visited have a copy of the *Interpretation of Dreams* by Imam Muhammad Bin Sirin in their possession.[13] A significant point to note about these manuals for dream interpretation is that they are translated and published by the Ahmadi community itself. This text is their own interpretation of the interpretations of dreams attributed to Ibn Sirin. As such, the text incorporates Ahmadi events, in particular the dreams of Ghulam Ahmad himself, into the text of Ibn Sirin. In the Ahmadi edition of the *Interpretation of Dreams*, the introduction, preface and short chapter, 'The Wonders of Dreams', integrates Ahmadi writers and translators into a text that is thought to have its origins in medieval Islamic thought.[14] While such practices have a long precedent in Muslim traditions and serve not only to show respect for the wisdom of earlier ages and to avoid the sin of *bid'a* (innovation), they also serve to project Ahmadi Islam back in time to a period several centuries before it came into existence and to assert that Ahmadi Muslims are continuing with the beliefs and practices of the Muslims of earlier times, not adding anything new and unwarranted. Such a position has political and not simply theological implications for the Ahmadi Muslim community today.

It is through dreams that ordinary members of Ahmadi Islam may come to a personal and unquestioned belief in life beyond this mortal one and also come to believe in divine predestination, aspects of which they may have a fleeting glimpse through their own dreams. In dreams, they may see or converse with deceased members of the family or receive a divine message to guide them when making important decisions in their lives.

While not everyone is fortunate enough to receive true dreams, and while some Ahmadis do not pay particular attention to dreams, there are some important moments in life when even the less devout may seek guidance through *istikhara* prayers. A key life cycle ritual when such true dreams seem to be particularly sought after is at the time of marriage, and many of the dreams I was told had to do with decisions about whether or not to accept marriage proposals or what kind of married life the couple could expect to share.[15] In what follows I set out a range of dreams and how they were interpreted at the time of the dream itself and, in some cases, also how they were reinterpreted years later. That dreams can be given one meaning at the time they are experienced and then revised in the light of events that may take place years later attests not to the arbitrary nature of the dream and its interpretation but rather to the belief held by individuals that the dreams are true but that people are not always able immediately to decipher them fully. The dreams, so long as they are not the result of physiological or satanic causes, thus remain true, it is the human interpretation of them that is limited and fallible.

One woman told me that her sister and her sister's in-laws were not particularly devout but that when a proposal for the marriage of the sister's daughter came along the family decided to ask a pious elder in the community to pray for them and ask for guidance on whether or not to accept the marriage. Following the *istikhara* prayer, the dream the pious elder received suggested that the marriage would not be a good one and so, despite the fact that both bride and groom were happy with the proposal, the marriage did not go ahead. Of course, as this marriage never took place, it is impossible to know if it would have been a successful union. This example suggests very strongly that even those who are not and do not consider themselves to be particularly devout may nonetheless put great store in the power of true dreams granted to devout persons when it comes to making important decisions.

Yet, in some cases, even when a less than ideal dream about a marriage is received following *istikhara* prayers the marriage may yet take place and in these cases pragmatic kinship considerations may outweigh a less than positive dream. Such was the case of a man who told me that when he was asked to consider his own marriage to a cousin, he prayed and received a dream which he asked his mother to interpret for him. In the dream the young man found himself at a well, and it took him a long time and great effort to get to the water at the bottom of the well. His mother interpreted the dream to mean it would take time, effort and patience to attain happiness in the marriage, symbolized by the water at the bottom of a deep well. The man wryly noted that both the dream and his mother's interpretation of it had turned out to be true and, several years after the marriage took place, he was still struggling to get to the water.

In yet another case, *istikhara* prayers and the dream that followed were used to justify and explain why a wedding was called off within days of when the ceremony was due to take place. In this instance, a young British Ahmadi woman had, in her own account of the incident, agreed to a marriage with her Pakistani cousin who was moving to the UK to be with his soon-to-be wife. The wedding date was set, invitations were sent out, the wedding hall was booked, the wedding clothes were ready and all the preparations had been made. With just a few days to go before the marriage, the woman decided that she could not go through with the wedding. At first her sisters, mother and father put this down to bridal nerves, but they soon realized that the woman was not going to budge from her decision. The repercussions for the family, more related to inter-family relations and reputation than to the financial loss that was by this stage inevitable, were unavoidable but were mitigated and to some degree accepted, when a senior and well-respected member of the family announced that following *istikhara* prayers she had received a dream which made it clear that this marriage should not go ahead. Here, no matter what some people may privately have thought, the authority accorded to true dreams was sufficient to provide a legitimate and to some extent face-saving way out of a marriage that the bride no longer wished to be part of.

And sometimes a dream following *istikhara* prayers may only make full sense to the dreamer some years after the dream itself. One woman told me of a dream before her own marriage which she had after *istikhara* prayers. In this dream, she found herself in a lush green park in the centre of which was a large marquee full of women. At the heart of the marquee was the khalifa, all dressed in white and surrounded by radiant light. The woman was holding a letter with Arabic verses on it. The women in the marquee parted to let her reach the khalifa and hand him her letter. After reading it, he said that the letter was a good one but it was not meant for her. In spite of this, the woman felt immensely happy and left the marquee feeling good. The letter in her hand blew away. In dreams, the colours white and green have positive connotations and the general emotional tenor of the dream was of one filled with happiness. The woman married and had, by all accounts, a happy but short marriage which ended when her husband died suddenly. After his death, the woman understood her dream to have been one that foretold a happy marriage but which also sought to prepare her for the end of her happiness, as she now equated the letter which blew out of her hand to the husband who was not destined to remain with her.

These marriage-related dreams were recounted to me by the people who either had the dreams themselves or had the *istikhara* prayers and the dreams that followed said for them. In some cases they prepared individuals for future happiness or hardship, while in other cases marriages that were destined to fail were thus avoided. In all cases, the dreams were believed to be true ones and hence were taken seriously, even if the individual the *istikhara* dream was intended for was not for an especially devout person. But not all dreams are true ones, and I end this section, a little anomalously, with a marriage-related dream that was not told to me by the person who dreamt it and which it was generally assumed was not the result of an *istikhara* prayer. This dream was recounted by a group of women who used it to show that not all dreams are true ones and that one needs to be alert to this possibility. The dream in question was the matter of some discussion as it involved the fourth khalifa at the point in his life when he had been recently widowed. A woman who was herself divorced with children, so the context for this dream narrative begins, sought the audience of the khalifa to share with him her dream. Such meetings are not uncommon as all Ahmadis can request and be granted such meetings and the khalifas are known to bless dreams that foretell good marriages among the faithful.[16] This dream, however, was one in which the widow saw herself as the spouse of the khalifa. The khalifa's response was to say the dream was, as the woman who told the tale to me put it, 'devilish'. Some dreams are indeed thought to be sent by the devil and in this case the woman had mistaken the dream for a true one but the khalifa had seen the truth of the matter and quickly dismissed the woman from his sight. Further discussion among the women showed that the divorced woman by sharing her dream with the khalifa had behaved in a manner that lacked decorum and modesty. One person suggested that by claiming to be a worthy wife to the khalifa, the woman had declared herself to be of the same spiritual standing and worth as the khalifa but this was evidently not so as in fact all she had done was to have 'lustful dreams of being with her "spiritual father"'. Dream narratives are never singular events; they are interpreted according to religious beliefs and cultural conventions. For Muslims, the dream itself is one part of a whole that includes the source of the dream and the status and moral condition of the dreamer, which have to be considered together when dream interpretation is undertaken.

However, not all dreams are received following *istikhara* prayers. In many cases people have dreams which they recall on waking and are so vivid and emotionally powerful that they cannot be ignored. Putting aside the dreams from the devil which *should* be ignored lest they come true, and those dreams that are simply the confused products of individual psychology, precisely those Freud considered worthy of study and which Muslims, using a different framework for classifying what is worthy of interpretation disregard, there remains a category of dreams sent to guide the faithful to prepare them for what is to come and to orient their actions and the manner in which they deal with future events.

As one might expect, the dreams that are most vivid and hence the ones most likely to be remembered are ones that the dreamer and the interpreters of dreams within the community can link to events in the life of the person who either has the dream or those the dream is about. Sometimes, the precise meaning of a dream only becomes clear to the dreamer with the passage of time. One such dream was recounted to me by an Ahmadi woman who described seeing her deceased grandfather in a dream she had when she was a child. The grandfather did not speak but beckoned her to follow him down a stairway that led into darkness. The next morning she told her father her dream and his immediate, somewhat anxious, response was to ask her if she had followed her grandfather. To the relief of her father she had not descended the staircase in her dream. A short time later, the woman's father died, unexpectedly. Years later this dream was still vivid for the woman and was a dream she now understood as one that was sent to warn and prepare her for a grievous loss to come, the death of her father. The meaning of the dream, however, while it may not have been clear to this woman in her youth was certainly clear to her father who understood that to follow his own deceased father into the depths was to join him in death. And, when I once recounted this dream to a group of Ahmadi women, it was equally clear from their expressions that they too understood what this dream was about. The only matter left unclear in the dream, in fact, was the identity of the person who was to follow the woman's grandfather to the grave. In other instances also, I was told that if a person you know is deceased comes to you in your dream and takes you by the hand to lead you away, you had better put your affairs in order, as your time on earth is coming to an end. Such dreams may be, as one person put it, 'frightening', but they are also in some ways reassuring. Death is not the end and one has been given the chance to leave this life in an orderly fashion, saying what needs to be said and doing what needs to be done in good time.

To see and even speak with deceased relatives in dreams is not particularly unusual. Hoffman (1997:47) relates that in a survey in Egypt in the 1990s, 50% of Egyptians said their deceased kin had visited them in their dreams, in many cases to ask for something specific to be done. These dreams were not considered out of the ordinary or especially religious in nature. Several Ahmadis told me of such dreams and also of how they can be a comfort to the bereaved. Not only do such dreams repeatedly reinforce the belief that death is not the end of life and that there are means of communication still possible between kin, they can also reassure the living that their kin have found peace. There is also justification in the Qur'an:

> for the belief that in the sleeping state, the spirits of the living and the dead are together in the divine presence. This is found in 39:42:

>> God takes the souls of those who die, and of those who do not die, in their sleep; then He keeps those ordained for death, and sends the others back.

Although the verse says that God takes the souls of those who die, not their spirits, most commentators . . . do not distinguish between the two, and take the verse as an indication that the human spirits are temporarily released from the body during sleep, and if God decides, He can make this separation permanent. Sleep is therefore analogous to death, and the condition and location of the spirit in sleep and in death are the same. Therefore, the spirits of the dead and the living are able to meet in the realm of *al-barzakh*, where the spirits dwell until the resurrection of the bodies on the Last Day.

(Hoffman 1997:46)

A recently widowed middle-aged woman told me how difficult she was finding it to adjust to life without her husband and how a dream her husband's sister had helped her to think about her future more positively. In this dream, the deceased brother, who had not been able to say goodbye to his close kin while still alive, told his sister that he was content and at rest. This dream was a great comfort to the widow and reassured her not only about her husband but also made it possible for her to begin to think about her work, her faith and her future in less bleak terms.

Another widow, a young woman, recounted a very vivid and unpleasant dream she had a short time before her husband's death. In her dream she is jumping from one stone to another to make her way across ground covered in a multitude of wriggling fish coming out of the muddy earth, thrashing about and struggling to breathe. In the dream she is trying to get to a tall, yellow, windowless building she can see far ahead at the top of a steep hill. The building is shaking. Eventually she makes her way up to the top of the building despite its narrow, claustrophobic corridors. Movement in this dream is difficult, either trying to avoid slipping on dying fish or constrained by the structure of the very building the dreamer has to navigate to deliver something she is holding. When she gets to the top of the building a man who looks like her husband, but who is much older than him, opens a door and asks her for what she has in her hand. He takes this from her and promptly shuts the door on her. The woman remembers thinking in her dream that it is strange for her to have struggled all this way and to be treated like this.

What was interesting about this case was not so much the dream itself as the choices the woman made when interpreting the dream. For some Ahmadis, the community's dream interpretation book is sufficient to work out what a particular element in a dream or a whole dream means. For others, people within the community who are considered to be skilled in dream interpretation can be called on to decipher particularly significant dreams. For the widow in this instance, a senior woman was asked to interpret the dream, but her interpretation was not one that met with the approval of the widow or her family. The fish were interpreted as women, with the implication that the husband had not always been loyal to his wife. The narrowness of the building and its height were interpreted as symbolic of the struggles the widow would now face in life. Rather than accept an interpretation that did not accord well with the marital relationship and nature of the husband as understood by the widow and her close kin, another female dream interpreter, a woman considered to be very pious, was consulted to see if a different reading of the dream was possible. In the event it was, and an interpretation of the fish out of water as signifying difficulties, stress and woes was forthcoming. The yellow colour of the building was recognized by all to symbolize sickness. This dream, it was also agreed, came from God and as with some of the dreams described earlier, it was sent to warn of the death that was soon to occur. A key point to note is that the same dream can be interpreted in different ways and the meaning is one that depends not only on the content of the dream but on the knowledge the interpreter also has of the person who had the dream. The dream and the dreamer are interpreted together as was, it is considered, the practice of Ibn Sirin about whom a popular story recounts the different interpretations he gave of the same dream brought to him by two men. In this tale each man dreamt of the call to prayer. For one man the interpretation was that he would go on *hajj* while for the other man the dream meant he was a potential thief. In each case the dream was interpreted according to a different verse in the Qu'ran and in relation to Ibn Sirin's assessment of the piety of the man who had the dream. The first was a righteous man and the second an impious one, hence the difference in the interpretations of the same dream (Amanullah 2009:103).

A final category of dreams which deserves more discussion but which I only briefly mention are those converts narrate they received, sometimes years before they had ever even heard of Ahmadi Islam or contemplated becoming Ahmadis. One such dream from a woman who converted from Christianity was recounted as follows:

> I constantly had a dream about a white lady. The dream was that the white lady started at the bottom of my bed and over the years she came nearer and nearer to me (I used to have the same dream constantly) and only appeared to me to be a white glowing shape. I never saw her face but I knew it was a lady. It was always glowing and brilliant white. Eventually over the years it came closer to the side of my bed and bent over me so that it was nose to nose to me. I then became aware that it was actually a face of a man. This really frightened me because all the time that I used to have this dream, I would wake up screaming, as I used to believe it was a sign that I was going to die . . .
>
> When I met Huzoor [the khalifa] I found out that he was the man who I had been seeing in my dreams. He told me that when the shadow bent over me that was where my heart was and that was God's way of telling me what He wanted [me] to do. He said that he could see I was shocked and that I needed to think about these things. He advised [me] to go away and think about what he had said and that it was up to me now to decide what I was going to do.[17]

These dreams, with hindsight, are recalled as significant and meaningful dreams that help guide the convert, but only when the time is right. Such dreams are sent to help the converts recognize the decisions they need to make to develop spiritually and are very similar to those recounted by *murids*, the disciples of Sufis, who recognize the Sufi leader they are to follow because he has appeared to them in their dreams long before they ever meet in person, or, if the Sufi saint is deceased, before visiting his shrine (Werbner 2003:135; Hoffman 1997:48).

The dreams recounted here work at different levels. For Ahmadi Muslims they provide continued guidance from God and his prophet at the level of the individual life as well as at the level of the community as a whole. Such dreams link ordinary Ahmadis to the khalifa, the spiritual head of the Ahmadi Muslims, as his dreams and theirs work to reinforce each other. In this way the prophetic charisma of the khalifa reveals itself as relational, in Weberian terms, where the charisma of a leader only exists when legitimated by followers who themselves experience charisma in attenuated form (Weber 1978:242).[18] Fortunate and deserving individuals may receive dreams of the future in which they see the khalifa-to-be and so are encouraged to dedicate themselves and their families to the service of the Ahmadiyyat. Together, these reinforce a belief in faith and in the Ahmadi community in particular, despite the hostility of other Muslims and the problems that many Ahmadis face because of their faith. Dreams serve as means to discover what may or will be and produce a sense of the world in which the 'mystical', or as Corbin (1966:406ff) put it, the 'imaginal' is ever present and the dividing line between the natural and the supernatural is not one that is impermeable or subject solely to scientific scrutiny. For Ahmadi Muslims, as for many other Muslims in the world today, there are things we cannot know about the future but which may be revealed to the deserving through prayer and dream.

In 1998 Tahir Ahmad, the fourth khalifa, published a 756-page book with the title *Revelation, Rationality, Knowledge and Truth*. This short title encapsulates in many respects the particular combination of logical rational scientific thought in the service of divine revelation which constitutes, for Ahmadis, the incontrovertible knowledge and truth to be found in Ahmadiyya Islam. It is in the merging of modern science and rational scientific processes with an unshakeable faith that science, logic and reason are only worthy when in the service of religion that makes it possible for Ahmadis to be both firmly grounded and successful in the disenchanted modern world while yet retaining a capacity for enchantment and belief in a transcendent realm which remains accessible to those who possess sufficient faith to recognize it. A page on the official website of UK Ahmadis, Al Islam, which describes this book provides an insight into just how the necessary combination of science and revelation is understood by Ahmadis as:

> any divide between revelation and rationality, religion and logic has to be irrational. If religion and rationality cannot proceed hand in hand, there has to be something deeply wrong with either of the two. Does revelation play any vital role in human affairs? Is not rationality sufficient to guide man in all the problems which confront him? . . .
>
> [The book] examines a very diverse and wide range of subjects including the concept of revelation in different religions, history of philosophy, cosmology, extraterrestrial life, the future of life on earth, natural selection and its

role in evolution. It also elaborately discusses the advent of the Messiah, or other universal reformers, awaited by different religions. . . .

The main emphasis is on the ability of the Quran to correctly discuss all important events of the past, present and future from the beginning of the universe to its ultimate end. Aided by strong incontrovertible logic and scientific evidence, the Quran does not shy away from presenting itself to the merciless scrutiny of rationality.

(www.alislam.org/library/books/revelation/)

The two realms, the enchanted and the rational, are perhaps best conceived, not as a case of one eliminating and replacing the other over time, but rather as both always co-existing and possessing permeable and blurred boundaries. In this view of enchantment and rationalization what matters is which aspect, the enchanted or the disenchanted, is foregrounded, to what extent this happens, and why this is so at any given moment. Enchantment is thus understood as a relative term and rational-organization may serve to permit the ordered, and occasionally less ordered, expression of enchantment into the social world.

While we may go about our everyday lives in the rational modern realm, therefore, the enchanted realm is never far and may enter the mundane world to rouse us from our disenchanted everyday existence at any moment. Constant reminders of the possibilities of other realms beyond our limited visible and material world can be made concrete and are to be found in mass produced material objects and modern media products themselves. The faithful may seek to find ways to preserve their experiences of religious and spiritual enchantment by possessing or consuming products imbued with the charisma found in holy persons and places.

And this may be achieved, in part, by technological means through what Bilu and Ben-Ari (1992) describe as 'manufactured charisma' in their study of lineage or clan charisma in modern Israel. In this context Bilu and Ben-Ari show how the unquestioned charisma and saintly status of Rabbi Israel Abu-Hatseira was transmitted at the time of his death to his rather less saintly son. The metaphor of 'manufactured charisma' is used to 'capture both the basic precariousness and the organizational basis of . . . charisma in contemporary societies' (Bilu and Ben-Ari 1992:673). This is a charisma that no longer depends for its transmission on word of mouth and informal networks, but rather on the mass reproduction of the images of the deceased Rabbi Israel Abu-Hatseira in photographs, on television, on key rings and other goods, and in the repeated retelling of his life story incorporating his many saintly deeds and prophecies published in monthly journals, in books and in children's literature. Together the 'newspapers, magazines, and television programs create an atmosphere in which a leader can appear to be everpresent and larger than life' (Bilu and Ben-Ari 1992:681). These mass reproduced images and tales serving to mythologize the life and deeds of the saint make it possible for devout followers to 'bring the saint home' by hanging photographs of him on the walls of their homes to keep him 'both visible and accessible' (Bilu and Ben-Ari 1992:681). Yet none of this would have the affective and religious meaning that it does for the devout in Israel if it did not develop from, and build on, pre-existing understandings of sainthood, culturally legitimated notions of charisma[19] and religious practices that derive from the North African homeland of Rabbi Israel Abu-Hatseira. In this case the relocation of North African 'folk veneration of saints among the Jews of North Africa' to Israel matters not simply as a continuation and mere repetition of faith practices but more precisely because it is 'a major, if not the major, cultural idiom and constituent in the collective identity of these people' (Bilu and Ben-Ari 1992:674).

For the Jews of North African heritage who have migrated to Israel, just as for the Ahmadis from the subcontinent who now make up the British Ahmadi diaspora, a key component of their collective religious identity draws on notions of charisma that have their origins in a home place that is becoming increasingly distant in time and is no longer a part of the lived experience of many devotees. Nonetheless, the connections with the source of their faith, the charismatic saint for the Jews of Israel and the promised messiah for the Ahmadis, can be brought into the home and made permanently visible and present through photographs, television programs and other objects that recall the charisma, lives and deeds of divinely inspired religious leaders and their descendants. Through such media and objects imbued with the potential for recalling charisma in mundane settings, the realm of the enchanted can be kept ever-present. In fact, I cannot recall visiting a single Ahmadi home, including those of people who do not consider themselves to be particularly devout, that did not have photographs of the promised messiah and the Ahmadi Khalifas adorning the walls of the sitting room and where, even if no one is paying immediate attention to it, MTA is often on the television providing a continuous background hum of pious and educational religious programming. For many London Ahmadis who knew the fourth Khalifa, Tahir Ahmad, and have fond memories of their meetings with him the regularly broadcast repeats of programs he made for MTA keep his words, his deeds and his presence very much alive. For those who did not come to know him personally during his life, the television programs make it possible to feel as if they know him.

Living in a home in which one is surrounded with material reminders of the enchanted and the charisma of religious leaders in the form of photographs, books and media products, creates not only a pious Muslim space within which everyday life can unfold but also allows for the possibility of the divine to enter directly into the quotidian. The fine line that exists between prosaic everyday life and the irruption of the potentially cataclysmic millennial into the mundane is one that can perhaps be understood with reference to a sermon the fifth khalifa gave in London in 2011. This sermon was delivered six years after the Danish cartoon controversy,[20] sparked by the publication in the *Jyllands-Posten* newspaper of 12 images of the prophet Muhammad which were considered disrespectful by Muslims, and just a few days after they were reprinted in France,[21] some three years after the global financial crash of 2008. These events were recalled by the khalifa in his Friday sermon on 4 November 2011[22] as part of a narrative enjoining Ahmadis to recognize the benefits that come from financial sacrifice for the *jama'at*. The sermon's rhetorical strategy was repeatedly to invoke past historical attacks on Ahmadiyyat and more generally on Islam to reinforce a message of ultimate victory in spite of current apparent weakness by declaring that 'none can contend with God's decree. They can observe that even today, each time the Community has been suppressed in any way at all, it has moved onwards and progressed'. Yet, in spite of the continuing belief in the ultimate success of the *jama'at*, worshippers were reminded of the consequences for all humanity of the offences committed against God by those who lack faith, for:

> the world is heading towards destruction anyway. In places natural disasters have occurred and in other places financial devastation is increasing. The reason for this is because people have forgotten God and are offensive about God's beloveds. They are daring God's sense of honour. The world needs to be alerted to fear of God. Ahmadis are doing this work. If the rest of the Muslims understood this, not only would they adorn their world and final end they would also be the recipients of God's blessings.
>
> (Friday sermon summary, 4 November 2011)

This was followed by a statement that resulted in panic buying and a fear of what the immediate future held for a section of the Ahmadi *jama'at*. A written summary of this part of the sermon in which the khalifa warned about possible food shortages, or perhaps worse, if the people of the world did not recognize their creator and pray to be spared punishment, reads:

> As an aside, Hudhur said there is no telling where the financial crisis will lead and how intense it will get. While there is no need panic, Ahmadis should definitely stock few days' dry food supply at home at all times as a precautionary measure. Hudhur explained that underdeveloped countries are used to such situations and people make some provision or the other but here [in the West] people do not know what such a crisis entails. The last crisis they faced was in WWII and their new generation has no idea of what can come to pass. Hudhur said while taking the precautionary step of stocking some food supply, we should also pray that may God enable the world to recognise their Creator and is saved from chastisement.
>
> (Friday sermon summary, 4 November 2011)

This stark warning, despite a clear request not to panic, from a khalifa believed to be chosen by god to lead the faithful, following as it did after a reminder of the publication of insulting cartoons of the prophet, the global financial crash and a warning about food shortages resulting from the sins of a world heading for punishment and destruction, so worried some members of the community that they rushed out to buy and stockpile rice, tins of food, and dry goods in enormous quantities. Some of those I spoke with at the time described family homes with corridors and rooms so crammed with boxes and cartons of food that they were no longer easy to move about in. The dividing line between a routine and mundane existence and a world in which divine retribution is always about to be meted out on the non-believers is a fine one for some Ahmadis who are living, as they consider themselves to be, in 'the latter days'. Needless to say, the Ahmadi leadership quickly took control of the situation and in some cases even visited people in their homes to reassure them that they could continue with their normal lives and do so without fear. In the greater scheme of things this was one small and swiftly contained incident, but it is one that speaks to a worldview in which the messiah has already come,[23] the latter days are upon us and the end, if not actually imminent, is already underway.

Thus, while Ahmadis can and do read books and watch programs produced by the *jama'at* to find answers to explain how logic and reason can be drawn upon to support their faith and even provide evidence of the truth of their beliefs, much of the deeply felt conviction that there is more to life than the visible material world around us comes from the experiences individuals themselves have and which connect them directly with forms of knowledge that they consider cannot be explained other than by a belief in the divine and in a life beyond this mortal one. Some of the experiences which convince believers that they can receive or seek guidance from the divine and through which the deceased and the divine can communicate by crossing from the enchanted realm to the mundane world take place in dreams. And through true dreams individuals may come into direct and unmediated contact with the divine.

Individuals who are fortunate enough to experience true dreams, or the family and friends of such individuals are also, because of these experiences, not only given proof of the truth of Islam but also of its continuing relevance for life today. The true dreams of pious but ordinary members of the *jama'at* also mean that the true dreams of the khalifas and other leading members of the *jama'at* are accepted as legitimate, but in their case as having implications not just for one person or one family, as is the case for ordinary people, but for the entire *jama'at*. Such

Figure 3.1 2018 UK Billboard 'The Messiah Has Come'

dreams are just one way in which the enchanted remains ever present and can guide the choices individuals make and even, when the khalifa has true dreams, guide the future direction of the *jama'at* itself.

I conclude this examination of the place of dreams among Ahmadi Muslims by briefly considering dreams about the fifth khalifa. I then discuss how a dream of the fourth khalifa has served to tie together the enchantment of prophecy and faith to a new institution requiring additional bureaucratic organisation.

Since 1908 there have been five successors, khalifas, to Ghulam Ahmad, and four of these were related to him as son, grandsons and, most recently, a great-grandson.[24] The khalifas themselves, although elected by a representative body of senior males in the Ahmadi organization, are all considered to have been pre-selected by God, and the election process is one that merely confirms a choice already divinely made. In the case of the present khalifa, this position is reinforced by the publication and internet availability of the dreams of members of the Ahmadi community and others who declare that they had dreams of the fifth and current khalifa prior to his election in 2003. One such document is entitled *Dreams Foretelling the Fifth Khilafat (Seen before the Elections)*. It is available in Urdu and English in hard copy in an Ahmadi journal and also electronically.[25] This particular selection includes 40 dreams by men and women and includes at least one dream as recounted by a non-Ahmadi who saw the fifth khalifa in his dream in 2002 – a fact which he only realized after the khalifa had been elected when he saw the new khalifa's photograph. In this respect, this dream by a non-Ahmadi of the future khalifa is reminiscent of many accounts told by Sufis who describe seeing their future spiritual guides in dreams long before they ever meet them in the flesh or visit their shrines.[26] The Ahmadi dreams foretelling the future khalifa are listed by author, date of the letter in which the dream was transmitted, and dream content. A typical example runs:

> In 1997 I saw a dream that you are visiting my home in Rabwah wearing 'Hazoor's' [the khalifa's] turban and are also dressed like 'Hazoor'. I address you as 'Hazoor'. I ask, where is the bodyguard? Then I ask how did this come to pass? You respond that it is a blessing of Allah upon yourself. For a moment I feel as if you are lost in the feeling of gratitude to your Lord. I touch your arm and that brings you around and you start walking again. In the dream I am told that your name is Masroor Ahmad. I had never met you before. I swear upon God that when after a gap of 10 years I was visiting Rabwah I saw you and found you as I had seen you in the dream. In the dream your countenance had a light to it that I have not seen before.[27]

Sometimes the same dreams appear in a variety of published and electronic sources so that, for example, the dream of the non-Ahmadi person who saw the fifth khalifa in his dream before he became khalifa appears not only in the dream collection cited here but also in the August 2008 edition of the Ahmadi eGazette, the *Al Islam eGazette*.[28] In this way, dreams are told and retold in a variety of media and in different contexts, sometimes summarized or reordered, but nonetheless each time reaffirming the intervention of the divine will through dreams. The sense of encompassment by a world beyond the mundane becomes pervasive. For those who are able to perceive it enchantment is all around. Ahmadis seeing, hearing and reading such dream material cannot but be convinced, not only as a consequence of the significance attached to dreams by their faith and by the Ahmadi hierarchy that controls official media output, but by the sheer quantity of such material. Khalifas as divinely chosen represent the best and only leadership choice for Ahmadi Muslims, so much so that the khalifa has the authority and power, should he wish, to overturn any decision made at a lower level in the organization. This power to overturn decisions made at lower levels in the organization, as well as the potential for revelation and divine inspiration, means that change can happen and innovation become incorporated into the movement when authorized by the khalifa himself, yet such changes may also be presented in the form of a traditional means – through dreams and the guidance they offer.

One example from the dreams and practice of the fourth khalifa will make clear how this process works. The fourth Khalifa, Tahir Ahmad, states in his biography that he had received divine revelations from his childhood, and as he grew older he 'experienced direct revelations from God' (Adamson 1991:52).[29] One of his dreams, in particular, led to the development of a new Ahmadi institution, the *waqf-e-nau*. In this dream, as recounted to me by two Ahmadi women, the khalifa saw an army of young Ahmadis who had gone throughout the world. This was an army of boys and girls who were changing the world, not through violence but through peaceful ways.

The khalifa interpreted his own dream in a series of Friday sermons where he said that unborn children were to be dedicated to this cause and to become a peaceful army. This dream, in 1987, became the *waqf-e-nau* scheme and was announced as a decisive new stage in the proselytizing mission of the Ahmadiyyat:

> On 13th April 1987 Hazrat Khalifatul Masih IV explained that very powerful divine inspiration suggests that with the dawn of the second century of Ahmadiyyat numberless venues will be opened for the domination of Islam and Ahmadiyyat for which a large number of upright devotees, well versed in spiritual and secular knowledge will be needed to cause a revolution in the field of preaching. To achieve this purpose Huzur announced a splendid initiative. The initiative is known as Waqf-e-nau. In response many people hastened to offer their children and the initiative was well taken by the Community. Such children are the asset of the Jamaat, who are destined to play an unprecedented role in spreading the name and the faith of the Holy Prophet (PBUH) all over the world.[30]

The children dedicated in this way, I was told, are occasionally selected pre-birth on the basis of a dream the mother-to-be has, and the children themselves are often described by their parents as special and having particular characteristics that make them suited to the role that has been divinely chosen for them. Given the emphasis on sex segregation and the more circumscribed life of females in the Ahmadi community, it was said to be evidence of God's divine mission that the majority of children dedicated to *waqf-e-nau* in the early years were born male.[31] Now that the scheme is more established, however, the numbers of male and female children dedicated to the scheme have somewhat evened out, though boys continue to outnumber girls.[32]

In this instance a dream, followed by a series of sermons,[33] led to the dedication of thousands of children over a period of some three decades and the requirement to set up schools, employ teachers and administer a new international institutional structure, including the annual conventions at which khalifas address the *waqf-e-nau*.[34] The khalifa's dream has also resulted in the dreams of women during their pregnancies and their conviction that their unborn child has, by divine will, been predestined to become a 'new endowment' for the transmission of Ahmadiyya Islam throughout the world. The dreams of these women which may, following an *istikhara* prayer, be in the form of a general feeling of tranquillity or as a good omen with the vision of the Qur'an covered in green cloth, also serve to reconfirm the truth and the authority of the original dream of the khalifa.[35] His true dream is thus reinforced and supported by their own true dreams.

Bureaucracy and rational organization in the service of faith: some histories and constitutions

In the final section of the chapter, and following the example of the *waqf-e-nau*, I consider in more detail some Ahmadi organizations, national and global, for women and for men, in order to give a more concrete sense of the ways in which Ahmadi institutions help to sustain what in Weberian what in Weberian terms could be characterized as an 'ethical salvation religion of brotherhood and compassion' (Weber in Kalberg 2005:246).

Ahmadi history recounts that the first constitution for an auxiliary organization was that of the *Lajna* (women's organization) established in 1922 in India. This followed closely on work by the *jama'at* to develop the educational provision available to girls that had taken place in the years immediately preceding and which was set up, following the example of the British education system in India, on modern lines. This was also one aspect of the institutionalization of Ahmadiyyat beginning with the education of children in segregated schools so that the content of the curriculum could be closely monitored to meet the community's religious requirements. Unlike other faith groups at the time, the Ahmadis did not take a collective position on the education of girls until the time of the second khalifa,[36] when the issue of female education became one that engaged the organization at the level of the leadership in formulating a community position and establishing schools and then later colleges to provide Ahmadi-approved education to girls and women.[37] The relative delay in dealing, as a community, with the educational needs of girls and women by comparison to other faith communities and sects in the Punjab was, almost certainly, the result of pragmatic and institutional rather than for religious or ideological reasons.

In 1915 the khalifa 'established the *Anjuman-i-Taraqqi-Islam* (the Committee for the Propagation of Islam) in which he outlined a plan of action whose goals' included 'found[ing] primary schools in the Punjab' (Jones 2008:201, citing Lavan 113). From this it is not explicit if the schools were to cater to girls as well as boys, but Walter was able to report that some work had been done on this front by 1918 (Walter 1918:117) and Powell, quoting the Ahmadi journal *Review of Religions*, makes clear that the education of girls was indeed one of the goals of the Ahmadis in the early twentieth century:

> [F]emale education should be made compulsory for the Community and wherever there did not already exist Ahmadia schools for girls new Ahmadia schools might be started and where the starting of the school was not practicable, Ahmadi girls might be educated in the Government Girls' Schools up to third standard of the primary schools compulsorily and that after this stage had been reached choice might be given to the individuals to pursue any course that they thought best to follow according to their peculiar circumstances and that where there were no Government Girls' Schools, girls be educated at home.
>
> (*Review of Religions* 1923:22/1–3:23 in Powell 2000:151)

This clearly suggests that by 1923 there were already some Ahmadi girls' schools established in the Punjab. Basic primary level education was all that was mandated by the Ahmadis at this time and while many girls did receive more education than this it is also very likely that the early age of marriage for girls and the financial and class position of the families themselves played a significant part in limiting the education many received.

As with the other reform movements that championed the education of girls from the late nineteenth century onwards, so too did the Ahmadi Muslim male leadership outline the requirements for Ahmadi girls and how best to educate them for their social and religious roles in the community (Powell 2000:134). The Ahmadis, despite entering the field of education for girls rather later than many other groups in the Punjab, entered under the direction and guidance of the leadership and was able to build on an increasingly bureaucratic organization which made implementation and success in terms of the provision of education more likely, more comprehensive, and more uniform across the community but particularly for those living in or near Qadian.

In terms of Ahmadi provisions for the religious and moral education of women, it was not until 1922, following on from the institutionalization of primary education for girls and still under the leadership of the second khalifa that a formalized Ahmadi organization was set out within a constitutional framework. This constitution laid out the structure of the Ahmadi women's organization which was made up of elected and nominated office bearers at national, regional and local levels. The *lajna* constitution for Ahmadi women continues today as the organizational and bureaucratic structure within which the women's auxiliary organization of the Ahmadiyya community functions.[38] The constitution of the women's auxiliary organization, the *Lajna Imaillah Silsila 'Aliya Ahmadiyya*,[39] consists of 204 paragraphs explicitly stating that women's religious and social education is necessary within a clear religious framework as part of the effort 'for attaining the objects of our creation', which leads to the 'spiritual, intellectual and moral uplift' of each individual woman. Such education is considered to be best when organized by women for women and girls, and takes as given the primary role of a mother in educating her children, for the 'future progress of the Jama'at is . . . greatly dependent upon the role played by . . . women' (*Lajna* Constitution, Aims and Objectives:2).

The women who are charged with delivering the aims of the constitution are themselves organized at the national, regional, and local levels with a clear hierarchy of offices. At the apex of the women's organization is the national president (*sadr*), who is responsible for new initiatives and the implementation of programmes to further the religious and social development of women and girls as well as the income generation required to continue existing programmes and fund new ones. The national president is also responsible for ensuring that any new initiatives or day to day instructions from the khalifa are also implemented. In the UK today, the national president has authority over more than 10,000 women and girls, a considerable budget, and oversight of the organization of many thousands of hours of voluntary labour offered by women for their faith.

The offices to be staffed by women volunteers in the 1922 constitution included president (*sadr*), vice president, general secretary, assistant general secretary, education secretary, a secretary for spiritual, religious and moral training, a finance secretary, a publications secretary, a physical health (sport) secretary and so forth running to some 18 positions. Pious practice was and is an explicit requirement for nomination and election to a position of authority within the women's organization as paragraph 115 of the constitution makes clear: 'No office of Lajna Imaillah shall be entrusted to a lady who does not observe purdah'. This is a regulation which, as an aside, also helps to explain why, as today across the world more and more Muslim women have returned, for a variety of complex reasons, to veiling, there has been no equivalent 'return to the veil' for Ahmadi women for whom this has been, since the inception of Ahmadiyyat, a core part of their identity and practice (cf. Mahmood 2005; McDonald 2006; Tong and Turner 2008:48 etc.).[40]

The explicit justification for this modern, rational and bureaucratic women's constitutional system was explained in a letter by the khalifa himself as serving the needs of the faith because 'the vigorous participation of Ahmadi women was as essential for the success of the Community as that of men' (*Lajna* Introduction). In his own words:

> The mistrust and mal-feelings against Islam which are being spread amongst children by the enemies of Islam can only be countered through the efforts of our women. Similarly the spirit of sacrifice can be produced only through the efforts of the mothers. Apart from their own spiritual, intellectual and moral

uplift, the future progress of the Jama'at is also greatly dependent upon the role played by our women in this respect.

(Hadrat Kalifatul Masih II 1922 cited in *Lajna* Constitution Aims and Objectives)

Here the very future of the Ahmadi *jama'at* is considered to rest on the efforts of the women, their sacrifices and their work to counter the enemies of Islam as perceived by the khalifa. To ensure the success of the women, however, the second khalifa organized them into a modern hierarchical bureaucracy which women staff and run for other women and which reports to and takes directives from the khalifa himself. Some women may have authority over other women but the khalifa retains authority over everyone in the *jama'at* and has the final say on which initiatives will, and which will not, be supported.

While there is no question of the importance to the *jama'at* of the work of women, their independent initiatives in many fields furthering Ahmadiyyat, the access women have to space within the mosque, events which are held by women and their control over funds, it may be considered that the prominence given to the role of women may have to do not simply with the Ahmadi interpretation of rights accorded to women in Islam but also to do with the particular place and time in which Ahmadi Islam came into being. For while Ahmadi Islam does seek to control women's behavior so that it accords with Ahmadi interpretations of Islamic teachings, the particular form this took in colonial India needs to be understood as part of a wider struggle for power in a context of religious competition in a period of rapid social change. In such a context, the new Ahmadi sect of Islam increased its chances of survival and growth by explicitly drawing in half its members, the female half, and using the knowledge and skills the more educated women already possessed to teach those who lacked such advantages not only how to become more pious through Qur'anic reading classes but also to transmit this knowledge to their children and so ensure that Ahmadiyyat would spread and continue over time. A return to the 'true Islam' was sought by utilizing modern organizational techniques. Ultimate authority and the power that comes with this, while delegated to women officeholders in the *Lajna*, is derived from the charismatic authority of the khalifa and is not independently held by any member of the *Lajna*.[41]

Yet, while the *Lajna* was formally instituted in 1922 and is thus officially the first auxiliary organization of the Ahmadi *jama'at* to have been set up, with the *Khuddamul Ahmadiyya* for men between the ages of 15 and 40 set up in 1938, and the *Majlis Ansarullah* for men over the age of 40 in 1940, in fact, there were earlier men's auxiliary organizations which served as precursors to these latter men's organizations (*Al-Nahl* 1990:4). Membership in the earlier men's organizations was compulsory for the men of Qadian but optional for all others save those who held offices in the organizations. The first of these precursor organizations was announced in 1911 with a limited remit aimed primarily at extending the missionizing of Ahmadiyya Islam. Members were exhorted 'to acquire knowledge, to pay greater attention to the communication of the word of God, to cultivate feelings of brotherhood, to serve the faith with single-minded dedication and to try to utilize fully all opportunities of conveying the Message' (*The Badr* 1911 in *Al-Nahl*

1990:4). It was this organization which made it possible for the first Ahmadi missionary, Choudhry Fateh Mohammad Sial, to travel to Britain in 1913.

With the establishment of the *Majlis Ansarullah*, participation became obligatory so that by 'the end of 1941, in the vicinity of Qadian alone, as many as 50 branches had been established' and further the branches 'were required to submit their monthly reports by the 3rd of each month. A report form too was prescribed' (*Al-Nahl* 1990:5; *Tarikh-e-Ahmadiyyat* 2018). In November 1940, a proposal to begin meetings with an oath of allegiance was adopted. The oath read:

> I solemnly pledge that to the best of my capacity and understanding and to my last breath, I shall continue to exert to establish, strengthen and spread Ahmadiyyat and true Islam and by the help and grace of God, I shall offer all possible sacrifices to see that Ahmadiyyat the true Islam stays supreme over all other faiths and spiritual orders and shall see that its flag continues to fly high and triumphant over all other flags and is never lowered. Amen O Allah! Amen O Allah! Accept this from us O Lord. Thou indeed art the Hearer, the Knower.
>
> (*Al-Nahl* 1990:6)

By 1972 the Ahmadi *jama'at* had spread internationally to such an extent that a division to oversee the branches of the Majlis Ansarullah which were now established outside Pakistan was set up and these branches were sent copies of the 'constitution and byelaws of the Majlis' (*Al-Nahl* 1990:7). This initiative was followed in 1979 with a tour by the *naib* (deputy) *sadr* of the European and American branches to activate and streamline their operations. It was only in 1989, some four years after the khalifa had moved to Britain to live in exile, however, that the auxiliary organizations in each country where Ahmadis were established were set up to have their own presidents who were henceforth to report directly to the khalifa as did the presidents of the auxiliary organizations in Pakistan. This very significant organizational change, a move which reflected the globalization of the Ahmadi *jama'at*, was announced in London by the fourth khalifa in a Friday sermon in which he stated:

> from now on each auxiliary organization in a country will have a Sadr of its own just as we have a Sadr for each auxiliary organization in Pakistan. And from now onwards these sadrs will send all their reports directly to Khalifatul Masih as do the Sadrs in Pakistan. All the current Sadrs who are elected as laid down, shall henceforth be Sadrs (of the subsidiary organizations) of Pakistan alone. The senior most office holders of the subsidiary Organizations in the rest of the world are designated from now on Sadrs in their own right. In other words, in England there will be Sadr Majlis Khuddamul Ahmadiyya, England, Sadr Majlis Ansarullah, England and Sadr Lajna Imaillah, England. So will be the case in other countries in the rest of the world.
>
> (*Al-Nahl* 1990:7, 16)

With this, the khalifa further consolidated his direct hold over the global Ahmadi movement.

The organization chart reproduced as Figure 3.2 sets out the structure of a national Ahmadi auxiliary organization using the example of the *Majlis Ansarullah Silsila 'Aliya Ahmadiyya* (for men over the age of 40).[42]

The organization chart makes visible the hierarchical organization structure with all committees of the *Majlis Ansarullah* receiving instructions from and reporting to the khalifa. The constitution of the *Majlis Ansarullah* sets out how

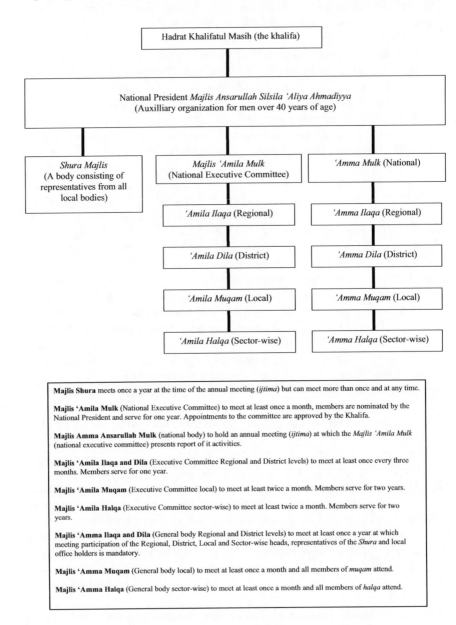

Figure 3.2 Organization chart of *Majlis Ansarullah Silsila 'Aliya Ahmadiyya*

members are to be elected to official positions, who is to be excluded from standing as well as how often meetings are to take place. Officeholders are required to keep records of meetings, outline which goals and targets set by the centre they have met and so forth. The constitution also sets out how many representatives from the regional, local and district bodies are to be sent to the national level meetings. Each month reports from the sector-wise (*halqa*) groups are sent up to the national level where the reports are collated and summarized for the khalifa to review. By this means all local groups of 50 or fewer members are incorporated into increasingly numerically and geographically larger units for each nation and ultimately into a global Ahmadi institution with a single leader at its head. This institutional model is one that is flexible and well suited to a growing organization as a region can split into two and local areas into wards with relative ease based on a simple headcount of members. London, for example, was a single region until the early 1990s when increasing numbers of Ahmadis living there made the split into two regions, London A and London B, necessary. Today numbers are such that the community based around the Baitul Futuh Mosque in Merton constitutes a region in its own right and the ward (*halqa*), the smallest unit, around the London Fazl Mosque, comprises just three local streets, while the Fazl Mosque area itself is a *muqami* (local) group, as are Putney and Wimbledon.

The monthly reports from each *jama'at* are produced by each officeholder for her or his particular remit. When they reach the national president, the reports are divided into their respective components and distributed to the different executive secretaries to work on. So the national *tabligh* (preaching) secretary, for example, will read through all the local *tabligh* reports, enter these into a spreadsheet and produce a summary for the national president to review before the khalifa is presented with the collated and summarized national level monthly report. Monthly reports in turn feed into end of year reports. The reports themselves record the number of meetings held, how many people attend, how well campaigns are going and so on.[43] Such a system would not be out of place in any business or similar organization, and as with any bureaucracy the amalgamation and abstraction of work done at the lower levels of the institution into a general report for the upper echelons generates a 'collective agency', producing apparently objective, rational data that can be used as evidence of the achievements of the *jama'at* (Hoag 2011:82).

The monthly reports which have to be filled in can be quite detailed, as Table 3.1 from a 2012–2013 UK *lajna tabligh* (preaching) form shows. This form makes clear that women are expected to attend the *jama'at* meetings and additionally also actively to engage with the wider community, both with individuals such as neighbours and through schools and local charities, in order to make Ahmadiyyat better known to the women they encounter. Wherever they are and whatever they may be doing, they represent the *jama'at* and are expected to participate in the social world around them. While the *lajna tabligh* form is necessarily outward facing and directed towards those who are not yet a part of the community, the *lajna tarbiyyat* (spiritual and moral training) monthly report form also reproduced here for the same year (2012–2013) shows how much emphasis is placed on the religious practices and development of each woman, and how the *jama'at* maintains a close interest in the spiritual development and duties of every woman.[44]

Table 3.1 Lajna Tabligh form

<u>TABLIGH REPORT</u> (To be filled in by Tabligh Secretary or Assistant)

Majlis: _____ **Region:** _____

Month: _____ **Tajneed:** _____

Report Filled In By: _____ **Telephone:** _____

Number of Bai'at(s) achieved this month ☐   Bai'at(s) achieved by:_____

Please make sure that you send a copy of the Bai'at(s) form with the report

ACTIVITY	No. of each	Please provide brief details of EACH event (attach extra sheets if necessary)
School Talk		
Exhibition		
Event L/K/A		
1-1 Sittings		
Literature: Books		
Literature: Leaflets		
Written to Media		
Tabligh Meeting		
Tabligh Workshop		
OTHER – please give detail		

Additional Tabligh Report – in relation to the 10% leaflet campaign	Total:
How many Lajna have become new school governors this month?	
How many Lajna are already existing school governors?	
How many Lajna have joined the PTA (Parent's Teachers Association) this month?	
How many Lajna are already part of the PTA (Parent's Teachers Association)?	
How many Non Ahmadi friends of Nasirat attended Nasirat classes this month? (*please state NON-AHMADI ATTENDANCE)*	
How many interfaith meetings have been held this month? (*please state NON-AHMADI ATTENDANCE)*	
How many interfaith meetings have you attended – organized by other agencies/ faith groups etc? (*please state how many LAJNA attended:)*	
How many bookstalls organized by the men have Lajna helped with this month?	
How many neighbours have been contacted this month by any member of the family in order to help via khidmate khalq?	
How many conversations have been held this month in which specifically being an **Ahmadi Muslim** has been mentioned?	
How many Lajna have to radio programmes (sic), **specifically in relation to issues concerning women in Islam,** this month?	
How many Lajna and Nasirat are using the email signature *www.ahmadiyya.org.uk*?	
How many organizations have been given the 10% campaign leaflet pack (as specified from the Central Lajna Tabligh Department)?	
How many leaflets have been given this month to your personal friends?	

Please indicate how many many contacts are under Tabligh at the moment:

Table 3.2 Lajna Tarbiyyat form

Tarbiyyat:

Month:_____ **Majlis:** _____

Total Tajneed:_____ **Secretary:**_____

Secretary's contact details (mobile, landline and email):_____

1.

How many Tarbiyyati sessions were held this month?	1	2	3	4	5
What was the attendance for each session?					

2. Love of Allah

How many members know the meaning of the attributes of Allah up to:	Attributes	Up to 20	Up to 40	Up to 60	Up to 80	Up to 99
	Members					

What steps were taken to promote the love of the Holy Prophet (saw), the Promised Messiah (as) and Khilafat?

_____

3. Salat

How many members offer 5 daily prayers?		Remind their husbands and children for Salat?		Observe congregational prayers at home?	
Was congregational prayer offered at any meeting?		Were etiquettes of Salat checked in members?		Were member reminded about voluntary fast and *nawafil*?	

4. Friday Sermons

How many listen to at least 3 Friday Sermons in a month?		How many mothers have their children listen to at least 3 Friday Sermons?		Were the Friday Sermons discussed in the meeting?	

NOTE: Please remember that no programmes should be held when Hazoor's (aba) live sermons are being broadcasted.

(Continued)

Table 3.2 (Continued)

5. Islamic Morals (please provide details)

a. Which vices were pointed out and discussed from either the list provided or other sources?

_____

b. Which moral values were pointed out and discussed from either the list provided or other sources?

_____

6. Jihad against un-Islamic customs (please provide details)

a. What un-Islamic customs were highlighted that take place at births, deaths, weddings and in other spheres of life?

_____

b. What Islamic practices were taught that should take place at births, deaths, weddings and in other spheres of life?

_____

7. Upbringing of children

How many mother's groups or coffee mornings were held?	Did you remind the mothers to pray for their children?	"How many members write regularly to Hazoor (aba)?"	How many members had family time/ discussion within their home?

8. Syllabus (please provide details)

a. Did you cover the monthly syllabus provided?

_____

9. Purdah
(to be asked quarterly, so include in December, March, June and August reports only)

Do all office bearers observe purdah?	Was a message regarding purdah at weddings given to members?	Have you explained 'Mehram' and 'non-Mehram' relationships?	How many members observe purdah?

a. What efforts were made for those who do not observe purdah?

_____

b. What advantages of purdah were discussed?

_____

c. What disadvantages of not observing purdah were discussed?

_____

10. Extra activities

Please report all extra activities done and use extra page if necessary.

It is hard to grasp from the outside just how much collective time is devoted to the preparation for meetings by members who have official roles to carry out and by those who are simply in attendance, and how much work is required to keep everything going, particularly given that almost everyone is a volunteer giving up what time they have after work, study, family and other responsibilities have been taken care of. And yet, despite the detailed organizational structure, the constitutions, policies and the sheer amount of work that volunteers do for the *jama'at*, bureaucracies, almost by definition, are never as rational and efficient as their self-representations would have us believe. Bureaucracies are of course, formidable situated, material, knowledge producing systems designed to shape practice, constrain individuals and produce a uniformity of outlook (Hoag 2011). Yet, much remains beyond the formal recording systems and some matters slip between documents when the needs of the organization at one level or another may benefit from such invisibility. As the time for completing the monthly forms comes around, I was told of the increased numbers of text messages and reminders from officials to *lajna* members asking them to attend meetings, visit schools, prepare materials and so on in order for this to be recorded in the monthly report sent to the centre. Rather than a material document for recording what is done, the forms thus become, at least for some women, the means of engendering the particular type of subject that is required for the institution (Hoag 2011:85). While some women find this encouragement a positive incentive, others may find it burdensome and may as a consequence choose quietly to distance themselves from regular and active participation in local *lajna* events. Others may continue to remain active in the *lajna* but on their own terms. The requirement, explicitly stated in the *Lajna* constitution, for example, that only women who observe *parda* can be elected for office seems to be undercut by section 9 of the *tarbiyyat* form, which asks the *tarbiyyat* secretary to state whether or not all office bearers observe *parda*. And this is a matter that arises, as I have met Ahmadi women in the UK who have held elected office yet do not observe *parda*. In one case, an articulate professional woman told me that her local *lajna* had asked her to stand for election because she was clearly competent but had also asked her to observe *parda* in order to be eligible for election. The woman replied that she would stand for election but would not observe *parda*. She was nominated and duly elected. In this case the evident abilities of the woman outweighed the formal requirement of *parda*, though presumably had another equally capable, willing and *parda*-observing woman been available she might well have been elected instead. Regulations in the documents prescribing some of the qualifications for office, piety included, play a role in the constitution of subjectivities, may prescribe forms of acceptable sociality and are central to the ways in which the institutions of the *jama'at* are imagined, encountered and in the case of this particular woman, resisted (Hull 2012:259–260).

The elections for offices themselves are conducted in what the Ahmadis describe as democratic fashion but where decisions reached by a local or regional group may be, and occasionally are, overturned by the khalifa. In one case where the person with the largest number of votes did not have her position ratified by the khalifa I was told that it might have been because the woman had young children and her role in the *lajna* would have been a very demanding and time-consuming one. Here, the interpretation by the women I spoke with of the khalifa's decision was that he had not wished to overburden a young mother. In another case I was told of an elected official whose resignation was not accepted by the khalifa despite the official's advanced age. The rationale given by my interlocutor on this occasion was that it was known the man in question had no family to care for him and that keeping him in post meant that at work he would be with people who would see to it that his needs were met. This, coupled with the descriptions of appointed officeholders that part of their remit, albeit unofficial, is to listen patiently to members of the community who come to their offices, to offer them cups of tea, and to be of service in a more 'social' rather than in a formal bureaucratic fashion, suggests that the Ahmadi bureaucratic machinery, for all the material appearance of efficient, objective and rational organization, retains elements of Weber's patrimonial administration in which efficiency by eliminating 'from official business love, hatred, and all purely personal, irrational, and emotional elements which escape calculation' (Gerth and Mills 1946:215; see also Rudolph and Rudolph 1979) may not always be the most important institutional goal.[45]

The election procedures themselves were described to me by several people. A woman on the national executive committee described the voting process for the *lajna* at the national level. Voting takes place in a large hall where representatives from each local *jama'at* gather and may involve 300 or more women. Each woman is permitted to vote only once for each office. A person who nominates another or seconds the nomination is expected to vote for the person she has nominated or seconded. Each person votes by raising her hand and this is visible to all present. Negative campaigning is not permitted. And a young man told me of the first time he voted when he was just 15 and a new member of his local level *Khuddamul Ahmadiyya* organization. His father was president of the local *Khuddamul* and the young man had missed not spending evenings with him as he was out virtually every night as well as often busy at the weekends with *jama'at* business. When the time came to elect a new president for the local *Khuddamul*, the young man's father was nominated to serve a second term and when it came to the vote the father was re-elected with only one vote, that of his own son, going against him. As voting is by a public show of hands everyone present saw how the son had voted and recognized that this was a vote by a son who just wanted to be able to spend more time with his father. The consequences for families of the demand on individuals' time is one aspect of the sacrifice that members of the *jama'at* are expected to make for their faith. This public and rather poignant playing out of a private drama between father and son captures sharply the ways in which the demands of faith can test the boundaries between the familial and the communal but it lets us see above all the kind of sacrifice some Ahmadis are willing to make in order to keep alive an ethics of brotherhood against a world of disenchantment.

Notes

1 The disenchantment of the world may not be an irreversible process, nor one that proceeds smoothly as magic as a means of salvation is eliminated from the ethical religions (Weber 2011:152–153).

2 For 'Weber, all legitimate social authority is rooted in charisma, but *because charisma is founded on a personal relationship between a followership and a leader, charismatic authority is inherently unstable*; that is, it cannot directly survive the loss of the leader. If the social organization is to survive, some form of routinization must take place; an orderly (or routine) determination of who legitimately wields power must be determined. According to Weber, the two principal types of routinization are traditional and rational-legal. In the traditional structure, a person is understood to inherit charisma in some way, often with mystical sanction (e.g. kingship). In rational-legal authority structures, a set of laws or rules serves this purpose. Real-world authority structures are usually of mixed character' (Swatos 1998:441).

3 In meetings to discuss dreams men often began by telling me that they, unlike many women, did not put much store in dreams when it came to their own lives but then they almost all began to share accounts of times when dreams had made a difference at a turning point in their lives. In one instance a dream was enough to make a skeptical khalifa agree that a young man who wished to devote himself to the *jama'at* should be accepted. The khalifa was hesitant to accept the man as a life devotee to Ahmadiyyat until the man recounted a dream he had recently had and which persuaded the khalifa that the decision to allow this man to work for the *jama'at* was the right one.

4 'While commentators have long debated the significance of this exact number, the general sense of the passage is clear: dreams are a legitimate source of divine knowledge' (Bulkeley 2002:8). Bulkeley adds: 'One common explanation is that the number 1/46th involves a doubling of the number of years (23) between the beginning of Muhammad's revelation and his death' (2002:13, fn 8).

5 See Hermansen 1997 for how this divinatory mode of experience worked, also Katz 1997. For contemporary examples, see Amanullah 2009 and Aydar 2009.

6 Oneirocritical Greek texts such as the second-century work of Artemidorus were translated into Arabic and elements of the methods and even interpretations of dreams resonate with later Muslim approaches to dreams foretelling the future (Price 1987; Lamoreaux 2002).

7 See also Kinberg 1985.

8 For example, Ewing 1994; Kilborne 1981; Hoffman 1997; Mittermaier 2010; Edgar 2007, 2010, 2016.

9 For example, in Corbin (1966) on Sufi traditions and practices.

10 Amanullah (2009:101) adds that as well as the greater likelihood of a dream being a true one if it is sent to the dreamer just before dawn, so too are dreams of the day time more likely to be true ones. The season when a dream is received also matters, with dreams during harvest time more likely to be true and the dreams of believers all said to be true at the end of the world.

11 The Arya Samaj is a Hindu revivalist movement established in the late nineteenth century.

12 Some people told me that whenever the family had a *mulaqat* (meeting) with the *khalifa*, the children present would be given some sweets by him which they were not allowed to eat but had to share out with other family members on the grounds, for at least one family, that the *khalifa* might have prayed over the sweets. This was described by them as *tabarruk*, though other Ahmadis have made it clear to me that this is not a practice they consider acceptable and that any gift of confectionary from a *khalifa* to children is no more than an act of kindness and is not to be considered as an offering imbued with his charisma or blessing.

13 See also Faruqui 1999. For a similar experience of finding the work of Ibn Sirin in many homes in Iran, see also Rahimian 2009:157. Some Ahmadis I met have photocopies of this dream manual, others now say they go online when they need to interpret a dream.

14 My copy is a global text. The work is said to be that of Imam Muhammad Bin Sirin, edited by M. A. Shahid, the Amir Ahmadiyya Jamaat Nigeria, published at the Fazl-I-Umar Press, Athens, Ohio, USA.

15 I was told such prayers are more likely to be said in the woman's family, as she will receive the marriage proposal and so has to decide whether or not to accept it.

16 One woman in this gathering interrupted the tale of the dream of the divorced woman to make sure that I was clear that while the khalifa may bless the dreams of those who are about to marry this does not mean that he guarantees these marriages will be successful. She reported that sometimes, when marriages that have been blessed in this way fail, people are disappointed because they do not realize that the blessing is just a blessing.

17 https://rationalreligion.co.uk/convert-stories/ahmadi-converts-western-background-3.

18 There are cases, however, where the dreams of potential charismatic leaders are institutionally subverted precisely to ensure that such dreamers do not become religious, social and political leaders on the basis of dream inspiration. Here the reverse of the case outlined in my chapter appears to be what takes place and reveals that charismatic dreams do not constitute the basis for any determinative predictions for their impact on the social order. For one such case in Papua New Guinea, see, for example, Robbins 2003. In yet other cases dreams can form the basis for the development of a theory of dreaming that encompasses elements of the charismatic, as in the work of Fabian 1966. In this latter case, however, Fabian was working with a Christian community which did not have an already established and available history of legitimate dream lore to draw upon. It is possible that the early Christian church eliminated dream interpretation as a valid and legitimate means of accessing divine knowledge in order to prevent challenges to its authority from charismatics who might challenge the rulings and institutions of the church.

19 Bilu and Ben-Ari (1992:674) describe this charisma as *zekhut avot* and compare it to the North African notion of *baraka*, or 'spiritual force' stating: '*zekhut avot* implies both divine grace and ancestral merit, connoting powerful inherited blessedness and ascribed virtue. . . . some of our informants explicitly stated that once holiness had recurred thrice in one family (that is, once three of its members had been acknowledged as sainted figures), it became a family possession "forever" '.

20 For an Ahmadi response, see Butterworth 2012. For academic analyses of the Danish cartoons and their aftermath, see, for example, Laegaard 2007; Blom 2008; Kublitz 2010; Veninga 2016.

21 Love 2011. And for an Ahmadi response to this, see Husain 2011.

22 Friday Sermon: Blessings of Financial Sacrifice by Ahmadiyya Muslim Community Delivered by Hadhrat Mirza Masroor Ahmad[at]. November 4, 2011. www.alislam.org/friday-sermon/2011-11-04.html.

23 In late 2017 the UK Ahmadiyya community posted billboards across London, Manchester and Glasgow with a photograph of Ghulam Ahmad and the message 'The Messiah has Come'. There was an immediate and concerted campaign organized by other Muslim groups to have the billboards removed as 'offensive' (Farley 2018; Cranmer 2018).

24 The first successor to Ghulam Ahmad was Nur-ud-Din (not a relative) who led the community for six years. The second successor was Bashir ud-Din Mahmud Ahmad, a son of Ghulam Ahmad (r. 1914–1965) and the third, khalifa Nasir Ahmad was a son of the second khalifa (r. 1965–1982). The fourth Khalifa, Tahir Ahmad, was the younger brother of the third khalifa (r. 1982–2003) and the current fifth Khalifa, Masroor Ahmad

(b. 1950, r. 2003–) is the great-grandson of Ghulam Ahmad. In Islam the khalifas were the direct descendants of the prophet, embodied both temporal and religious power and thus theoretically ensured the legitimacy of government (Robinson 2005).

25 Published in Urdu in December 2005 in the Ahmadi journal *Badr*, and in English at www.alislam.org/topics/khilafat/dreams.pdf.

26 For example, in Hoffman 1997:48.

27 Dream of Mr Ikram Cheema of Germany as written to Hazoor (dream 2 in *Dreams Foretelling the Fifth Khilafat (seen before the elections)*).

28 15 August 2008:18–19, www.alislam.org/egazette/eGazette-Aug2008.pdf.

29 Ahmadis told me that he received disturbing dreams prior to the events of 9/11 and that their import only became clear to him after the attacks on the twin towers in New York. Cf. the 9/11 dreams of Muslims in Edgar (2007).

30 www.alislam.org/books then Tehrik-e-waqf-e- nau-2008033NW.pdf.

31 See Faruqui 1999.

32 At age 15, the children who have been dedicated are invited for an interview at the mosque and asked if they themselves wish to be *waqf-e-nau*. If they do not, the mosque wishes them well with their lives and they are free to live as they wish; if they do, they are given guidelines about appropriate career paths to follow and are expected to devote a period of study to religious training. See also Hadi 1997:288–289 on this.

33 A collection of these sermons is available as an electronic document with the title 'The initiative of Waqf-e-nau: a collection of Friday sermons by Hazrat Khalifatul Masih IV (in Urdu language)': www.alislam.org/books then Tehrik-e-waqf-e-nau-2008033NW.pdf.

34 In 2006, according to the concluding *Jalsa* (convention gathering) speech USA delivered by the khalifa on 3 September there were 534 *Waqifeen-e-Nau* in the United States and in a press release of 1 August 2004 it is stated that the *Waqf-e-Nau* scheme had 28,300 members (http://alislam.org/jalsa/usa/2006/JSUSA20060903-EN.html). On sacrifice, in a Friday sermon 22 September 2006 delivered by the khalifa, it was said that such children have 'offered themselves on the precept of Ishmael (on whom be peace) therefore these fathers [the fathers of the Waqfeen-e-Nau] need to demonstrate the model of Ibrahim (on whom be peace)'. It should be noted that the command of God to Abraham to sacrifice his son is, for Muslims, said to have come in a dream (Bulkeley 2002:6). By 2018 the khalifa was able to state that in the UK alone there were some 2,500 female members of the Waqf-e-Nau scheme and that this amounted to 44% of the members in the country. With 3,200 male members in 2018 the UK had a total of 5,700 such children, many of whom have now reached the age of 15 and so can renew their 'pledge freely and independently' to sacrifice their lives in the cause of Ahmadiyyat (*Review of Religions* April 2018:34).

35 Not all children are pledged following a dream. Many women simply choose to dedicate their children as they consider this in the best interest of the child and the *jama'at* as well as a reflection of their commitment to Ahmadiyyat.

36 www.alislam.org/library/history/ahmadiyya/54.html.

37 'In 1928 Nusrat Girls High School was established and in 1951 Jamia Nusrat (Women's College) started functioning in Rabwah. Ahmadi girls were thus enabled to get University education close to their homes. Religious instruction was also given in these schools' *A Brief History of Ahmadiyya Movement In Islam* www.alislam.org/library/history/ahmadiyya/57.html. The girl's high school was established in India and the college in Pakistan. In 1949 Nusrat Girls High School was also established in Rabwah. In 2011 the school was said to educate 2,500 girls (*Rabwah Times*, 22 October 2011). www.rabwah.net/nusrat-girls-highschool-risking-lives-for-education/.

38 In this respect it is worth comparing the bureaucratic organization of the *Lajna Imaillah* in colonial India in the 1920s requiring the participation of Ahmadi women, setting up executive and general committees with nominated and elected members, and office bearers with the call by contemporary feminist Muslims in the United States and

Canada, for example, for more leadership positions to be made available to women within mosques and for equal access to mosques for women (e.g. Wadud 2006; Nomani 2006). See CAIR: 'according to data from the national survey of mosques conducted by CAIR . . ., the trend towards inclusion is not as widespread as the standard demanded by Islam. . . . many mosques relegate women to small, dingy, secluded, airless and segregated quarters with their children. Some mosques in Canada and the United States actually prevent women from entering. . . . some Islamic centers and mosques . . . discriminate against women by denying them the rights of membership, voting, or holding office. These practices are unjust and degrading' (2005:5).

39 The Ahmadi translation of Lajna Imaillah is 'maidservants of Allah', www.alislam.org/books/pathwaytoparadise/LAJ-chp4.htm.

40 I recognize the complexity of the debate on 'veiling' and even the difficulty of selecting a suitable vocabulary to describe what has been happening, certainly with some considerable post-9/11 impetus in the west and elsewhere, but do not discuss the matter here.

41 For a Christian take in this vein on the uses made of female piety, see Parish 1992.

42 This organization chart is derived from the 2011 *Constitution of Majlis Ansarullah Silsila 'Aliya Ahmadiyya* for the US-based Ahmadi. See also the 2018 *Constitution of the Khuddamul Silsila Ahmadiyya 'Aliya Ahmadiyya* at https://khuddam.ng/wp-content/uploads/2018/04/MKAConstitution.pdf.

43 This summary of how reports at national level are produced from the many local level reports was described to me by former members of the UK national *lajna* executive committee and may, of course, vary over time and across different national auxiliary organizations.

44 For the *Lajna Tarbiyyat* syllabus for 2016–2018 see: http://lajna.org.uk/wp-content/uploads/2017/01/Tarbiyyat-Syllabus-2016-2017.pdf.

45 Offices have hospitality budgets to cater for those who come to seek advice or simply to have someone listen to them.

4 Asylum and the Ahmadi diaspora

This chapter is primarily concerned with examining the history of Ahmadi asylum seekers who have sought refugee status in the UK. It focuses in particular on the social and political circumstances that have fueled the Ahmadi flight from Pakistan, and on the ways in which those working for, and officials representing, the British government and government institutions, politicians, and the Ahmadi *jama'at*, have dealt with the rise in numbers of those seeking asylum and how this has developed over time. To set this discussion in a broader historical and social context, the first part of the chapter offers a brief survey of migration patterns that were common to Ahmadis and other South Asians before the rise in the numbers of Ahmadi asylum seekers which began in the mid 1980s.

There are many reasons why people migrate from one country to another, and over the course of the twentieth and twenty-first centuries the reasons for international migration to the UK by members of the Ahmadi community have changed in some general but also very stark ways. Some of the changes in migration patterns can be understood as responses to changing British government immigration regulations and asylum practices and of the Africanization policies in East Africa from the late 1960s. For more recent decades they are also a consequence, at least in part, of what has happened in Pakistan and can be understood as responses to the political and social situation of Ahmadis there. First, I briefly outline the history of short-term migrants who came to Britain to work or study for a few years in the early to middle decades of the twentieth century. These were the pioneer sojourners who paved the way for the later post-war permanent settlers, the migrants who established perduring family lives in the country. I then consider in more detail the asylum claims of South Asian Ahmadi asylum seekers who have arrived in the UK since 1984 and the British Ahmadi institutional rationales for gathering objective data on the plight of Ahmadis in the subcontinent. The examination of these forms of migration and how the Ahmadi *jama'at* has responded to them offers valuable insights into the complex nature of the Ahmadi diaspora and the transnational networks that have resulted from the complicated migration history of the South Asian Ahmadis[1] who find themselves in the UK today. The chapter concludes with a discussion of recent Ahmadi engagements with British politicians in All Party Parliamentary Group meetings and in British parliamentary debates.

From temporary sojourners to asylum seekers

For much of the twentieth century the reasons the Ahmadis came to the United Kingdom were the same as for members of other South Asian communities. Those who came early in the twentieth century did so in small numbers, typically as missionaries or students without any expectation that they would settle in the UK.[2] The missionaries could expect to be reassigned after a few years to other posts in other countries, as the needs of the *jama'at* required, and the students would be expected to return home once their studies were completed. Moles, for example, notes that there were just six Ahmadis in the UK in 1913: three were students and three worked for the *jama'at* (2009:69). Seven years later, in 1920, the number of Ahmadis in the UK had risen to about 100, and 94 of these were thought to be converts. It is unclear if these converts were also migrants, but some were likely to have been native British citizens (Moles 2009:71, fn 21).

Others in the pioneer sojourner generation came not on *jama'at* business or as students, or to settle in the UK, but to work for a brief period and return home economically more secure than when they had left. This pattern of short-term employment and short stay was not unusual: the small number of South Asians who were in the United Kingdom in the first decades of the twentieth century and earlier – from the 1700s onwards – were, for the most part, present as relatively menial workers, ayahs if women and lascars, who sometimes jumped ship to work as peddlars, if men. Some members of the Ahmadi social and educational elite, such as Zafrulla Khan, came to the UK to study law and others to study medicine and dentistry in the early years of the twentieth century (Moles 2009:69). In this respect they were following established paths also taken by non-Ahmadis such as Ameer Ali, who had come to England to study law over 30 years earlier in 1869, before returning to India to follow a career in the legal profession (Visram 1986). Atypically, Ali retired to the UK in 1904, and in 1909 he was appointed to the Privy Council, remaining the only Indian on the Council until 1919. He was also a founder and president of the London All-India Muslim League in 1908, and an example of how a very small number of Muslim men who were loyal to the Raj could reach positions of relative distinction from which to set out the political aspirations and espouse the cause of Muslims in India from the heart of the British empire itself (Visram 1986:98–100). Despite the labourers, students and missionaries, the numbers of South Asians in Britain in the early decades of the century remained small, with the Indian National Congress survey of 'all Indians outside India' estimating that in a country of 44 million, the Indians in Britain numbered just 7,128 in 1932 (Visram 1986:190).

From the mid-twentieth century, however, and along with many other South Asians, Ahmadis began to arrive in larger numbers, primarily for work. Even so, the number of Ahmadis was only a very small fraction of all the migrants coming from South Asia. As with the earlier pioneer sojourners, it was usually single men who arrived first and, to begin with, they assumed that their stay in the UK was going to be of relatively short duration. This was often a means for men, as representatives of larger kin groups, to contribute to the welfare of those who remained at home as the remittances they sent back were significant in helping extended family networks to thrive. Often these men would come to Britain, work long hours in less than ideal conditions for a few years and then return to their homes to be replaced in the labour force by other men from the same kin group (Ansari 2004; Ballard 1987, 2003, 2005, 2006).

The majority of Indians who found themselves in the United Kingdom at the outbreak of World War II were of Punjabi origin, from rural backgrounds and unlikely to have numbered more than a few thousand by the end of the war in 1945 (Ballard 2003:199–200). As the post-war UK economy picked up, these men found themselves in a strong position to find work and to help kinsmen and fellow villagers also to come to Britain, through chain migration, to take advantage of the shortage of indigenous workers available for post war reconstruction and the economic boom that followed.[3] Even so, 'by 1959 there were only 149 Ahmadis in the UK: while some were Pakistani male migrants who had come to the UK in search of better economic opportunities, many of the Ahmadi migrants were young students from abroad' (Moles 2009:74).

From the mid-1960s the South Asians who had settled in East Africa and who, as British subjects, had a right to enter the UK, were forced to leave their homes during the enactment of Africanization policies in countries such as Uganda and Kenya.[4] Among these East African Asian migrants were Ahmadis who still have, in some cases, family links and fond memories of childhoods spent in Kenya, Uganda and Tanzania. The migrants who came directly from South Asia were less likely to have had formal secondary or tertiary level education, while those who arrived via East Africa were more likely to be fluent in English, have university degrees and professional qualifications and careers. They also differed significantly from those who came directly from South Asia to the UK in terms of their more liberal attitudes towards female education, paid employment for women and household composition (Shaw 2004:278). The migrants who arrived from East Africa were more likely to travel as family groups and so came with different support needs and networks as well as resources for establishing family life.[5] The Ahmadis arriving from East Africa significantly increased the Ahmadi population in the UK at this time, possibly even doubling the size of the community (Moles 2009:78). The arrival of so many in such a short period of time also put a considerable strain on the Ahmadi leadership. As Moles (2009:78) notes:

> the East Africans . . . first arrived in the London Mosque, at times even at a rate of 50 people a week, and were housed in rooms that were turned into dormitories. However, they only stayed for a couple of days before the community leaders were able to find them temporary accommodation at the other members' homes, mostly in Croydon and Southall, which were conveniently located near the airports for potential initial employment. However, not all East African Ahmadis stayed in these two areas, but moved elsewhere, such as Gillingham, when they found other employment or set up their own businesses. Because many East African Ahmadis knew each other, they tended to settle in the same areas so as to establish similar social networks that they

had had in East Africa. Unlike many Pakistani Ahmadis, the East Africans were educated and financially better off, and therefore, after an initial adjustment period, it was easier for them to find better jobs and to buy themselves houses. Their good socioeconomic standing also meant that the Ahmadiyya community became more middle class by nature. Currently many members of East African origin are in important leadership roles within the community.

One Ahmadi woman I spoke with recalled arriving in the UK in 1965 from Kenya. She said that her father saw the direction the country was headed in and decided to leave sooner rather than later. The family had been in Kenya for four generations and were British citizens, so her father chose to come to England rather than go to Pakistan because he wanted to ensure that his children received good educations. Over the following years this woman, now in her late sixties, recalls that her home was full of the 'aunties and uncles we helped when they arrived because some came with almost nothing as they had to leave in a hurry'.

Chain migration based on ongoing reciprocal relations and commitments between kin and neighbours in South Asia and the UK, and the more complex migration histories of the twice migrant[6] South Asians who came to the UK via East Africa, resulted in a transnational South Asian diaspora that was internally diverse in terms of faith, languages, educational and class backgrounds as well as migration trajectories. Save for the shared religion, this diversity in terms of class, education and even language differences applied within the Ahmadi community just as much as it did across other South Asian communities in the United Kingdom.

From the 1960s more women and children also began arriving from Pakistan to join male kin already in the UK. This was in response to the British government's newly introduced immigration restrictions in the 1962 Commonwealth Immigrants Act and the further restrictions introduced in the Commonwealth Immigrants Act of 1968. From this point on, Pakistani migration to the country was mainly comprised of the wives and dependent children of men already domiciled in the country. This phase of migration for family reunion purposes continued into the 1980s (Shaw 2006:210; Charsley and Benson 2012:868).

Shaw notes that from 1961 to 1971 the Pakistani population of the UK more than quadrupled, rising from 25,000 to 119,000 and then doubling again in the following decade. This period was marked by the establishment of Pakistani family life and culture in British society. The Ahmadis in the UK, just as the non-Ahmadi South Asian Muslim population of Britain, now turned their attention to the best means of raising children in the secular West and so set up Qu'ran classes, built mosques and community centres, and in other ways developed strategies to maintain their cultural and religious values and practices in the diaspora (Shaw 2006:211). And also, like other South Asian communities which have made socioeconomic gains over the years and across the generations, the Ahmadis have found ways to succeed professionally and economically while yet retaining their distinctive religious and cultural identities. This is a feature of the South Asian diaspora Ballard (2003:203) describes as the development of the bi- and multi-cultural competences through which South Asians in the UK have 'developed fluent capacity to participate in arenas exclusively organized according to the conventional expectations of members of Britain's dominant ethnic majority', without necessitating, however, 'an abandonment of their own ancestral roots, expectations and loyalties . . . the vast majority of settlers have continued to organize their domestic lives *on their own terms*' (italics in original).[7]

In more recent years, even migration for family reunification purposes has become more difficult because of increased immigration restrictions, imposed partly as a consequence of a rise in populist anti-migrant rhetoric in the media and the electoral advantages to be gained by politicians seen to be tough on incoming migrants who are often elided in the popular press and popular imagination with illegal immigrants and welfare 'scroungers' (Leudar et al. 2008; Gabrielatos and Baker 2008). Today, therefore, with very few migration options available, those who migrate from the subcontinent to the UK often arrive as spouses of an already settled migrant (usually of South Asian descent and a domiciled British citizen) or as asylum seekers. This is as true for Ahmadis as it is for any other community of South Asian heritage in the UK. 'Pakistan accounts for more marriage migrants than India and Bangladesh combined. In 2000, over 10,000 Pakistani nationals (4720 males and 5560 females) obtained entry clearance to join partners who are British citizens' (Shaw 2006:211). These numbers have declined since 2006 with just 5,735 visas issued to spouses from Pakistan in 2016 (GOV.UK 2017:6). This is in line with the general downward trend in spousal migration to the UK (Blinder 2017:2). Many of those who arrive as spouses are consanguineal kin, often cousins, of their UK spouse (Shaw 2001, 2006:212ff).

However, even the right of a legal spouse to enter the UK has not always been a straightforward matter. The 'primary purpose' immigration rule was, from 1977, used to deny entry to a person seeking to marry or join a spouse in the UK if the entry clearance officer considered that the marriage was entered into in order to obtain admission to the United Kingdom. As Menski (1999:83) notes, the primary purpose rule:

> was gradually fine-tuned during the late 1970s and early 1980s, especially after 1983, as an effective key element of British immigration controls regarding the entry of foreign spouses. It was designed to target Asian family formation in Britain, seeking to slow down, if not totally prevent, the addition of new family members from overseas through marriage.

The primary purpose rules were widely considered to be unnecessary, applied inconsistently and impossible to implement fairly (Pannick et al. 1993). After reviews and legal challenges, the requirement to prove that a marriage is genuine was finally waived in 2002 (Home Office 2002). This did not, however, mean that bringing a spouse into the United Kingdom became a more straightforward matter, nor that the potential for gendered and ethnic discrimination encountered by those seeking to bring marital partners into the UK was now at an end (Carver 2016; Charsley and Benson 2012).

To reinforce just how much times, attitudes and official procedures have changed since the mid-century and how much harder migration has become for Muslim Pakistanis one now senior Ahmadi woman told me about her parents' arrival in the UK in the 1950s and their first encounter with British immigration officials. She was a baby at the time, so the story she recounted was recalled from her parents' accounts of the family's move to London which was for her father – a banker by profession – a career advance. Her mother, as was and is the case for many devout Ahmadi women, wore a veil covering her face which left only her eyes visible when in public. She had no photograph in her passport. On arrival in the UK, the immigration officer looked through the woman's passport and asked about the missing photograph. The husband calmly motioned towards his wife and said to the immigration officer 'that's how she appears in public, what is the use of a photograph for her?' The bemused immigration officer, perhaps encountering such a situation for the first time, simply waved the family – including the veiled woman with no photograph in her passport – through and into their new life in Britain.

As of 2018, by contrast, the process for bringing a spouse into the country requires a domiciled spouse, one with British citizenship, indefinite leave to remain, or a refugee or person granted humanitarian protection in the UK, to sponsor a fiancé or spouse. In order to do this, the sponsor, among other things, needs to prove that she or he earns at least £18,600 per annum before tax (more if there are children) and the fiancé or spouse will need to attend an interview before a visa is granted. Carver notes that when the £18,600 income requirement was introduced for the UK sponsor in 2012, 47% of the UK working population at the time would have failed to meet the income threshold needed to sponsor a non-EU spouse. Given the gender gap in pay in the UK, female sponsors would have been disproportionately affected by this. Furthermore, as members of ethnic minorities are more likely to earn less than their counterparts, this too would have been an additional factor militating against the likelihood that a sponsor of South Asian heritage could meet the income requirements, particularly given that these also had to be demonstrated to subsist over a minimum five-and-a-half-year period (Carver 2016:2769–2770). In addition, British citizens and those with indefinite leave to remain also have to pay substantial fees to apply for visas for a dependent; the fee is waived in the case of refugees. This does not, however, mean that the process for family reunion in the case of refugees is straightforward or readily achievable. The British Red Cross considers that the current process can leave vulnerable family members at risk because of the restrictions, complexities and requirements of the application process itself (Gower and McGuinness 2018:12).

What these changing patterns of migration, shaped at least in part by changes in visa regulations over the twentieth and twenty-first centuries, mean in terms of the broader Ahmadi diaspora today is that it is a complex and varied diaspora. There are individuals who have been in the UK for several generations and are the now well-established and British-born children, grandchildren and great-grand-children of those who came as missionaries or migrant workers before the 1970s, the twice migrants from East Africa who arrived in the 1960s and 1970s as well as those who have arrived in greater numbers, many as asylum seekers, since 1984 when Ordinance XX in Pakistan made it increasingly difficult for many Ahmadis to continue to live in safety in their country of origin. Additionally, there are also those, mainly of South Asian heritage, who arrive in the UK from other European countries where they have been previously domiciled and have acquired citizenship. Among these latter, many are from Germany, and German and Punjabi are likely to be the main languages they speak. But these migrants, if they first arrived in other European states as asylum seekers, are no longer in this position when they arrive in the UK and are therefore not discussed in the following section.

Ahmadi asylum seekers

To become a refugee who can then, perhaps, begin to think about seeking family reunification, an asylum seeker has first to be recognized by the Home Office as a person in need of international protection on the basis of one of the five UNHCR grounds for granting refugee status. The 1951 Convention Relating to the Status of Refugees, modified by the 1967 protocol, defines a refugee in Article 1(A)(2) as someone who:

> owing to well-founded fear of being persecuted for reasons of race, religion, nationality, membership of a particular social group or political opinion, is outside the country of his nationality and is unable or, owing to such fear, is unwilling to avail himself of the protection of that country; or who, not having a nationality and being outside the country of his former habitual residence, is unable or, owing to such fear, is unwilling to return to it.
>
> (UNCHR 2010:14)

In what follows, I examine the situation of Ahmadis who claim asylum in the UK. I outline the ongoing persecution in Pakistan, which is the prime reason why Ahmadis flee the country today, and also the processes and difficulties faced by asylum seekers once they have decided to seek refugee status. But my primary focus is on how the interventions and strategies of the Ahmadi *jama'at* have developed over time in response to the difficulties experienced by Ahmadi asylum seekers in their efforts to obtain either refugee status or humanitarian protection.[8] Obtaining refugee status or humanitarian protection often requires individuals to appeal against the almost routine initial refusals of their asylum claims.[9] The delays in the determination of asylum cases are often expensive and stressful for the individuals seeking refugee status. They leave people unable to move on with their lives, to settle down and find work, and are disruptive of the lives of children whose educations may be compromised while cases are pending.[10]

Among the materials I draw on to discuss the asylum process are legal determinations available in the public domain promulgated by immigration judges on Ahmadi cases; the UK Home Office Country of Origin Information Reports (COI), now known as Country Policy and Information Notes (CPIN), and other Home Office materials produced to assist asylum case workers to assess the credibility of asylum seekers and to help them determine if cases meet the threshold to qualify for refugee status; reports from US and Canada immigration departments among others, and from human rights organizations and British government and Ahmadi funded fact-finding missions detailing the situation of Ahmadis in Pakistan; interviews with members of the Ahmadi community, including Ahmadi solicitors specializing in immigration matters, a former Ahmadi asylum and immigration tribunal judge, and those who were themselves asylum seekers or who have family members who were asylum seekers; and my own first-hand experience, from 2005 to 2011, preparing country expert reports, commissioned by solicitors representing asylum seekers to provide the immigration courts with objective information about the conditions in the asylum seeker's country of origin.[11]

During the six years I wrote reports for asylum seekers from India and Pakistan, I worked on cases involving both religious and gender-based forms of persecution (e.g. Balzani 2011). A small number of these reports, some 13 in total, related to Ahmadi Muslims or, to be more precise, to individuals claiming asylum because of a connection to Ahmadiyya Islam which they considered put them at serious risk of harm if they did not leave Pakistan to seek refuge in a safe country. In 10 of the 13 cases men were the ones seeking asylum, though in several of these cases spouses and children were also part of the asylum claim in some way. In one case, a man sought asylum not because he was Ahmadi but because, despite identifying as a Sunni Muslim, he had been accused of being Ahmadi and so was, he claimed, at risk just as any Ahmadi would be if brought to the attention of the Pakistani authorities and anti-Ahmadi organizations like Khatm-e-Nabuwat. In the case of this particular man, as for so many others in Pakistan, while he was clear that he himself was not an Ahmadi, he knew that some of the families in his extended kin network were. Ahmadi Muslims often have Sunni kin in Pakistan and relations between such kin may vary from passive acceptance to a refusal of social interactions to open hostility.[12] In another case a woman sought asylum because her husband had become an Ahmadi while she and her daughters had not converted, and this resulted in abuse and threats from the husband, including attempts to marry the daughters off to Ahmadi men against the wishes of the daughters themselves. In yet other cases, people said that they had been threatened because they had successfully proselytized and converted others to Ahmadiyya Islam, and in one case an individual was also at further risk because, for complex reasons, the person had been excommunicated from the Ahmadi community. In this situation, the individual claimed that there was a fear of persecution and risk of harm not only on religious grounds for being an Ahmadi, but also because the excommunication meant that no Ahmadi, including close family who remained within the Ahmadi fold, would offer any support or assistance should the individual be forced to return to Pakistan. One Ahmadi man fled Pakistan after a business trip to Saudi Arabia during which he took the opportunity to make an *umrah* pilgrimage to Mecca. In this case the asylum seeker dated his persecution from the time his work colleagues found out about this and attacked him on the grounds that such a pilgrimage is only for Muslims. Some claimed asylum because they had converted to Ahmadiyya Islam in Pakistan, and when this was discovered they were accused of apostasy. Others were targeted because business-related disputes in which the faith of the asylum seeker was, in effect, simply the weapon used to gain advantage over the Ahmadi and win the dispute, even if it meant driving the Ahmadi out of business and out of the country. One man found himself, as Ahmadis increasingly have been in recent years, accused of terrorist related offences because he possessed Ahmadi publications that were deemed to constitute 'hate literature' (see also PHRG 2017:24). Another person had, after arriving in the UK, met and married an Ahmadi, which meant that this individual's asylum situation was now even more complicated than it had been when the person came to the country. Asylum in this case was sought both for the reasons that brought the individual to the UK in the first place, and also for reasons resulting since arrival. And one person, whose immediate family had all obtained refugee status several years earlier, found himself at risk of deportation because he had been found guilty of committing a crime in the UK. As this brief overview demonstrates, while all these people were seeking asylum, their particular circumstances and experiences were very varied. However, all the cases, in one way or another, centred on the individuals' faith as members of the Ahmadiyya Muslim community.

1984: a turning point

Before I consider some of the issues faced by Ahmadi asylum seekers in the UK in recent years and how the Ahmadi *jama'at* has engaged with Ahmadi asylum seekers and the immigration authorities, I begin with the arrival in England, in April 1984, of Tahir Ahmad, the fourth Ahmadi khalifa. His journey into exile from Pakistan marked a turning point for the Ahmadi diaspora and it is from 1984 that more and more Ahmadis have left Pakistan and sought asylum, mostly in the UK, Germany, the US and Canada. By 1984, or thereabouts, there were already, according to the UK national president of the Ahmadiyya Association, some 10,000 Ahmadis in the UK, and most of them, according to the Ahmadis, were British citizens at this time (HO 1984–5:325/617).[13] However, some well-informed Ahmadis I have spoken with consider the figure of 10,000 is high and would significantly reduce the estimated number of Ahmadis in the UK in the mid-1980s. Those who came to the UK had done so in part because of a long history of transnational migration, because of family connections, as well as because of the deep links between the UK and the subcontinent. But they now also began to arrive to be close to their spiritual leader and the living centre of their faith.

In 1984, however, the prospect of an extended, or possibly permanent, stay in the UK by Tahir Ahmad was not one that the British authorities were relishing. While it was recognized that the Pakistan Martial Law Ordinance of 1984, which in effect criminalized followers of Ahmadiyyat, amounted to religious discrimination, at the time it was considered that it was not 'being strictly enforced or that there [was] any all-out persecution of Ahmadis in Pakistan' (HO 1984–5:325/617). By early 1985 the immigration situation of Tahir Ahmad had changed from that of a visitor to the UK to one where he had 'applied, with the personal support of Mr Mellor, the MP for Putney, to be allowed to remain further as a minister of religion'.[14] A letter, dated 25 April 1985 from Lunar House, Croyden, the headquarters for UK visas and immigration, noted that '[t]he Foreign and Commonwealth Office were consulted and, although not entirely happy at the prospect of Tahir Ahmad extending his stay here, raised no objections'. The letter goes on to explain that because 'Tahir Ahmad is the head of the movement he is not an ordinary "minister of religion"', there was 'no good reason why he should not be treated as such'. The 'usual entry clearance requirement' was therefore waived and he was allowed to remain until 18 March 1985.

The option of allowing him to extend his stay as a minister of religion[15] was a legitimate, but also diplomatic, way of avoiding the inevitable negative repercussions with Pakistan which would have arisen had he been granted refugee status. As the letter acknowledged:

> [h]ad we attempted to refuse the application there would have been a right of appeal and Tahir Ahmad might well have sought asylum here, making it very difficult in the present climate in Pakistan to insist on his return there. He is therefore here under the Rule as a minister of religion, and although this gives the prospect of settlement in four years' time, it is a much less contentious status than asylum.

In this latter situation, the British government would have risked undermining the politically necessary cordial relations 'to further United Kingdom interests'[16] that had been established with Zia ul Haq, the ruling military dictator, and would have acknowledged that the British government accepted that persecution of Ahmadis was indeed taking place in Pakistan. This would also have been counter to the official line being taken by the British government which was to downplay the severity of the immediate and potential future consequences of the Martial Law Ordinance of 1984, and officially to accept that the Pakistan government's intention was, in fact, to protect the Ahmadis from persecution by extremist elements.

The British position was clearly stated in letters sent by Baroness Young, the Minister of State for Foreign and Commonwealth Affairs, in response to enquiries made by MPs following letters and visits from their Ahmadi constituents across the country:

> We are aware of the recent measures introduced by the Pakistan Government, restricting Qadiani activities, in particular Martial Law Ordinance of 26 April. We understand your concern about the renewed agitation against Qadianis in Pakistan. However, we note that the Pakistan Government have not acceded to the more extreme demands made during the recent agitation, for example, the Qadianis should be dismissed from all government posts.
>
> You may wish to know that at our request our Ambassador in Islamabad has recently discussed this matter with the Pakistan authorities, making the point about Pakistan's international standing. . . . They emphasised that there was no question of permitting persecution of the Qadiani community. Their aim was to defuse the situation and to protect the Qadianis from extremist

elements, some of whom had been arrested. The Pakistan authorities also indicated that any violence or further action against Qadianis would be severely dealt with.

> (letter to David Mellor from Baroness Young,
> 15 May 1984 in FCO 1984 37:3833)

Baroness Young's assessment here follows closely the evaluation by Sir Oliver Forster, ambassador to Pakistan from 1979 to 1984, offered in a restricted telegram sent to the FCO on 4 May 1984. The telegram accepts at face value the disingenuous claim made by Pakistani ministers that by passing anti-Ahmadi legislation the Pakistan government was in fact 'protecting Ahmadis'. Sir Forster explains that at a function with the Minister of the Interior and the President's Adviser on Minorities, and including the Finance Minister, he was told 'there was no intention of allowing a persecution of the Qadianis, as happened in earlier years, and that *the measures that had been taken were basically for the protection of the Qasianis*' [*sic*] (italics added) (FCO 1984 37:3833). Forster added that the Pakistan ministers went on to say:

> there had been a sudden upsurge of anti-Qadiani feeling (they were not sure who or what had touched this off) which the government judged could well get out of hand if they did not move quickly. Accordingly, they had acted to defuse the situation by passing the ordinance restricting Qadiani activity.

> (Ibid.)

In effect, this amounted to saying that in order to prevent extremist agitations calling for Ahmadis to be discriminated against, the government of Pakistan had passed legislation designed to discriminate against Ahmadis.[17]

This marked a distinct change of strategy from earlier official responses to anti-Ahmadi agitations as when, for example, Pakistani judges had investigated the anti-Ahmadi violence that erupted in the Punjab in 1953. The report which resulted from this earlier inquiry had made explicit the malice of religious leaders and the machinations of politicians in fomenting unrest for their own religious and political ends (*Report of the Court of Inquiry* 1954). And while, in 1984, the notion that legislation that discriminated against a segment of the population was actually a form of protection for that community may perhaps have been what the British authorities believed, or considered it politic to believe, 'some of the more extreme demands made during the . . . agitations' which were not acceded to at the time were, in fact, granted in the years and decades that followed. For example, the Khatm-e-Nabuwat conference speakers who (as widely reported in the Pakistani and British national press at the time) were instrumental in escalating the disturbances of 1984, demanded not only the removal of all Ahmadis from government posts but also the removal of the name Rabwah from the town bought and built by the Ahmadis post-partition. Today there are in Pakistan no Ahmadi senior officials in government, those who remain in the military are denied promotions, and Rabwah was renamed Chenab Nagar, against the wishes of the residents, in the Punjab Assembly on 14 February 1999.

Tahir Ahmad was never able to return to Pakistan and died in the UK on 19 April 2003, some 19 years after his enforced flight to avoid arrest. The following afternoon Masroor Ahmad arrived in London from Pakistan, with some 200 or so other senior Ahmadi men who were either already in the UK or who came from across the globe, to take part in the selection of Tahir Ahmad's successor. On 22 April Masroor Ahmad was elected as the fifth Ahmadi khalifa and with this found himself, as had his predecessor, unable to return to Pakistan. His wife and children soon joined him in the UK and had to begin to adjust to a life that none of them had ever expected to lead. In Masroor Ahmad's case, as in that of his predecessor, the option of the right to remain in the UK as a minister of religion was available but required a tier two visa, which also meant that the post he sought would need first to be advertised in the UK to see if any suitable applicant was already in the country. This was clearly not going to be the case, and in the event I was told that Masroor Ahmad, because of his position as leader of the Ahmadiyya Muslim community, was granted indefinite leave to remain by the British authorities in an exceptionally short period of just a few months.

Such expedited avenues to indefinite leave to remain, options for the very highly placed and indisputably at risk members of the *jama'at*, are not, however, available to the majority of Ahmadis who arrive in the UK and seek asylum on or soon after arrival. For these latter, negotiating the asylum system can be a long drawn-out and costly affair. And yet, the flight of Ahmadis from Pakistan to seek asylum in the UK was not unforeseen. One of the concerns repeatedly raised and discussed in the FCO and HO papers during the mid-1980s was the fear that the situation in Pakistan might result in the arrival of increasing numbers of Ahmadi asylum seekers. As the Home Secretary, Leon Brittan, wrote to Sir Geoffery Howe on 29 April 1985:

> It appears that the anti-Ahmadi laws are not being enforced rigorously and, as you know, I do not at present consider that the fact that a person is an Ahmadi from Pakistan is of itself ground for asylum here. The few Pakistani Admadis [*sic*] who have so far sought asylum here have been refused; but should individuals arrive here in the future who have suffered direct persecution in Pakistan on account of their religious beliefs or should the discrimination against Ahmadis in Pakistan develop into persecution then the number of those arriving in this country with a strong claim to asylum could increase significantly.
>
> (HO 1984–5:325/617)

This concern was one that had been highlighted a year earlier by the British Consulate General in Karachi, in a letter dated 9 May 1984 and headed 'The Qadiani Sect', quoting a report from a routine 'Dear Department' letter of 29 April that had raised 'the possibility of our receiving a number of applications for political asylum from members of the Qadiani Sect'. The letter made clear that no such applications had actually been received but expressed the fear that such applications might follow shortly because of the 'out-lawing of the sect by Government decree', and also because of a visit from a Mr Hifazet Syed who apparently, after detailing a series of 'outrages against Quadianis', had added:

> that under the new law, Qadianis could be imprisoned without trial, merely for claiming themselves to be Moslems – which they believed themselves to be although their belief in the last prophet being alive and well and living in London is unacceptable to orthodox Islamic theologians.
>
> (FCO 1984 37/3833)

It is not clear from this if it is Mr Syed who did not understand the Ahmadi position on prophets and whose lack of understanding on the matter was being correctly quoted, or if it was the British official reporting this exchange who misrepresented the Ahmadi theological position. From the report, however, what is clear is that Mr Syed was a solicitor seeking advice on how best to advise his Ahmadi clients who were considering applying for political asylum.[18] The letter writer, I. H. Davies, asked for advice on how to handle potential asylum seekers who applied for entry clearance and wondered if they should be granted the 'earliest-possible interview date' or if such a course of action would simply encourage queue jumping. He further wondered if Mr Syed's request to waive the 'Visa Applied For' stamp in the passports of those seeking political asylum could be granted as 'such a stamp in a passport could alert the authorities to the applicant's intention to leave the country, with the possibility of unfortunate repercussions'. He then added that not putting the stamp in a passport might result in 'deliberately suppressing a useful signal' (FCO 1984 37/3833). It is not entirely clear if this 'useful signal' was for the benefit of the British or the Pakistani authorities, or perhaps it was meant for both. It was clearly not a signal that was going to be 'useful' for the Ahmadi seeking a visa to leave the country because of persecution.

Asylum and the Ahmadiyya *jama'at*

Save in exceptional instances the Ahmadi *jama'at* has been reluctant to intervene on behalf of individuals seeking asylum. This is made clear in a letter from 2007 on behalf of an asylum seeker in which a senior official from the Ahmadi *jama'at* writing to the solicitor dealing with the case states:

> The Ahmadiyya Muslim Association UK (the 'Association') does not normally write letters of support for asylum applicants. Each Ahmadi Muslim is required to pursue his or her claim. The Association does not have the resource to verify each FIR[19] or aspect of persecution suffered by each Ahmadi applicant. However, according to our records, there have been about three thousand asylum applicants whose membership the Association has confirmed to the Undersecretary of State for the Home Office over the past 22 years. Contrary to Home Office fears this number is a paltry number when compared to other refugees and the actual persecution suffered by

the Ahmadiyya community in Pakistan. There is a huge majority that bears atrocities, personal attacks and violence . . . but lack the strength, resolve or means to do anything about it. Only a handful whose persecution has been most severe has been able to find its way beyond Pakistan. Out of this number, the Association may have elaborated on less than 50 cases since 1985 on the particular circumstances of an individual applicant. . . . The Association does not consider such letters to be letters of support but merely a recital of the facts known to the Association at that time.

(extract from letter, asylum seeker's file, 2007)

Those the Ahmadiyya Muslim Association (AMA) writes on behalf of are members whose services to the community are very well known or whose risk of further persecution is deemed to be inevitable if the person is returned to Pakistan. In one interview I was told that the Ahmadi *jama'at* had, exceptionally, paid for the legal costs of one of their members because he was considered to have already endured such appalling violence that the *jama'at* had a moral obligation to support him.[20] This man was a survivor of the 2010 mosque attacks in Lahore. I was told that the *jama'at* had paid in the region of £60,000 in legal fees to support the asylum claim of this particular individual.

In most cases, however, while individuals do not expect to have letters written by the Association which 'elaborate on . . . the particular circumstances of an individual applicant' (Ahmadi asylum seeker's file 2007), they can and do ask the association to verify that they are indeed Ahmadis. This matters as some claims can be refused if the immigration interviewing officer, the case owner,[21] does not believe that the asylum seeker really is an Ahmadi. And one of the reasons an asylum seeker might not be considered a genuine Ahmadi is because many of those who flee Pakistan use the services of agents who obtain fake passports for them to travel on. This situation has arisen because Pakistani passports list the faith of the holder and this can sometimes make international travel difficult for Ahmadis.[22] This is particularly so if an Ahmadi has come to the attention of the authorities, has had an FIR issued against her or him, or has been threatened by Khatm-e-Nabuwat. The passports agents procure for Ahmadis cost, in 2018, between 500,000 and 1 million Pakistani rupees (about £3,200 and £6,400 at 2018 rates of exchange) – a significant amount of money in Pakistan. But these fake passports may also cost the asylum seeker credibility with the immigration case owner who may use the fake passport to cast doubt on other aspects of the asylum seeker's claims made in the witness statement. This might happen, for example, if a case owner uses Section 8(2)(b) and (3)(b) of the Asylum and Immigration (Treatment of Claimants, etc.) Act 2004 to state that the use of a false document, or one that does not belong to the asylum seeker, to enter the country is evidence of the use of deception to pass immigration control and thus damages the credibility of the asylum seeker. In effect, an asylum claim can be damaged and may even be rejected on grounds that have nothing to do with the persecution a person may have suffered but rather with the means an asylum seeker used to flee the country where the persecution took place (cf. also Good 2011:112–113).

Though having said this, an Ahmadi asylum seeker who does travel on a genuine passport may well find that this too can be used against him as happened in the case of one asylum seeker I prepared a country expert report for after his initial claim for refugee status was rejected by the Home Office. In the Reasons for Refusal letter the asylum seeker received explaining why refugee status was not granted, one reason he was given for the denial was because 'you were able to leave Pakistan on your own passport without any problems, which is unlikely to be the case if the authorities are interested in you'. For some of those, including myself, who worked on asylum cases as solicitors or expert report writers, there was a lurking suspicion that whatever an asylum seeker stated in an interview or presented as evidence to support a claim might be disputed by a case owner who would scour the Home Office's own 'objective' country of origin information material or use immigration regulations to refuse claims (e.g. Tsangarides 2010:42; Good 2011; Kelly 2006).

For their part, the AMA recognizes the problems that would arise if any Pakistani asylum seeker could simply claim to be Ahmadi and gain refugee status on this basis. The AMA has therefore, as I was repeatedly told, worked with the Home Office to provide a list of questions that immigration case owners can ask those who claim to be Ahmadi to ascertain if the interviewee really is an Ahmadi. For obvious reasons the exact questions and their approved responses are not made widely available, but I was told that they might be along the lines of 'can you tell me the name of the third khalifa's wife?' The answers to such questions are thought to be a matter of general knowledge within the *jama'at*, but not for a person who might falsely be claiming to be Ahmadi in order to gain refugee status in the UK.[23]

In addition to being able to answer Ahmadi designed and Home Office accepted questions about Ahmadiyyat, any Ahmadi individual can, as noted earlier, ask the Ahmadi Association to verify for the Home Office that they are indeed members of the *jama'at*. This is a formal bureaucratic procedure which is recognized by the UK authorities. In brief, because all Ahmadis are registered with their local mosque wherever they reside, it is possible to verify if a particular person really is a member of the *jama'at*. The Ahmadi community verification process is global in reach and administratively well organized so that lines of communication and procedures are in theory, and in practice also most of the time, uniformly followed, no matter where the request for verification comes from. The UK system for verifying whether an individual is a member of the Ahmadiyya *jama'at* is described in a Home Office *COIN: Pakistan, Ahmadis* (Home Office 2018:57–59), and requires an Ahmadi to complete a 'Particulars of the Ahmadi Applicant' form, with information, including name, positions held in the community and reasons for leaving Pakistan, with relevant dates.[24] The form is then sent to Rabwah for processing and involves passing the information on to the individual's local *jama'at* in Pakistan to have the details about the individual confirmed. In the past the forms would be gathered together and sent in a bundle to be delivered by hand with a member of the *jama'at* who was known to be planning to travel to Pakistan and could be trusted with *jama'at* business. With advances in technology later forms were faxed to Pakistan and nowadays the forms are scanned and emailed, making the whole process faster and more efficient than was previously the case. If the verification process reveals that an asylum seeker is not an Ahmadi the person is asked, by the *jama'at*, to withdraw the application. The highest authorities in the *jama'at*, the Nazir Umur 'Amma (executive director of Public and General Affairs), Wakilu Tabshir (executive director of Foreign Missions) in Rabwah and the Additional Wakilu Tabshir London (the executive in charge of the UK Chapter of the Director of Foreign Missions), collate information that is received about individuals. Information is relayed to the Home Office only via the Secretary Umur 'Amma (Public or General Affairs) UK or by the national president or the vice president UK. Ahmadis may also ask to have particular events or activities that took place in Pakistan confirmed by their *jama'at* in Pakistan to support an asylum claim in the UK and a specific procedure for this is also set out.[25]

The AMA can issue a letter reproducing the information on the applicant received from the headquarters in Rabwah. The letter contains a file reference number, the name of the applicant, date of birth, nationality, and UK Border Agency's reference number. The letter is signed by the Secretary Umur A'ama UK (General or Public Affairs Department), although sometimes it can be signed also by another person within that department or by one of the five national vice presidents of the AMA. The letter is issued to the applicant's solicitor and a copy can be provided to the asylum seeker for his records. Letters for converts are issued after at least two years of initiation and . . . will contain the exact date and place of initiation in the UK.

(IRB Canada 2013)[26]

It is perhaps worth noting just how much personal information relating to individual Ahmadis the bureaucracy of the AMA has access to. Once a member of the Ahmadi Muslim *jama'at* has completed a 'Particulars of the Ahmadi Applicant' form and has been verified as a member of the community, the person is, in the UK, US and Canada, issued with an AIMS (Ahmadiyya Information Management System) card which provides the member with a unique AIMS number. The AIMS card provides individuals with verification of their position within the *jama'at*. In the UK, the Ahmadi member is asked to go to the Baitul Futuh mosque in London to have a photograph taken for the AIMS card which also includes the person's name and the branch where she or he lives. The AIMS card has the dimensions and feel of a credit card with a bar code on the bottom right, a membership number above the bar code and the person's name above that (Home Office 2016:37). Children under 15 have AIMS cards without photographs. However, possession of an AIMS card does not automatically mean that the person is currently a member of the *jama'at* as those against whom there are disciplinary proceedings may have their membership suspended or ended (IRB Canada 2013).

Through the AIMS card, an individual within the community can be quickly identified by those with access to the internal electronic data system. This was made very clear to me by a woman I know who had been living in the USA and was registered with a mosque in the United States but had returned to live and work in the UK where her natal family was based. On arriving at *jalsa salana* in the UK a few years ago she found herself questioned about why she had not asked to be reassigned to a local UK mosque and, most disconcertingly, realized the Ahmadi official she was talking to – a complete stranger – had access to information about her *chanda* (charitable donations) records and could list her relatives, her precise relation to each of them, state what their marital status was and access other personal information. The AIMS cards gives access, therefore, to considerable amounts of information held by the *jama'at*, not just on the card holders but also on their kin.

As a final point on the AMA's direct engagement with the Home Office I briefly note the relationship between the AMA and the Home Office, each year around the time of the annual Ahmadi *jalsa* in England. Many thousands of Ahmadis from all over the world come for this event to Hampshire, where the Ahmadis have purchased a farm large enough to accommodate the Ahmadis and visitors who attend. For some Ahmadis requiring visas to enter the UK, senior officials from the AMA UK meet with British officials in the United Arab Emirates to process the visa applications together. I was told that relations between the Ahmadis and the British visa officials are cordial, and that they are often able to resolve differences but that not all applicants are successful. Those likely to find their visa applications rejected are Ahmadis with relatives who are either asylum seekers or who have been granted refugee status in the UK. And for its part the AMA also advises visiting Ahmadis not to overstay their visas or to use their visa for purposes other than attending the *jalsa*. A 'Directives for Guests and Workers' document from the 2009 *jalsa* includes the following 'Advice Regarding Visa':

> Please observe the other laws of this country during your stay here. Make sure that you leave this country before your visit visa expires. Those who obtained the visa to come to Jalsa must utilize the entry clearance for the Jalsa alone strictly.[27]

Beyond verifying that a person is indeed a member of the *jama'at*, the AMA does not provide a great deal of assistance to new arrivals in the UK. They are told to handle their asylum applications on their own, and advised to claim on arrival at the airport or as soon after as possible in order to 'have credibility' with the UK Border Agency, a branch of the Home Office. The *jama'at* does not offer assistance with accommodation for new arrivals to the UK, and only if absolutely necessary will such persons be granted a three- to six-day stay at the mosque. This is because the mosque is not resourced to deal with individuals or families who need longer accommodation. Nor does the *jama'at* recommend lawyers for asylum seekers to go to when preparing their asylum claim. While there are Ahmadi solicitors, and some of these specialize in asylum and immigration matters, the *jama'at* is wary of directing asylum seekers to these solicitors as they are not responsible for the actions of any individual solicitor (some of whom are reputed to have made a lucrative living from asylum cases), nor can they take responsibility for or intervene in cases where refugee status has been denied.

Officials I met with at the London mosque were also quite pragmatic about distinctions between different kinds of migrants: economic migrants who do not meet the UNHCR Article 1(A)(2) standard for refugee status and those described to me as 'religious persecution' migrants who deserve asylum on these grounds. For those in this latter group I was told different people have 'different intensities of faith'. I took this to mean that while some individuals can demonstrate that they are active and committed members of the *jama'at*, for others obtaining objective evidence to support their claims about their faith is harder. Of course, a person can have deep faith without being actively involved in mosque affairs or even attending prayers on a regular basis, and in one case I recall being told by a person who had been excluded from the Ahmadi *jama'at* that she was born an Ahmadi and would die an Ahmadi, no matter what the official *jama'at* position on her was. And as far as meeting the threshold for refugee status in terms of religious persecution is concerned, even someone who is not particularly devout but who is targeted in Pakistan for simply being an Ahmadi, an identity position one might have from birth, would seem to have a prima facie claim to refugee status on grounds of religious persecution.

Ahmadi asylum claims and the reasons for refusal letter

Asylum seekers individually make claims which may repeat elements that are, unsurprisingly, also found in the claims of other asylum seekers who flee from the same or very similar forms of harm and persecution. This does not mean the asylum claims are untrue or unfounded, simply that at particular times and for particular reasons many individuals may go through the same or very similar difficulties. Equally, as case owners and immigration judges start to deal with more cases which share many similarities they begin, while still required to keep in mind the specifics of each individual case, to reach more standardized and consistent decisions based on a shared body of knowledge. In this section I consider two of the standard reasons given in decisions to refuse asylum claims by Ahmadis and how each standard response, over time, was challenged and eventually recognized as problematic. The outcome of the challenges vindicated the position taken by the Ahmadi *jama'at*. Yet this has not meant that more Ahmadi asylum cases now succeed, as in the time that it took to challenge the most frequent reasons given for refusing asylum it has become much harder for Pakistani Ahmadis even to reach the UK to claim asylum.

During the six years ending in 2011, when I prepared country expert reports, there were two particularly common reasons regularly given by the Home Office for routinely rejecting asylum applications made by Ahmadis. The first was that the person applying for refugee status was not an 'exceptional Ahmadi', by which the Home Office seems to have meant not a prominent proselytizer or high-ranking official within the *jama'at*. As such the Home Office simply assumed the 'unexceptional Ahmadi' could return to Pakistan, relocate to a part of the country where she or he had not previously experienced persecution, and by this means evade the risk of future harm or persecution. The second reason given for rejecting asylum claims was that Rabwah was a safe haven, a majority Ahmadi town in which Ahmadis can find refuge. In the cut-and-paste language so often found in the 'Reasons for Refusal' letters sent to inform asylum seekers of their failed claims, one 2007 example reads:

> 45. You have not claimed to be a prominent member of your local Ahmadi community, and have not claimed to be involved in any preaching or proselytizing.
>
> 46. Therefore it is asserted you have related your alleged fear of return only to certain areas within Pakistan. Irrespective of any other comments regarding the merits of your claim, you do not qualify for recognition as a refugee. This is because there is a part of Pakistan, namely Rabweh [*sic*] in which you do not have a well-founded fear of persecution and to which it would be reasonable to expect you to go.

While this quote is taken from one particular 'Reasons for Refusal' letter, identical or nearly identical quotes could have been just as easily taken from many other cases for which I produced expert reports.

On the first point, that not being a prominent, high-profile or very active member of the community sufficiently diminished the likelihood of risk of persecution on return to Pakistan, the category and language of the 'unexceptional' Ahmadi became, over time, one of the elements taken into consideration in the decision making of the Asylum and Immigration Tribunal itself and was used by the Secretary of State to argue against the necessity of granting refugee status. In what follows, I set out some of the history and use of the term 'exceptional Ahmadi' and similar expressions through asylum appeals which fall into the class of cases known as country guidance cases.

Some asylum cases decided before immigration judges become country guidance cases when the immigration judges rule on matters that 'are meant to establish authoritative assessments of objective or "background" evidence about countries of origin, in relation to issues which recur in numerous appeals' (Yeo, cited in Good 2007:234). In principle, such country guidance should eliminate 'variable or haphazard' decision making, thus avoiding inconsistency in decision making by individual immigration judges (Good 2007:234). These country guidance cases, however, are not best understood as 'factual precedents' as 'further evidence [can] show that the original decision was wrong or . . . expose other issues which require examination' (Good 2007:234). In short, the country guidance cases are meant to facilitate standardized decision making on matters which arise time after time in asylum hearings and stand until they are replaced by future country guidance rulings.

In a country guidance Determinations and Reasons document from 2005 ([2005] UKAIT 00033) which set out the decision of the Tribunal after hearing an appeal brought by the Secretary of State against an asylum seeker known as KK, the term 'unexceptional Ahmadi' was defined as 'a man who is of the Ahmadi faith' but:

(i)   Has no record of active preaching and is not a person in respect of whom any finding has been made that there is a real risk that he will preach on return;
(ii) Has no particular profile in the Ahmadi faith;
(iii) Has no history of persecution or other ill-treatment in Pakistan related to his Ahmadi faith; and
(iv) Has no other particular feature to give any potential added risk to him (e.g. by being a convert to the Ahmadi faith).[28]

One senior Ahmadi, himself writing a country expert report on behalf of an Ahmadi asylum seeker in 2006, tried to explain the inadequacy of the 'exceptional' and 'unexceptional' categorizations as follows:

[W]ith the passage of time I have observed that certain misconceptions about the Community and its beliefs have emerged or have been invented by the decision makers in the UK in the absence of any formal representation from the Community and or the experts e.g. 'exceptional Ahmadi', 'unexceptional Ahmadi', 'ordinary Ahmadi', 'publicly preaching Ahmadi' and 'low level or high level preaching Ahmadi' including all level of authority in Rabwah. I therefore, find it essential to clarify and rebut such notions of the decision makers and bring into the light the real state of facts on the ground, *only for advancing the interests of justice, fairness and without any allegiance to any particular person or body whatsoever as an expert in this area to assist the court only.*

(emphasis in original)[29]

The report writer elaborates further on this matter later in the report:

Anti-Ahmadi legislation only requires an Ahmadi to be accused of preaching and or posing like a Muslim 'directly or indirectly'. He needs not to be a qualified preacher or of a high profile or with any other qualification. The rest of blasphemy penal provisions follow the same pattern, hence in order for an Ahmadi, in Pakistan, to be caught by these widely drafted statutory provisions it is not important:

•   To whom he preaches, whether to outsiders or Ahmadis;
•   Where he preaches, whether openly in public places or discreetly behind closed doors including showing sermons on the Muslim Television Ahmadiyya;
•   The level and extent of preaching;
•   His visibility to those outside his faith or to hostile elements; and
•   His knowledge, qualification and status in the religion or the society.

Hence an Ahmadi could be targeted without any of the reasons but simply by malicious allegations triggered by the fanatic hatred, personal rivalry and jealousy of the opponent.

It appears, however, that this was not at the time a sufficiently convincing argument as the distinction made in the UK between 'exceptional' and 'unexceptional' Ahmadis continued to be used by the Secretary of State to limit the number of Ahmadi asylum seekers granted refugee status over the coming few years. The matter of the usefulness of the 'exceptional Ahmadi' category was finally raised in a country guidance case in 2008, (UKAIT 00033) in terms that begin to align with the understanding of the Ahmadi expert report writer cited above:

> 86. The Secretary of State accepted that the concept of the 'unexceptional Ahmadi' in *KK* was no longer a useful test. Analysis of the position of Ahmadis in Pakistan had been complicated by the 'preaching' test which both representatives and the Tribunal now agreed was an unhelpful way of viewing a wider obligation to propagate the Ahmadi faith (da'wa). Similarly, the evidence did not support a finding that occupying one of the Ahmadi community rôles such as Nazim, Motamid, Sardar, or being a Quddam was risk-free. Each case would turn on the risk factors for the individual Ahmadi and his profile with Khatme Nabuwwat or other potential persecutors.

And yet, despite this, in another country guidance case in 2012 dealing with a number of individual applications for asylum,[30] the distinction between 'exceptional' versus 'unexceptional' Ahmadi was once again raised by the representative for the Secretary of State because the Ahmadis seeking asylum had been targeted for persecution on account of their business or work. The Secretary of State's representative further stated that distinctions could be made to discern whether or not a person's faith and demonstration of this faith was a 'core' or 'peripheral' aspect of a person's identity, taking the position that only those Ahmadis for whom it could be demonstrated that their faith and their practice of faith were core to their identity should be considered for refugee status. Some of the lawyers representing the Ahmadis appealing against the refusals of their asylum applications, however, disagreed and argued that:

> Attempting to divide Ahmadis into categories of ordinary and exceptional or proselytising and quiet misses the point and is legally flawed. The Tribunal should be cautious of questioning the importance to Ahmadis of calling themselves Muslim or calling their mosques 'mosques', using the azan and similar. There is no authority or support for the Secretary of State's distinction between core and peripheral aspects of a religious faith or the practice of a religion and the Tribunal should reject this proposed approach.
>
> (paragraph 276 [iv])[31]

Ultimately in 2012, the country guidance recognized that, for Ahmadis, legislation in Pakistan not only prohibits 'preaching and other forms of proselytizing but also in practice restricts other elements of manifesting one's religious beliefs, such as holding open discourse about religion with non-Ahmadis, although not amounting to proselytizing' (paragraph 119 [iv]).[32] The country guidance also accepted that if:

> an Ahmadi is able to demonstrate . . . it is of particular importance to his religious identity to practice and manifest his faith openly in Pakistan in defiance of the restrictions in the Pakistan Penal Code (PPC) under sections 298B and 298C, . . . he or she is likely to be in need of protection, in the light of the serious nature of the sanctions that potentially apply as well as the risk of prosecution under section 295C for blasphemy.
>
> (paragraph 120[i])[33]

Further, such Ahmadis were not to be expected to curtail or hide their religion, or any desire to openly manifest it, to avoid 'a risk of prosecution' in Pakistan. This still allowed for those Ahmadis who did not practice their faith or who did so on a restricted basis, and who could not demonstrate to the satisfaction of an immigration tribunal that on return to Pakistan they would 'practise and manifest their faith openly', to be unlikely to be granted refugee status. Crucially, however, the 2012 country guidance also recognized that even if a person was not likely to manifest her or his faith actively and openly in Pakistan, such a person might nonetheless be in need of international protection if 'that person would nevertheless be reasonably likely to be targeted by non-state actors on return for religious persecution by reason of his/her prominent social and/or business profile' (paragraph 127).

Additionally, the tribunal recognized, in its judgments in some of the appeals it heard, that while it considered Ahmadi women in general not to be at particular or additional risk qua women, it did accept that they might, like men, preach and manifest their faith but, because of the gender norms in place in Pakistan, in ways that were distinct, and often more private and low key than men. This was not taken as evidence of a lesser risk of persecution on return or of a lesser right to international protection. In effect, the country guidance in 2012 came round to the position that the Ahmadis themselves had long argued and which at least one of them had included in the 2006 expert report quoted earlier.

The matter of Ahmadi rights to asylum on the basis of persecution on grounds of faith and lack of internal relocation options in Pakistan, however, was not settled once and for all in 2012. A submission to the All Party Parliamentary Group (APPG-UK) in 2015 by the Ahmadi Human Rights Group, the Human Rights Committee, noted:

> From the information we have and according to reports we receive from other organisations and individuals, particularly those claiming asylum, the guidelines set out in MN [2012 Country Guidance Case] are not being followed and cases are being pushed down the Tabligh (preaching route). All too often there is a general pattern of refusing cases due to adverse credibility when

the circumstances are not fully appreciated, the situation of Ahmadis in Pakistan, MN not being followed and not fully considering the evidence of the Ahmadiyya Muslim Association UK.[34]

The country guidance case of 2012 has also had limited application because the absolute number of Ahmadis who have entered the UK as asylum seekers in recent years is so small. One estimate from a well-placed Ahmadi officeholder put the number of Ahmadi asylum seekers from 1984 to April 2018 at about 6,900, or just over 200 per annum, of whom approximately 80% became refugees, while the remainder were either deported or fled to another country.[35] It has in fact become increasingly difficult in recent years to even get to the UK for a variety of reasons, including the 'upstream' delegation of border entry surveillance to airline staff. This delegation of immigration control to airline staff has led to a situation in which:

> much of the UK's immigration control is in practice carried out by private carriers such as airlines and security companies contracted by airlines and other carriers. The threat of carrier sanctions on private companies, including a £2000 fine per improperly documented passenger brought to the UK, means that individuals suspected of intending to claim asylum in the UK are classified as a threat and therefore likely to be refused boarding. Identification of such risky passengers is based on little more than ad hoc profiling by carriers, and the use of 'gut feeling' to intercept individuals suspected of travelling irregularly or of intending to destroy their travel documents before arriving in the UK.
>
> (Reynolds and Muggeridge 2008:5)[36]

As a consequence of this, today's Pakistani Ahmadi asylum seekers are more likely to find their way to Sri Lanka, China, Thailand and Malaysia, countries where living conditions are poor and it can take three to five years for cases to be processed. As of 2015, according to the AMA, no Ahmadi in these countries had been resettled in the UK despite provision for this through the Gateway and Mandate Schemes.[37] The former scheme was launched in 2004 to resettle 750 persons per annum who had found themselves in protracted refugee situations, and the latter was launched in 1995 to permit the resettlement of refugees with close family members in the UK (UNHCR 2018).

While the country guidance of 2012 may in practice help relatively few Ahmadi asylum seekers to resettle in the UK, there may nonetheless be other ways in which such country guidance can serve the Ahmadi community's broader goals. In addition to the rulings on Ahmadis who openly practice their faith, or who may be targeted by non-state actors for reasons which may have to do with the prominence of an individual because of their business or other secular positions held, another significant ruling in the 2012 country guidance, at paragraph 124, states:

> The option of internal relocation, previously considered to be available in Rabwah, is not in general reasonably open to a claimant who genuinely

wishes to engage in paragraph 2(i) [i.e. preaching, proselytizing or openly practicing their faith] behaviour, in the light of the nationwide effect in Pakistan of the anti-Ahmadi legislation.

This too was a finding that Ahmadis had long campaigned for but which I discuss in the following paragraphs in relation to another aspect of how the Ahmadi *jama'at* keeps the issue of persecution in Pakistan an active and publicly debated one in the UK. In this case, the work of the *jama'at* is not limited to dealings with the Home Office and the immigration services for the benefit of Ahmadi asylum seekers; it is also more broadly conceived as a means, by influencing the British government and British government policy with regards to Pakistan, to influence and encourage the government of Pakistan to ameliorate the conditions for Ahmadis who live in Pakistan. This strategy of discrete intervention takes two forms: the funding of independent human rights reports and participation in parliamentary debates about the situation of the Ahmadis in Pakistan and the UK. Though the reports and the debates are independent of each other, they are part of a coordinated effort to raise awareness of the Ahmadi cause, with the reports to some extent also providing an information resource for the debates.

Parliamentary reports and debates

One strategy pursued by the Ahmadis to keep the issue of Ahmadi discrimination and persecution ever present in official and political circles includes collating and making publicly available up to date information about their situation in Pakistan.[38] To this end, fact-finding missions composed of experts whose methods and conclusions it would be difficult to impugn are funded by the Ahmadis to produce substantial and carefully researched reports such as the 2010 *Report of the PHRG* [Parliamentary Human Rights Group] *Fact Finding Mission to Pakistan to Examine the Human Rights Situation of the Ahmadiyya Community*; the 2015 *A Beleaguered Community: On the rising persecution of the Ahmadiyya Muslim Community*; and the more recent 2017 *Ahmadis in Pakistan Face an Existential Threat: the growing violence, legal discrimination and social exclusion since 2015*.[39]

However, the first of the UK reports on the Ahmadiyya community in Pakistan by the PHRG in 2007, *Rabwah: A Place for Martyrs?*, does not appear to have been funded by the Ahmadis (PHRG 2007). This suggests that the Ahmadis may have recognized, after this report was produced, the potential value to the community of up to date research undertaken by non-partisan researchers. The willingness to pay the expenses of the researchers in the later 2010, 2015 and 2017 reports, therefore, is one way in which the Ahmadi *jama'at* can provide support, at a remove, for Ahmadi asylum seekers as objective evidence from these reports also makes its way into the materials used to support individual asylum claims.[40] These reports are, additionally, a means by which the Ahmadi community keeps the issue of discrimination and persecution in Pakistan constantly present in the political and public domain in the UK. As such the reports keep some visibility and pressure on Pakistan in an attempt to work towards improving the conditions for the Ahmadis who remain there and who cannot or choose not, for whatever reason, to leave to seek a place of safety elsewhere.

The 2007, 2010 and 2015 reports had forewords written by the distinguished British politician Lord Avebury,[41] while the 2017 report includes a foreword by a former UN Special Rapporteur on Freedom of Religion or Belief and also, for good measure, a quote from Prince Charles on the global scale of religious persecution. The contents of the reports are produced by non-Ahmadi human rights workers, researchers and others whose work cannot be easily dismissed by immigration judges as self-serving or biased. And this matters when seeking refugee status as immigration tribunal judges will readily discount any material they consider to be advocating on behalf of an individual or to be lacking in objectivity. Insofar as these reports can be quoted by solicitors, expert report writers and others in support of the claims of individual asylum seekers, they serve as objective and impartial evidence.

The connections between these human rights reports and the situation of Ahmadi asylum seekers is made explicit in the 2007 PHRG report *Rabwah: a place for martyrs*? This report is described in the preface by Lord Avebury as commissioned directly in response to the increasing numbers of Ahmadi asylum applications which were being refused because immigration judges assumed that the asylum seekers could return to live in Rabwah in safety. As Lord Avebury states:

> In recent years, the PHRG has noted that an increasing number of Ahmadis, trying to escape the persecution in which they are trapped in Pakistan, have sought asylum in the UK, and although many have succeeded, our impression was that an increasing proportion were being refused. In a number of cases the reasoning was that, while the applicant might have had a well-founded fear of persecution within the meaning of the Refugee Convention if he returned to his locality of origin, he would be safe enough if he migrated internally to the city of Rabwah, founded by the Ahmadiyyah community and inhabited by a majority of Ahmadis. The anecdotal evidence we had from Rabwah was that life in Rabwah itself was severely restricted and that residents were subject to the same conditions, including occasional violence and intimidation, that occur elsewhere in Pakistan, and there was no real safety in numbers.
>
> (PHRG 2007:iii–iv)

The purpose of the research carried out for the report was precisely to investigate the situation on the ground in Rabwah, and while Lord Avebury states that the report itself 'draws no conclusions, allowing the facts to speak for themselves (PHRG 2007:iv), he ends his preface (discussed in Chapter 1) with the categorization of the town as 'a ghetto' and 'a dead-end' that is 'at the mercy of hostile sectarian forces whipped up by hate-filled mullahs and most of the Urdu media' (PHRG 2007:iv).

Beyond such prefaces, the language of these reports is, as one would expect, for the most part measured and, some direct quotes notwithstanding, information is fact-based and presented straightforwardly with supporting references. The PHRG reports are, therefore, extremely valuable and largely reliable sources of information about the Ahmadi community in Pakistan and I draw upon them heavily in my own account of life in Rabwah in Chapter 1. But some of the testimony I discuss there about the everyday life of Ahmadis in Pakistan was derived from Ahmadi participants speaking at a meeting of the APPG for the Ahmadiyya Muslim Community in 2018. This cross-party parliamentary group was established, initially, in response to the Lahore mosque attacks of 2010; it is one of a number of Parliamentary venues where the Ahmadi *jama'at* has been able to raise awareness of the conditions of Ahmadis in Pakistan. In the following paragraphs I consider the Westminster Hall debates, APPG meetings and House of Commons debates in order to show some of the ways in which the UK Ahmadi *jama'at* works with British politicians to effect change in Pakistan.

The violent attacks on two Ahmadi mosques in Lahore in 2010 may be considered a critical event as understood by Das (1996), a moment of social suffering so overwhelming it has the potential to upset routine understandings of the way things are, to compel new discourses, and to re-shape how 'communities construct themselves as political actors' (1996:2). This particular critical event also took the ongoing violence against the Ahmadis in Pakistan from a local matter to a globally reported incident drawing the world's media to Lahore and Rabwah. British counter-terrorism officers, for example, were on site at the Baitul Futuh mosque in London while the attacks in Lahore were still ongoing, and the impact of the violence in Pakistan, filmed for television news, was keenly felt in the UK.[42] Immediately following the Lahore attacks, the police presence and general security at UK Ahmadi mosques were stepped up. The attacks served also as a primary impetus for the organization of the Westminster Hall Debate[43] on the Ahmadiyya Community, the first ever parliamentary debate in the UK on the community, held on 20 October 2010.[44] Siobhain McDonagh, the MP for Mitcham and Morden, made the motivations behind the debates clear in her opening statement, in which she also made explicit the role she hoped British parliamentarians would play in influencing future events in Pakistan:

> I am extremely sorry to bring this community's concerns to the House at this particular time. The circumstances that led me to ask for a debate are extremely sad. On 28 May, nearly 100 Ahmadiyya Muslim worshippers were brutally murdered in two separate attacks in Lahore. However, what makes the story especially poignant is not just the fact that the Ahmadi are so peaceful but that their murderers were also Muslim. What I hope to do today is to examine why the attacks took place, then ask whether there is anything that we in Britain and the wider community can do to prevent such atrocities happening again in the future. Finally, I want to assess what the implications are for Britain of how the Ahmadiyya community in Pakistan is treated and what we can do about it.
>
> (Hansard 2010)

The visibility of the violence against Ahmadis made possible by the live media transmission of the attacks as they unfolded in Lahore was central to the shift in how British parliamentarians viewed the situation of the Ahmadis in Pakistan. The impact of the global media cannot be underestimated, as McDonagh went on to say in the debate itself: 'the loss of life and the prolonged and bloody siege prompted widespread condemnation and global media coverage, and it is the reason why we have asked for this debate'. She also argued that asking for the debate to help Pakistani Ahmadis on behalf of her Ahmadi constituents additionally served the goal of protecting the general British public from future violence:

> If we do not persuade mainstream politicians in Pakistan to stand up for the Ahmadi Muslim community, we risk further Islamicist militancy. Moreover, if the militancy continues in Pakistan, it not only threatens Ahmadis but the whole international community. After all, any increase in Islamicist activities also affects us here in the UK, so it is in our own interests for the Government to seek to persuade Pakistan's Government to show more tolerance to the Ahmadi Muslim community.
>
> (Hansard 2010)

The scale and duration of the attacks in 2010 not only spurred action in the diaspora, it also elicited some muted condemnation and sympathy in Pakistan itself (Saleem 2010). This, however, was so quickly and so forcefully condemned by anti-Ahmadi organizations that it compelled even national political leaders to find ways to retract their initial statements of empathy with the victims of the mosque attacks. Just days after the attacks, Nawaz Sharif, the leader of the Pakistan Muslim League-N (PML-N), described Pakistani 'Ahmadi brothers and sisters' as an 'asset' to the country in which they were citizens (*Dawn* 10 June 2010). He was immediately rebuked by a range of organizations, including Jamiat Ulema-i-Islam, Jamaat-i-Islami, Wafaqul Madaris, Jamiat Ahl-i-Sunnat and Al-Hadith and Khatm-e-Nabuwat, who were insulted, among other things, at the thought that an Ahmadi could be the 'brother' of a Muslim and considered Sharif's words also to be a 'violation of the Constitution' (*Dawn* 10 June 2010). It was left to a PML-N spokesperson to clarify on Sharif's behalf that 'Nawaz Sharif said what the Quaid-i-Azam had already stated, that all Pakistanis were brothers irrespective of their religion, language or caste', and that those who were attacking him were simply exploiting the situation for their own ends (Ibid.). Even such muted public statements of sympathy for Ahmadis, as fellow citizens, in the wake of a terrorist attack are made at the speaker's risk and routinely silenced in Pakistan.[45]

The same was not the case in the UK, and the Westminster Hall Debate allowed MPs to make explicit requests to the British government to intercede on behalf of the Ahmadis in Pakistan. In response Alistair Burt, then Parliamentary Under Secretary of State in the Foreign and Commonwealth Office, described his regular exchanges with Pakistan's Federal Minister for Minorities, Shahbaz Bhatti, and praised the work he was doing to reform the blasphemy laws. A few months later, in March 2011, Bhatti was assassinated by the Taliban al-Qaida Punjab who scattered leaflets insulting Bhatti's attempts to tackle the blasphemy legislation as they fled the scene of his killing (Walsh 2011). By the time of the most recent APPG meetings in May 2018 the Ahmadis themselves were no longer asking for the reform of the blasphemy laws, considering this to be unachievable in the current political climate.

The Westminster Hall debate in 2010 touched on many of the issues which continue to exercise ministers and politicians, and also the Ahmadiyya Muslim community members, both in the UK and in Pakistan. Such matters included the use of UK taxpayer monies to fund development programs, including educational ones, in Pakistan, and how these might be better monitored to ensure that no British funds are being used to produce textbooks that incite discrimination and violence against Ahmadis and other minorities. Other issues included forms of anti-Ahmadi discrimination that are commonplace in Pakistan but which have now also found their way to the UK, such as boycotting Ahmadi shops, refusing to serve Ahmadis in non-Ahmadi shops and restaurants, and handing out inflammatory leaflets (that allegedly included statements such as: '*Kill a Qadiyani and doors to heaven will open to you*').[46]

It was clear to the speakers in the 2010 Westminster Hall debate that the tactics and strategies of those who discriminate against the Ahmadis in Pakistan had made their way to the UK, and that the best way to ensure peace in the UK was by working to ameliorate conditions for the Ahmadis and other minorities in Pakistan. Pakistan's long historical and political connection to the UK, its geo-political importance, the numbers of Ahmadis now settled and others seeking asylum in the UK, and the importation of forms of discrimination against Ahmadis originating in Pakistan are intertwined issues that directly connect the British Pakistani diaspora and British authorities to Pakistan. This makes what happens in Pakistan a matter of considerable significance to the British authorities which deal with the consequences of anti-Ahmadi ideas and practices in Pakistan as they then play out in the streets, on air and in the mosques of the UK.

The Westminster Hall debate in 2010 was soon followed by the formation of an APPG for the Ahmadiyya Muslim Community. The APPG for the Ahmadiyya Muslim Community has since met several times, most recently in 2018. And another Westminster Hall debate on the Persecution of Religious Minorities in Pakistan, which included a good deal of discussion of the Ahmadiyya community, took place in 2016, just weeks before Asad Shah, an Ahmadi refugee settled in Glasgow, became the first Ahmadi to be murdered in the UK for simply being an Ahmadi. In 2015 two more APPGs were established, one on international freedom of religion or belief, and the second on Pakistani minorities. Both have extensively discussed the Ahmadi situation in Pakistan, and in 2016 the APPG for International Freedom of Religion or Belief published a report on Pakistan and UK government policy which included a substantial amount of material on the plight of Ahmadis in Pakistan.[47]

In 2018 another series of APPG meetings for the Ahmadiyya Muslim Community was held, and the situation in Pakistan for Ahmadis was debated in the House of Commons on 24 May 2018. From 2010, therefore, there has been a significant increase in the amount of parliamentary time devoted to the Ahmadis, and the issues concerning the Ahmadis have moved from Westminster Hall and the discussions of informal groups of members of both houses to the centre of government in the form of a debate in the House of Commons itself.

This increasing visibility of the Ahmadiyya Muslim community in political circles over recent years is indexed by the visits of the khalifa himself to attend Parliament, as he did for the first time on 22 October 2008 when a special parliamentary reception and lunch was hosted for him by the MP for Putney, Justine Greening.[48] Along with the khalifa on this occasion were MPs from all parties, members of the House of Lords, including Lord Avebury, the Uganda High Commissioner, and several senior Ahmadi representatives, both women and men. The 2008 invitation was repeated in 2013 when the khalifa returned to the Houses of Parliament for a reception to celebrate the centenary of the Ahmadiyya Muslim *jama'at* UK and on this occasion the deputy prime minister, Nick Clegg, and the then Home Secretary, Theresa May, were among those present.[49] Both these events, the first to commemorate the centenary of the Ahmadi khilafat in 2008, and the second the centenary of the Ahmadi presence in the UK in 2013, were important occasions permitting the Ahmadis to make symbolic statements about their place at the centre of the state and to showcase the welcome they receive in Britain. Both occasions owed their success in no small part to the long-established Ahmadi practice of inviting MPs and local people of influence to Ahmadi events, such as the *jalsa*. Over many years, these invitations have helped to build networks and trust between politicians and the Ahmadis. The presence of an Ahmadi member of the House of Lords, Lord Ahmad of Wimbledon, also facilitated the welcome of the khalifa in Parliament.

Today's British Ahmadis are thus not only local constituents who, by voting for their elected representatives, can shape the future of the country; they are also among those who stand for election and serve in the Houses of Parliament, thus directly influencing what happens in government. Over the course of the last century the Ahmadis have moved from being a virtually unknown sect establishing itself at the margins of the capital city to producing elected officials and representatives serving in government and on government committees such as the Community Engagement Forum set up in 2015 to help tackle extremism. Lord Ahmad, a British-born Ahmadi and at the time also Minister for Countering Extremism, along with two other Ahmadiyya Muslim representatives, were three of the 26-member group in the first Community Engagement Forum meeting.[50]

I now take a closer look at one of the debates on Ahmadi issues during the 2018 APPG meetings.[51] The debate, which focused in particular on education, elections, asylum and British government funding for development in Pakistan, can serve as a lens through which to understand the interactions between British politicians, UK-based Ahmadis and Pakistan, focusing on the situation in Pakistan that generates Ahmadi asylum seekers as well as anti-Ahmadi practices in the UK, and what can be done about this.

The APPG inquiry into the denial of freedom of religion and human rights violations of Ahmadi Muslims and other religious communities in Pakistan

I discuss took place in Portcullis House on 23 April 2018. The meeting was chaired by Siobhain McDonagh, MP for Mitcham and Morden. I was present at this first meeting which focused on the historical context of the ongoing persecution against religious communities in Pakistan. Two Ahmadi representatives had flown in from Pakistan to attend the meeting. The first was Mr Mujeeb ur Rehman, a senior advocate of the Supreme Court of Pakistan, who spoke about the Ahmadi situation in Pakistan and answered questions posed by members of both the House of Commons and the Lords during the two-hour session. The second Ahmadi representative was born in Rabwah but had spent much of his youth in the UK, returning to Rabwah after completing his university education in London.

After a brief historical outline of the situation for the Ahmadis in Pakistan the meeting moved on to questions about the current situation and what British MPs and the British government could do to assist. One question asked by Zac Goldsmith, MP for Richmond Park and former brother-in-law of Imran Khan who was elected as the twenty-second prime minister of Pakistan in August 2018, was whether there was a political party in Pakistan today able to bring about the changes needed to make the Ahmadis safe in their own country. The answer was, perhaps inevitably, given in the negative. Further, Mujeeb ur Rehman also made it clear that there was no point at present even trying to repeal legislation such as the Second Amendment to the Constitution of Pakistan of 7 September 1974 declaring the Ahmadis to be non-Muslim.[52] The position in the country had so hardened against the Ahmadis since that time that the only pragmatic approach to take at present, he argued, was to focus on subordinate legislation that might be amended, drawing less attention and inciting less opposition than the repeal of the Second Amendment inevitably would.

The secondary legislation that could be tackled included that dealing with the separate electoral lists for Ahmadi voters. Under Zia ul Haq non-Muslim communities were placed on separate electoral lists and required to vote for non-Muslim candidates. In 2002 General Musharraf abolished the separate electoral list for all communities, save the Ahmadis, and thus made the Ahmadis the only community to be discriminated against in this way in Pakistan.[53] The electoral list issue was a pressing one at the time of the APPG meeting as the country was going to the polls on 25 July, just three months after the parliamentary meeting. The issue for Ahmadis is that:

> Under Pakistan's election law, Ahmadis are effectively denied the right to vote and are disenfranchised unless they declare themselves as non-Muslims, which effectively would mean giving up their faith. The Electoral Commission of Pakistan has decided that Ahmadis can be permitted to vote only under a separate register and by self-identifying as a non-Muslim minority. This requirement to deny their faith to vote has caused their disenfranchisement from politics for more than 30 years, and worse still the separate Ahmadi electoral register is publicly available, making it much easier for extremists to target them.[54]

As the Ahmadi representatives expressed it in the APPG meeting for Ahmadis in Pakistan, one right, that of being able to self-identify as Muslim, is challenged by another right, the right to vote. The Ahmadis have chosen to prioritize their identity over citizenship rights and so are disenfranchised. Worryingly, the younger of the representatives then made it clear that because the Ahmadis have not voted in elections in Pakistan since the 1970s, younger generations of Ahmadis no longer even feel the loss of a fundamental right they have never experienced. And yet, as this Ahmadi analyst also noted, if the Ahmadis were able to vote they would have sufficient numbers to make a decisive impact on 25 to 30 seats in the Punjab. And if 25 to 30 politicians needed Ahmadi votes to win their seats, then they might be encouraged to pay some positive attention to the Ahmadi community and its needs.

The way in which the Ahmadi issue is implicated today in the wider political landscape of Pakistan was also explained in the APPG meeting in discussions relating to the 2017 protests in Pakistan over changes to the Elections Reform Bill 2017. The changes involved minor revisions to the language in clauses relating to the finality of prophethood and the omission of clauses 7B and 7C of the Conduct of the General Election Order 2002, which mandated a separate voters list for the Ahmadiyya community (Ahmad 2017; Shahid 2018b). In response, a newly formed Barelvi[55] Islamist religious political party, the Tehreek-e-Labbaik Party (TLP), launched a protest decrying the changes as blasphemous. The government quickly reversed the changes but not in time to prevent TLP supporters blockading roads in Islamabad and calling for the sacking of the law minister (Ahmad 2017; Sayeed 2017). These widely reported and socially disruptive protests were described by one Ahmadi representative at the APPG meeting as marking a change in the Pakistani anti-Ahmadi protests insofar as past organizations were not predominantly Barelvi ones and this recent development was therefore, as he put it, 'more impactful' given that most Pakistani Sunnis are Barelvi. However, the same representative also considered that this religious political party was being supported by the Pakistan military as part of a strategy to weaken the government in the run up to the elections.[56] The Ahmadi representative went on to say that after the sitting government lost the next election, as it was expected to and in the event did, the military would withdraw support and the TLP would weaken as a political force. In this reading of the anti-Ahmadi protests in Pakistan the community was a pawn in the power struggle between the ruling party and the military, with the TLP strategically deployed by the military against a soft target, the Ahmadis, to achieve their political ends.

Whatever the case may have been and whoever was supporting the TLP to whatever ends, the anti-Ahmadi protests by the Barelvi TLP made the immediate situation for the Ahmadis in Pakistan even worse than they already were, and this is one more mark of the hardening of attitudes against them in the country. As those present at the APPG meeting were informed, prior to the 1974 legislation declaring the Ahmadis non-Muslim, there was no general consensus on this issue in Pakistan and opinions among non-Ahmadis varied. The official position on the Ahmadis as non-Muslim was settled in 1974 and question then became one of what rights, as non-Muslims, Ahmadis should have in Pakistan. And today, the APPG meeting was told, the issue has moved on from a discussion about what rights Ahmadis should have to questioning if they even deserve to live in Pakistan at all.

Part of this hardening of attitudes in Pakistan has to do with the anti-Ahmadi content of educational textbooks in schools, and this was another area in which the Ahmadi representatives thought the British parliamentarians might assist their cause. When asked if the British government, which spends more on aid to Pakistan than to any other country,[57] should withdraw funding if the Pakistan government does not work to improve the situation for the Ahmadis, the response from the Ahmadi representatives was a decisive 'no'. The Ahmadis did not want any funding to be taken away from Pakistan but rather to have what the money was spent on closely monitored and for more, perhaps, to be channeled into inter-faith causes.

In relation to printed materials and religious literature the Ahmadis described how they have been impacted by what happened following a terrorist attack on a school in Peshawar in 2014 which left over 150 people, mostly children, dead. In response to this attack the government of Pakistan established the National Action Plan to tackle terrorist organizations. As part of a strategy to prevent future terrorist attacks, the National Action Plan included provisions to crack down on hate literature. Unfortunately for the Ahmadis, the Punjab Provincial Assembly set up a board of clerics, the Mutahiddah Ulama Board, to define what constituted hate literature, and they advised that all Ahmadi literature, including newsletters, periodicals, CDs, websites and all the books by Ghulam Ahmad should be banned under this legislation. One of the Ahmadi representatives at the APPG meeting described how he was called by fellow Ahmadis in the middle of the night and told to remove all his books from his shelves because they feared raids were imminent. This was not an unreasonable course of action to follow given that Ahmadis have had their printing presses and homes raided, and those arrested face a military court and a mandatory five year prison sentence.[58] According to an Ahmadi website which tracks anti-Ahmadi materials and which collates information on acts of violence against them, the Mutahiddah Ulama Board, while finding Ahmadi literature to constitute 'hate' literature, simultaneously found that material produced by Khatm-e-Nabuwat was not hate literature because:

> As Mirzais/Qadianis/Lahoris have been declared non-Muslims in the Constitution of Pakistan and they are forbidden by law to use Islamic terms [*sic*] but they continue to use these in violation of the law, and the Khatme Nabuwwat literature that is produced in their rebuttal and designates them *Kafir* is in no way in the category of hate material. Thus the Home Department, the Police in general and the Government of Punjab in particular should take no action whatsoever against the Khatme Nabuwwat literature, its drafting, printing, distribution and sale. It was unanimously recommended that the Home Department should issue a notification in this regard.[59]

Again, as in the case of seeking amendments to electoral legislation, the Ahmadis encouraged the APPG members to support the call to overturn the provincial banning order which would thus allow them access to their own religious literature once more. As the process by which the ruling that all Ahmadi literature is hate material can be overturned is clearly set out, and as a provincial rather than a federal level ruling, the Ahmadi representatives considered that this might be a more achievable goal than repealing other explicitly anti-Ahmadi laws at the present time in Pakistan.

Some of the questions raised and information provided during the discussions at the APPG meeting in April generated material that found its way into the House of Commons debate held the following month on 24 May 2018. Participating in the APPG meeting is, therefore, one way in which Ahmadi representatives can shape debate, and ultimately perhaps also government policy relating to issues in Pakistan through the democratic process in the UK. At present the Ahmadis do not vote and hence have no political representation in Pakistan itself but, as one representative made clear in the APPG meetings, the Pakistani authorities listen most of all to the British. This, he stated, is so well understood by representatives of all countries that even when Canadian officials or officials from other countries visit Rabwah to find out first-hand about conditions there they inevitably ask 'have you spoken to the British about this?' And while, given the context, one might imagine that the Ahmadi representative wished to encourage the British parliamentarians by such flattery, the statement is also true given the historical connections between the UK and Pakistan, the large UK-based Pakistani diaspora, the level of British development funding for Pakistan and trade connections between the two nations.[60]

The politicians who spoke in the debate in the House of Commons on 24 May 2018 repeatedly referenced, as in many previous debates, the need to work to defuse and eradicate extremism in Pakistan in order to help arrest the spread of such extremism in the UK. It was clear that they were aware that what happens in Pakistan will make its way to the UK, and often sooner rather than later. Several MPs also made the now well-rehearsed point that Ahmadis experience discrimination in the UK from other Muslim groups. As MP John Spellar asked: 'is it not also a problem that some of that hatred comes here from other countries? We have seen attacks on individuals – we have seen incidents in Glasgow and elsewhere, even if they do not lead to murder – as well as calls for boycotts on businesses owned by Ahmadis?' Siobhain McDonagh agreed but added that the issue was broader than simply the importation of discrimination from outside, noting that 'local authorities need to look to themselves as well, because Ahmadis are also excluded from most SACREs – standing advisory councils on religious education – in English councils, so some of these things are very close to our respective homes'. And this explicitly raised an issue in Parliament which some Ahmadis also discussed at length with me as a matter they consider infringes on their rights to self-define and participate in local government in the UK.

Although not explicitly discussed in this parliamentary debate, one of the SACRE cases known to Siobhain McDonagh, and the one she was perhaps thinking of as she spoke in the debate, went on for several years before it was finally resolved in Birmingham. In brief, Birmingham Council found itself embroiled in a controversy beginning in 2012 over the issue of allowing Ahmadi representation on its SACRE committee, the interfaith group local councils consult on how religious education is to be delivered in schools.[61] The Muslim representatives on the Birmingham SACRE committee stated that they would only agree to the participation of the Ahmadis on the committee if they were prepared to identify themselves as non-Muslim and they also threatened to walk out if their demands were not met (Porter 2016). The Ahmadi response was to claim that the Labour-led council, if it acceded to the demands of the Muslim faith leaders, would have failed to promote and protect religious tolerance. Further, the Ahmadis argued, this was divisive and an example of unlawful religious sectarianism of a type that had made its way to the UK from South Asia. After a campaign that lasted some five years, involved a wide range of stakeholders, engaged legal advisors and required many meetings, the Ahmadis were eventually co-opted, in spite of the continued resistance of the Muslim representatives, onto the Birmingham SACRE Committee A in 2017.

Other examples of discrimination against Ahmadis in Pakistan which have made their way to the UK and were also raised in the House of Commons debate included the 'editing out of any Ahmadi Muslim's contribution to Pakistan's history'. And in this respect the life and work of the Nobel Prize–winning Ahmadi physicist, Abdus Salam, was specifically mentioned as having been deleted from Pakistani schoolbooks. These schoolbooks, it was further suggested, might possibly have been funded by British aid monies. This issue too, however, is not confined to Pakistan but has made its way to none other than Oxford University, as was also noted in the same House of Commons debate. Ahmadi student societies across the UK have over the years repeatedly stated that university Muslim student societies regularly undermine their activities and the recent Oxford case was just one in a long series of such instances. At Oxford University in May 2017, as reported in the *Cherwell*, an Oxford University student weekly newspaper, a documentary on the life of Abdus Salam was screened by the Oxford University Ahmadi Muslim Student Association (OU-AMSA). The AMSA had sought to co-host this event with the Pakistan Society (PakSoc). However, communications between AMSA and PakSoc appear to have been intermittent and misunderstandings clearly arose over a period of a few months leading up to the screening. The last minute action to advertise and offer to co-host the screening on the part of the PakSoc was considered to be no more than an attempt at 'face-saving' by AMSA, an accusation strongly denied by the PakSoc spokesperson (Morris 2018).[62] As with the right to take part in British local government groups such as SACRE, or to screen films at university, the difficulties experienced by Ahmadis in the UK are examples of the forms of exclusion and discrimination which Ahmadis consider to be local versions of the exclusionary and discriminatory practices imported, as it were, from Pakistan. The difference between Pakistan and the UK, however, is that in the UK the Ahmadis can, and do, use the systems and processes in place to challenge any form of discrimination and exclusion they experience.

Towards the end of the parliamentary debate Mark Field, Minister of State for the Foreign and Commonwealth Office (FCO), responded to the issues that had been raised in the debate by the various speakers. In response to the issue of whether or not British development funds were being used in the production of school textbooks that might promote intolerance, Field stated that he would need to look into the matter and reply in writing at a later date. He also made clear that the British government was actively seeking to develop trade and maintain good relations with Pakistan, in part at least because of its geographical neighbour, Afghanistan, 'its relationship with China, and the sense in which the United Kingdom is a trusted partner at a time of uncertainty in that part of the globe'. It was part of the British strategy, he stated, to work quietly with the Pakistani authorities to keep communication channels open and maintain good relations between the two countries, 'in private, rather than through megaphone diplomacy'. MPs earlier in the debate had asked about when the British might show their 'teeth' and make clear to Pakistan that the trade advantages it enjoys through the UK and EU, such as GSP+ (Generalized System of Preferences) status which grants developing countries preferential reduced tariffs or duty-free access to EU markets,[63] could be at risk if Pakistan did not abide by international conventions concerning discrimination in regard to employment and occupation. The response to this from the FCO was not altogether unexpected.[64] Field noted that the:

> Department for International Development has its biggest single programme there [Pakistan], and efforts are being made to work with British Pakistanis to develop trade connections for the future. It all involves a huge amount of work, but that is not in any way to downgrade the work that we do in standing up for the Ahmadi community. I will take the opportunity to ensure that we raise that issue more extensively.

While trade and issues of geopolitical security may thus be prioritized, the minister also mentioned that he had raised relevant minority issues with the Pakistan Ministry of Human Rights, and that he had also written to the Foreign Minister, Khawaja Asif. Additionally, he noted that his ministerial colleague and 'man of deep faith' Lord Ahmad, himself an Ahmadi Muslim, had 'raised this issue as recently as February with the Pakistan Minister of Interior'. And yet, it was also made clear in this debate that when British parliamentarians had recently spoken of the Ahmadi issue with the deputy high commissioner of Pakistan, they had left the meeting with the impression 'that there did not seem to be an acceptance that there was, in fact, an issue for the community'. The Liberal Democrat Tom Brake added: 'after reading out some quite detailed evidence, we were asked to provide more evidence to demonstrate that there was a problem'. So, while British ministers may be working quietly and conscientiously with their Pakistani counterparts to raise the Ahmadi issue without harming trade and risking wider geo-political understandings, it remains possible for senior diplomats such as the Pakistan deputy high commissioner to leave British MPs with the impression that the Pakistan government does not consider there to be an Ahmadi problem in Pakistan today. And while the situation is clearly very different to that in 1984 when British ministers and politicians, who sought to keep their good working relations with General Zia, were sufficiently reassured that the government of Pakistan was, by passing anti-Ahmadi legislation, actually working to protect the Ahmadis, the necessity the British government has to maintain links with Pakistan today means that pressing the Ahmadi issue with their Pakistani counterparts is one that diplomats and ministers may opt to shy away from if they can.

Picking up on points made by several others during the debate, Field also recognized the consequences for the UK of acts of persecution that take place in Pakistan when he stated that: 'Incidents of religious persecution in Pakistan have a tangible impact on community relations in the UK, and we are working hard to reduce the risk of extremist influences being projected into our own communities'. And indeed examples of such 'extremist influences projected into' the UK were graphically described during the debate when Zac Goldsmith outlined how the UK registered charity, Khatam-e-Nabuwat had publicly congratulated Muslims after the murder of Asad Shah in 2016. Goldsmith went on to say:

> Appallingly, that organization has been an affiliate of the otherwise respected Muslim Council of Britain. The MCB has since set up a panel to look at the group, but why on earth do we need a panel when the group has quite openly and brazenly celebrated the murder of people whose version of Islam they do not like? Even calling a panel to examine such a phenomenon is an insult. To add to the insult, two of the members that have been put on to it have strong ties to the very group it is investigating. One of them gave a speech shortly before, saying:
>
> > having any sort of ties with them − Ahmadis − is far worse than being addicted to drugs and alcohol. . . . I am humbly requesting you, do not meet them or your faith would suffer from an incurable cancer. . . . Leave this place with the promise that not only will you sever all ties with the Ahmadis but also with anyone who sympathizes with them.
>
> Well, I guess that includes all of us in the Chamber today.

Concern about Ahmadis languishing in refugee camps around the world was also raised during the debate and a request was made to the Foreign and Commonwealth Office minister to confirm that he would ask the Home Office 'whether this country can take in more Ahmadi Muslims who are sitting forgotten in refugee camps', and to 'revisit our guidance on how Home Office officials are trained to consider asylum applications by Ahmadi Muslims from Pakistan'. These matters were not explicitly dealt with by Field in his response to questions and issues raised during the debate, though he did discuss measures that might be taken to improve the screening of visa applications for individuals seeking permission to enter the country to make sure that they were not inclined to contribute to radicalization or promote violence and sectarian division in the UK.

Even if the language of the FCO minister was to suggest that quiet diplomacy behind closed doors, boosting international trade with Pakistan and increased diligence over the granting of visas to immigrants were the priorities for government, the debate was not unimportant. The very fact a debate took place at all marked a significant step forward in the visibility of British Ahmadis and also in the public recognition that the community is persecuted and discriminated against in Pakistan and elsewhere. As McDonagh concluded, '[n]one of us should underestimate the power and importance to the Ahmadi community of a debate of this sort taking place in the British Parliament, on the Floor of this Chamber. It means that they are recognised and heard – and they desperately need to be heard'. The debate ended by passing a resolution stating:

> this House notes with concern the rising tide of persecution of Ahmadi Muslims in Pakistan, Algeria and other countries around the world; further notes the effect that hate preachers have on radicalising people internationally and in the UK, through the media, social media and otherwise; notes with concern the past activities of hate preacher, Syed Muzaffar Shah Qadri, who radicalised Tanveer Ahmed, who in turn murdered Mr Asad Shah in Glasgow in March 2016; calls on the Government to make representations to the Governments of Pakistan and Algeria on the persecution of Ahmadis; and further calls on the Government to make more stringent the entry clearance procedures to the UK for hate preachers by ensuring that entry clearance hubs and the Home Office have adequate numbers of Urdu speakers to monitor visa applications and online radicalisation.

Conclusion

Over the last 106 years, the Ahmadi population in the UK has risen from a transient six individuals in 1913 to a settled community of 25,000 to 30,000. For much of that time the reasons for Ahmadi migration, both short-term and permanent, paralleled those of other South Asian communities and grew in response to developments in British migration regulations limiting future settlers from the subcontinent, as well as because of the Africanization policies in newly independent East African countries. Since 1984, with the arrival of the fourth Ahmadi khalifa in London, the Ahmadi population in the country has grown more rapidly and a significant proportion of those who have arrived since this time have come as asylum seekers. The Ahmadi diaspora in the UK is, in no small measure, a product of the political events that have taken place in Pakistan.

As the Ahmadi community in the UK has become established and as their numbers are now sufficiently large for them to organize and carry out strategic interventions on behalf of the wider Ahmadi community, they have worked, both individually and particularly at an organizational level, to make the needs of Ahmadi asylum seekers better known to the Home Office, asylum and immigration tribunals, and to the government through their MPs. Articulate and well-informed Ahmadi representatives have developed lasting individual contacts and relations with officials and politicians, and they have understood the value of objective and well-researched studies to advance their cause. Human rights reports such as those discussed earlier serve several functions. They record the plight of Ahmadis in Pakistan today and hence will become in due course historical documents, they are used as supporting objective evidence for individual asylum seekers, and they also serve to provide data British politicians can draw upon when discussing current and future British-Pakistan relations.

While the UK-based Ahmadis work with local institutions, local MPs and on national issues, it is clear that there is also a global Ahmadi strategy. For example, US-based Ahmadis will work on publicizing the same issues as the UK Ahmadis, networking and reaching out to their own elected representatives, producing reports and making visible the plight of Ahmadis in the subcontinent to relevant local and national bodies wherever Ahmadis are settled. And while in the 1930s Home Office records show that the Ahmadis were not well known to the British authorities, today they can be found at the heart of the British establishment, in government, at both local and national levels. In the early twentieth century there were very few South Asian Muslims able to influence government policy or, like Ameer Ali, in positions of institutional authority. Today British Ahmadis have achieved considerable organizational capacity and visibility. This has meant that over the last decade, in addition to the publication of several human rights reports, there have been debates in Westminster Hall about their situation in Pakistan and elsewhere, an APPG devoted to them has been established, and a debate was held in the Houses of Parliament. Through such reports and by their attendance at APPGs British Ahmadis can represent and speak for Pakistani Ahmadis who remain otherwise without voice and representation in Pakistan.

Notes

1 I make this distinction as while the UK Ahmadi community is primarily of South Asian heritage there are also members from West Africa, North Africa and of white European descent. These latter remain for the present time a numerical minority in the UK and are not a focus of this chapter.

2 For more on transnational religious networks established by Muslims in late nineteenth- and early twentieth-century Britain, see Ansari 2008:46ff.

3 Ballard (2003) notes that the South Asian migrants came from relatively few places in the subcontinent and many of them were Muslims, Sikhs or Hindus from the Punjab, the others being Gujaratis, 80% of whom were Hindu and 20% Muslim, and Bangladeshis, mainly from Sylhet, who were also Muslim.

4 'In 1971, the number of Asians from East Africa resident in the UK was about 45,000. However, with more expulsions from African countries, the number of East African Asians in 1981was estimated at about 180,000' (Anwar 1998:5).

5 This point is also made by Ramji 2006 discussing Hindu Gujarati twice migrants. One woman in the 'mother' generation interviewed about the move to the UK said: 'We came as a family from Uganda and we stayed as a family in London. This made it easier for all of us, I was here to help my family settle and we were all around to support one another. I think it was very hard for women who had to wait until their husbands called them over, this took many years' (2006:712).

6 Bhachu coined the term 'twice migrant' in 1986 to describe migrants who moved 'to Britain throughout the 1960s after their jobs had been "Africanized" in the decolonization process in the three East African countries of Uganda, Kenya, and Tanzania. These migrants had come from different parts of India, though predominantly from the Punjab . . . and from Gujarat in . . . India from the 1890s onward. As settlers in East Africa for often over a century, they were experienced at the game of migration and the management of their minority status before they migrated for a second and a third time' (Bhachu 2016:1). Bhachu defines twice migrants as 'people who have initially moved from a country of origin to a destination in which they have settled and then, having been part of an established diaspora as settlers, have made a second or third move, rapidly reestablishing their networks and their social, cultural, and economic capital in new economies' (Bhachu 2016:1).

7 Ramji (2006:717) describing Indian migrants notes in similar fashion that 'a trait of the Indian diaspora is that in the cultural domain Indians tend to preserve their identity while in the economic domain they are quick to integrate'.

8 'Humanitarian protection (HP) was introduced in April 2003 to replace the policy on Exceptional Leave to Remain. . . . HP is designed to provide international protection where it is needed, to individuals who do not qualify for protection under the Refugee Convention. It covers situations where someone may be at risk of serious harm if they return to their country of origin but they are not recognised as refugees because the risk is not of persecution for a reason covered by the Refugee Convention' (Home Office 2017:6).

9 Though I have come across occasional exceptions to this with people granted asylum on arrival at a UK port and in one case a man granted asylum by an immigration judge after he was asked why he did not have any objective evidence of persecution such as a newspaper cutting naming him as a target of anti-Ahmadi violence. The man, a well-educated professional, told the judge that they both knew such newspaper reports could be easily forged and that even without such 'evidence' his case was genuine and he was in need of international protection. The man was granted asylum and now advises fellow Ahmadi asylum seekers to 'just tell the truth'. In this particular case, however, the evidently middle class position and clearly articulate, rational and reasonable response of the asylum seeker may well have established a rapport across cultural divides with the tribunal judge which worked in the favour of this man but might not work quite so well with less educated, less cosmopolitan and less articulate asylum seekers who might find establishing their credibility in a court room setting more difficult to achieve.

10 Study bans were part of the Immigration Act 2016 (McClenaghan 2018). However, on 9 May 2018, the Home Office issued new Bail Guidance stating that asylum seekers must be permitted to study.

11 For more on country expert reports, see Good 2007, particularly chapters 6, 9 and 11.

12 One woman, interviewed in London in 2018, told me that her father and his brothers were Ahmadi but that her father's sisters were not. When she visits her Sunni Muslim paternal aunt in Pakistan she is warmly welcomed and accepted but also requested not to let visitors or affinal kin of her aunt know that she herself is Ahmadi. In this case the immediate consanguineal Sunni family are accepting of their Ahmadi kin but do not wish to have to deal with the consequences that might result from affinal kin and acquaintances learning of their Ahmadi relations.

13 In a letter dated 17 September 1985, sent on behalf of the national president, Ahmadiyya Association, UK to the Home Office, Immigration Department. The fact that some members of the Ahmadi community were both Pakistani and also British citizens, including prominent men such as Zafrulla Khan, is highlighted in Home Office files in letters from MPs such as David Mellor. The point being that any attack on British Ahmadis in Pakistan would be a matter for the British government to deal with (FCO 1984 37:3833).

14 The London Mosque, then headquarters of the UK Ahmadis, is in Putney. David Mellor was Conservative MP for Putney at the time, hence many of his constituents were Ahmadis.

15 The conditions for a person seeking to stay in the UK as a minister of religion included then, as now, the undertaking not to have recourse to public funds (www.ukimmigration.com/ministers_of_religion). After four years of continuous work as a minister of religion a person can apply for permanent residency.

16 Quoted from a letter from the Home Secretary, Leon Brittan, dated 29 April 1985 (HO 1984–1985 325:617).

17 In a similar vein the MP for Mitcham and Morden, Siobhain McDonagh, in a debate in the British Houses of Parliament on 24 May 2018 described the persecution of Ahmadis in West Java with an updated version of this approach to the 'Ahmadi issue', stating: 'But perhaps the persecution is best illustrated by the calls from the governor of West Java, who claimed there would be no violence against the Ahmadiyya community if there were no Ahmadi teachings or practices. The "problem", he suggests, "will disappear if the belief disappears."' www.theyworkforyou.com/debates/?id=2018-05-24a.1040.0.

18 It is clear from the paragraphs that follow that I. H. Davies did not give Mr Syed all the information he had about political asylum, for example, that it was possible to travel to the UK without a visa and seek political asylum on arrival. He added, however, that he did not give him this information as he assumed he would already know this (FCO 1984 37/3833).

19 An FIR is a First Information Report, the written allegation of a crime reported to the police. It is in response to an FIR that the police investigate crimes and may go on to make arrests.

20 London, 26 April 2018.

21 The New Asylum Model was introduced by the Home Office in 2007 to speed up asylum claims. Every asylum seeker is assigned a specific member of the UK Border Agency staff (the 'case owner') to oversee a case from the point an application for asylum is made to the final decision.

22 The Home Office (2018:19–20) *COIN Pakistan: Ahmadis,* states:

> 5.5.1 A person's religious affiliation must be declared when applying for a passport and/or national identity card (CNIC). When applying for a passport or CNIC, those wishing to be listed as Muslims must sign a declaration denouncing the Ahmadiyya Muslim prophet. This effectively prevents Ahmadi Muslims from obtaining legal documents and puts pressure on them to deny their beliefs in order to enjoy citizenship rights, including the right to vote. . . . However, the USCIRF 2013 report noted that individuals who refused to sign the declaration when applying for a passport still received one, although in a note dated 8 June 2018, the IHRC informed CPIT that the Ahmadiyya Muslim Community in Pakistan confirmed this was not the case. The IHRC noted that an Ahmadi cannot legally obtain a passport without signing the declaration and, if they sign it, they are effectively declaring themselves Muslim, which is in breach of the PPC.
>
> 5.5.2 According to a NADRA official, consulted by the British High Commission . . . in June 2018, no mention of the person's religion is made on Machine Readable Passports. If a person has a valid passport and visa there are no travel restrictions against any minorities. In contrast, the IHRC stated in its note to CPIT, dated 8 June 2018, that information gathered during its fact-finding missions and interviews with the Ahmadiyya Muslim Community in Pakistan, had identified numerous instances when Ahmadi travellers faced great harassment and difficulties at Pakistan airports. Lahore airport was reportedly notorious in this respect. Ahmadis were restricted from participating in the Hajj due to the passport application requirements to record one's religious affiliation.

23 This concern, that a non-Ahmadi may be granted asylum by claiming to be Ahmadi, is one that other immigration and asylum courts have recognized, as for example noted by Vatuk for the US (2011:26).

24 In an interview in April 2018 I was told that the 'Particulars of the Ahmadi Applicant form' requires a photograph for men but not for women. When I asked why this was the case, I was told that there was enough written information on the form for a photograph not to be required for a woman and that this was also because the form would pass through many male hands as it went through the verification process.

25 For more on this see Home Office 2018:57–59 and Asian Human Rights Commission and International Human Rights Committee 2015:85. See also IRB Canada, RESPONSES TO INFORMATION REQUESTS 2013. 'Ahmadi Membership Verification'.

26 In similar vein for Germany Zia Shah (2014) rebutted the accusation that the Ahmadi *jama'at* is in the 'asylum business' stating the German Ahmadi *jama'at* provides certificates on the status of the individual within the community; alerts the authorities to anyone seeking asylum by falsely claiming to be an Ahmadi; does not specify which lawyers asylum seekers should use to pursue their cases; does not provide mosque accommodation for asylum seekers etc. This suggests that while national *jama'ats* fine-tune their dealings to fit with local legal and administrative circumstances there is a globally agreed general framework they all work within in terms of how the Ahmadi *jama'at*, as an institution, approaches and manages asylum seekers. There are, however, rare cases of particularly determined individuals who appear to be able to fool not only the UK Border Agency but also the Ahmadis they come into contact with. Some years ago I was told of a pious woman who had converted to Ahmadiyyat and sought asylum in the UK. This woman lived for years as an Ahmadi gaining enough trust to become a finance officer in the *lajna*. As soon as her refugee status was granted she simply disappeared. No one has seen or heard from her since. The assumption is that the woman was pretending to be an Ahmadi to gain asylum in the UK. To maintain such a deception for so long while interacting with so many Ahmadis must have taken extraordinary levels of skill, focus and perhaps, desperation.

27 This should perhaps be understood in the context of HO concerns about Ahmadi overstayers as detailed in, for example, FCO 1988. 37/5244 Ahmadiyya Muslim Community. In this document it is clear that the HO and AMA were in communication, the former concerned about how many Ahmadis might be using the *jalsa* as an opportunity to get to the UK (though these concerns were considered slight by some of the British officials who discussed this matter) and the AMA position that very few Ahmadis overstayed their visa. The AMA even went so far as to provide the HO with a list of the 12 overstayers they had identified.

28 Paragraph 3.

29 The purpose of the last clause highlighted in bold was to confirm to the immigration tribunal that the report writer, in this case also a member of the Ahmadi community, was aware that his primary duty and obligation was to the court and not to the individual asylum claimant. And this duty is in the UK one that 'elevates the expert's duty to the court in the first place' (Good 2007:137). Report writers are also to be clear that their role is not to act as an advocate and in practice any report writer who appears to be advocating on behalf of a client may find the judges simply dismiss the entire report. Comprehensiveness and transparency are also required of report writers so that evidence which might detract from the claimant's case should be included in the report and the writer is expected to make clear the limits of her or his knowledge and the sources for all material included in the report (Sutherland 2009; Good 2007:137). The value of a report, from the point of view of the judges, is that it should provide them with information in areas in which they are not expert, and do not have the skill or experience required to help them decide on the truth when determining the outcome of a case.

30 MN and others (Ahmadis – country conditions – risk) Pakistan CG [2012] UKUT 00389 (IAC).
31 Ibid.
32 Paragraph 2(i).
33 Paragraph 3(i).
34 HRC 2015.
35 If the figure of 6,900 is correct and if the one quoted from a 2007 report written by an Ahmadi country expert of no more than 3,000 asylum seekers from 1984 to 2007, a 23-year period, is also correct, it means that some 3,900 Ahmadi asylum seekers arrived in the UK from 2007–2018. Such a figure would put the average annual number of asylum seekers over 11 years at 354.5, while the figure for the previous 23 years averages at 130 per annum. Given the increasing difficulties for Pakistani asylum seekers trying to enter the UK this rise in numbers seeking asylum per annum supports the AMA's own assessment of the worsening situation in Pakistan.
36 The measures taken to safeguard the UK's borders are set out in a Cabinet Office 2007 report, *Security in a Global Hub: Establishing the UK's new border arrangements*.
37 Paragraph 18 of the Ahmadi 2015 written 'SUBMISSION TO APPG for International Freedom of Religion or Belief', where it is also noted that Canada, unlike the UK, has a formal resettlement programme in place for Ahmadi Muslims. https://appgfreedomofreligionorbelief.org/media/APPG-UK-Submission.pdf.
38 For example, at www.persecutionofahmadis.org, which includes monthly reports, breaking news and a section on non-governmental organizations and foreign reports.
39 These reports explicitly declare the source of funding for the research necessary to produce the reports. For example, the 2015 report states: 'The expenses of the mission were met by the Ahmadiyya Muslim Community. The members of the mission have not received and will not receive any compensation for their time'.
40 The strategy of securing the services of professional non-Ahmadi experts in support of the Ahmadi cause is one that goes back to colonial times. An interesting parallel situation, for example, was the funding of the work by the Australian geographer Oskar Spate in the 1940s employed by the Ahmadiyya community to work on the boundary issue prior to partition. For Spate's insights into the boundary commission and both public hearings and behind the scenes events to do with the partition of the Punjab see also in Chester (2009:62–65, 67, 69–70, 100–101). In his 1947 article Spate goes as far as to say 'I found myself acting in effect as an unofficial advisor to the Muslim League, and considered myself – perhaps on inadequate grounds – as an expert witness' (1947:201).
41 Lord Avebury was also the first recipient to be honoured at the Ahmadi Peace Symposium, in 2009, with the Ahmadiyya Muslim Prize for the Advancement of Peace. See Bates (2016) for an obituary of Lord Avebury.
42 During the attacks in Lahore a British Ahmadi and Putney resident, Mr Muhammad Bilal, who was visiting Pakistan and in one of the mosques at the time of the attack was killed. The London community felt the loss not only as an attack on their fellow Ahmadis but also as one that was very close and personal because of the loss of one of their local members too.
43 Westminster Hall Debates offer MPs an opportunity to raise issues and receive a response from a government minister.
44 The transcribed debate is at: https://hansard.parliament.uk/Commons/2010-10-20/debates/10102039000002/AhmadiyyaCommunity.
45 And in 2018, in the lead up to the Pakistan elections in July, it was reported that Bilawal Bhutto, the chairman of the Pakistan People's Party, and grandson of Zulfiqar Ali Bhutto who amended the county's constitution to declare the Ahmadis non-Muslim in 1974, had deleted a tweet from 2013 in which he appeared to support the right of an Ahmadi man to read the Qur'an after the man had been arrested for doing precisely this (Rehan 2018).

46 This matter was widely reported in the print media and on national television. Whether the particular quote on a leaflet mentioned in the Westminster Hall debate even existed was taken up by anti-Ahmadi campaigners who challenged the Channel 4 News reporter to provide evidence for the claims made. The 5 December 2010 Channel 4 report is at www.channel4.com/news/hate-crime-investigation-into-threats-against-ahmadi-muslims. The 8 December 2010 BBC report is at www.bbc.co.uk/news/av/uk-11947734/ahmadiyya-targeted-by-hate-campaign. The position questioning the reporting of the hate leaflets is at www.qern.org/channel-4-and-bbc-hate-campaign/.

47 APPG 2016. *Freedom of Religion or Belief in Pakistan & UK Government Policy: APPG for International Freedom of Religion or Belief.*

48 For the Ahmadi press release: https://alislam.org/press-release/UK_Parliament_Khilafat_Event.pdf.

49 For the Ahmadi press release: www.alislam.org/library/press-release/historic-reception-takes-place-at-houses-of-parliament-to-celebrate-ahmadiyya-muslim-jamaat-uk-centenary/.

50 In: www.parliament.uk/business/publications/written-questions-answers-statements/written-question/Commons/2016-01-04/20784/. In 2018 Lord Ahmad was the Foreign Office's Minister for Human Rights and Freedom of Religion or Belief. Other Ahmadis have been elected as local councilors (in one case also serving as a mayor) and some have stood, not always successfully, as prospective members of Parliament. The people I spoke with included those who were active members of the Conservative, Labour and Liberal parties and thus crossed the mainstream political spectrum.

51 Full debate at: https://hansard.parliament.uk/Commons/2018-05-24/debates/B2B8FC6E-7F7F-4BFC-8C7A-107F94D1B9FB/AhmadiyyaMuslimCommunity.

52 On this see, for example, the Asian Human Rights Commission 2016.

53 The Human Rights Watch 2018 report notes: 'In 2002, President Gen. Pervez Musharraf abolished the separate electorate system and restored the original joint electorate scheme with one major amendment. Through an executive order, he created a separate category for Ahmadis. Executive Order No. 15 states that elections for the members of the National Assembly and the provincial assemblies shall be held on the basis of a joint electorate, but the "status of Ahmadis [was] to remain unchanged." As a result, Pakistani citizens have been moved to a single electoral list, leaving only Ahmadis on a "non-Muslim" list. The new Election Act 2017 retains the provisions regarding the status of the Ahmadis'.

54 MP Liz McInnes speaking at the APPG (2018:37) International Freedom of Religion or Belief. https://appgfreedomofreligionorbelief.org/house-of-commons-debates-the-persecution-of-ahmadis/.

55 See Khan (2011:3) on the Barelvi Muslims of Pakistan. A group with its origins in 'the Indian town of Bareilly, which was the birthplace (and thereby the last name) of Ahmed Raza Khan Bareilly, a pioneering scholar and revivalist of the latter half of the nineteenth century whose teachings greatly influenced modern religious thought across the subcontinent'. Modern Barelvis consider themselves: 'orthodox Sunnis, or "Ahl-e-Sunnat wal Jamaat" (Followers of the Traditions of the Prophet and Congregation) who adhere to true Islam as it was originally practiced by the Prophet and his companions as well as by various saints (wali) throughout history' (Ibid.:4).

56 Such a view appears to be one that historian Ayesha Jalal also shares as she made clear in an interview with Ashraf (2018).

57 DFID spent £463 million in 2017 on Pakistan in bilateral aid. Syria was second with £352 million. https://fullfact.org/economy/uk-spending-foreign-aid/. In DFID's Pakistan Profile report for July 2017 the Punjab Education Support Programme is allocated £75.4 million, more than any other single programme. https://assets.publishing.service.gov.uk/government/uploads/system/uploads/attachment_data/file/636548/Pakistan1.pdf.

58 This information is collated from several sources, including the IHRC/AHRC 2017 'Fact-Finding Report', in the UK Home Office June 2018 *CPIN: Pakistan, Ahmadis*.

59 In 'The Government of Punjab bans Ahmadiyya books and publications', which states that this quote was from the *Daily Ausaf*, 14 February 2015. www.persecutiono-fahmadis.org/the-government-of-punjab-bans-ahmadiyya-books-and-publications/

60 This does not mean, of course, that Ahmadis based in other countries do not seek to make their case heard. For example, as shown on YouTube, 'U.S. House of Represent-atives Testimony: Persecution of Ahmadiyya Muslim Community in South Asia' www. youtube.com/watch?v=e6DT57f7Y3w. In this film Amjad Mahmood Khan is shown testifying before the US House of Representatives on 21 March 2012 and making very similar points as were made in 2018 during the UK APPG. He also suggested that tackling frivolous accusations of blasphemy by tightening up the procedures by which a FIR is filed would be a small step in the right direction. American House Representa-tive, Tom Lantos, asked the Ahmadi spokesperson on this occasion, as did the British MPs and Lords some six years later, what their government could do to 'encourage the Pakistani government to reform' the blasphemy laws. And, as in the UK, the Ahmadi representative was clear that the outlook was bleak when it came to the reform of these laws because of entrenched opinions and attitudes against the Ahmadis.

In relation to the repeal of separate voter lists which Ahmadi representatives were seeking British government support on Ahmadis have also been working with US poli-ticians to achieve the same goal as is made clear by Speier and King, co-chairs of the Congressional Ahmadiyya Muslim Caucus, (2018) who state: 'Notably, reform of the passport regime and the electoral process can be achieved through purely administra-tive and executive action by Pakistan's government: neither issue requires legislative action. Restoring the franchise to Ahmadis, for example, would require only rescind-ing Pakistani Presidential Order No. 15 of 2002 ("Executive Order No. 15"), which uniquely excludes Ahmadis from the joint electoral rolls, and requires them to be reg-istered on a separate supplementary voter roll. We cannot afford to let another five-year election cycle pass before the critical issue of restoring the full and free right to vote for Ahmadi Muslims is resolved once and for all'.

61 Birmingham SACRE Minutes 15 October 2012.

62 Other demeaning acts to humiliate Ahmadi students both in Pakistan and in the UK include not allowing Ahmadi students to use cutlery that other Muslim students are using. An Ahmadi man now in his thirties told me of a time he went to an Islamic Society event at his university in London and although he was not asked to leave when it came to the refreshments he was expected to use plates and cutlery that had been set aside for him and no one else to use. It is commonplace in Pakistan for Ahmadi children to be prevented from using shared utensils in schools and to be expected to provide their own. These practices separate Ahmadis from others in ways that are very reminiscent of the treatment of Dalits in India. Such discriminatory practices are ones that were already being called for in the mid-twentieth century as noted in the *Report of the Court of Inquiry* (1954:140) 'At Gujranwala printed leaflets were broad-cast demanding that Ahmadis should be treated as untouchables and separate utensils provided for them at food and drink shops'.

63 As described in the EU Joint Staff Working Document 2016 report 'The EU Special Incentive Arrangement for Sustainable Development and Good Governance ('GSP+') covering the period 2014–2015' https://eeas.europa.eu/sites/eeas/files/european_com-mission._2016._report_on_the_generalised_scheme_of_preferences_during_the_period_2014-2015.pdf.

64 For an EU assessment on Pakistan and its GSP+ status, see the EU Special Incentive Arrangement for Sustainable Development and Good Governance (GSP+) assessment of Pakistan covering the period 2016–2017. This notes ongoing issues in Pakistan with regards to religious minorities, human rights, discrimination in the workforce, etc. http://trade.ec.europa.eu/doclib/docs/2018/january/tradoc_156544.pdf.

5 Home from home

Mosque building and urban planning in a global city

In March 2013 a British tabloid newspaper[1] published a colour photograph of what the text referred to as a 'mega-mosque'.[2] The image was taken from a perspective designed to emphasize the building's dominance over the surrounding environment. With its marble-white dome in the centre and minaret to the right, the mosque takes up two thirds of the photograph and dwarfs an iconic red London bus in the foreground. The caption read: 'New landscape: Merton's mosque, which dominates the skyline of the south London suburb . . . can accommodate 10,000 people'. The photograph thus juxtaposes stereotypical symbols of Islam, a dome and minaret, with another easily recognizable symbol of the capital city, the red double decker bus, to make visible the message that the former now looms over the latter, calling into question our assumptions of what London is, should be and is becoming, and just who is in a position actively to transform the city's landscape into something we are told 'is not English any more'.[3] The accompanying article further locates this image as a visual referent for what the author describes as the 'polite apartheid' threatening social cohesion in the UK as a result of 'over-rapid immigration in recent years'.[4] This image, then, is not just about Islam and the religious buildings of diasporic faith communities in the capital city, it is about migrants elided swiftly in the article with asylum seekers and a perceived lack of social integration in a Britain that is no longer as white as it once was, even if some of the recent arrivals are, for the record, described as 'model immigrants' who work, pay their taxes and are law-abiding. The newspaper article is also about what London, a global city, has become and how those who fashion the city to meet their needs no longer do so solely on the basis of class identities but on ethnic and religious ones which, in some cases, have come to supercede the earlier class-based identities of the industrial city. For, as Cesari (2005:1016) states:

> While the industrial city brought an end to ethnic and cultural differentiation and gave rise to more universal categories such as the working class, salaried employees, private employees and civil servants, the global city tends to reinforce and preserve ethnic differences. . . . The development of ethnic business, like all forms of self-employment in the service sector, provides economic opportunities to those who newly enter the great metropolis. Within this new principle of urban organisation, the forms of socioeconomic

integration can no longer be understood solely in terms of class. More and more, class tends to be combined with ethnicity.

And key aspects of many ethnic identities include both a religious and a trans-national component which further serve to challenge the nostalgic vision of a supposed homogenous Christian and white society, such as the one portrayed in the newspaper article I started the chapter with. These identities, however, 'are not straightforwardly given, but worked at through language and action, and . . . these identities do not just take place, but also make place', which means that we 'need to understand the way in which inter-ethnic relations may be the emerging outcome of "everyday" spatial influences' and interactions (Clayton 2009:483). Some of these interactions may even take place thousands of miles away yet their effects can be felt locally. Further, urban city spaces can be conceived of as dynamic, in process and as the outcome of competing discourses, practices and power relations between different ethnic and religious communities as well as between these and the official bureaucracies which mediate disputes and adjudicate on the built environment. The account of the living conditions in Rabwah given in the first chapter, in particular the comparison of life in the Ahmadi town with historical descriptions of life in a ghetto, sought to frame and help explain the forces that have shaped the Ahmadi diaspora. In this final chapter I approach the complex process of mosque building in the global city of London as an instance of the making of place, a home from home for the Ahmadi community.

Some of the processes, discourses and interactions involved in the process of mosque building noted earlier were made visible in the planning applications and protests against the building of the mosque in the photograph described above, the AMA's Baitul Futuh Mosque. This mosque, built on the derelict site of a former industrial Express Dairy bottling plant in Merton, a borough on the outskirts of southwest London, is considered a post-industrial development success by the local council. It is listed on a council website as a local tourist attraction and is located in one of the less affluent parts of a borough which contains some very upmarket locations as well as several considerably more deprived wards.[5] The mosque provided Merton Council with a virtually cost-free urban regeneration project as the Ahmadis undertook to raise the funds for the redevelopment of the site themselves; and its location, by a railway track and fronting a large main road, also served to facilitate planning permission as minority religious buildings in the UK are increasingly denied planning permission on amenity grounds if the chosen sites are not already in built up areas (brownfield sites) and also on main thoroughfares, served by public transport or otherwise suitably removed from residential housing.

However, despite the clear regeneration potential at low cost to the Council, the mosque from the very first proposal for its construction was at the centre of many debates, including whether or not it can even be called a mosque. Examining what the building represents for Ahmadiyya Muslims, for other Muslim groups and for non-Muslims, together with the transformation of the local environment that has resulted from it, allows for complex and nuanced understandings of local

Figure 5.1 Baitul Futuh Mosque

manifestations, and refutations, of Islamophobia in the context of wider concerns over mosque-building in Europe. It also contributes to the understanding of how everyday forms of racism are submerged in the language of 'amenity' in town planning regulations. In addition, the mosque and the debates surrounding it make visible how local issues arising from international migration and sectarian inter-Muslim conflicts between Sunni Muslims and Ahmadiyya Muslims, stemming from a very particular historical political context in Pakistan, are now played out in places of worship in southwest London. More positively, it allows for the study of inter-community engagements, local economic regeneration, and the participation of Ahmadiyya Muslims in local, regional and national community developments and politics. The latter is particularly clear in relation to the professional middle class Ahmadis who are active in local and national politics. However, while some Ahmadis are educated and active in many professions, a large number of Ahmadis, including those more recently arrived from the subcontinent and others who have arrived, in particular from Germany, may well be among the less affluent members of Merton Borough and for these individuals and families, seeking employment, housing and schooling for children may present challenges typical of those faced by new immigrants and members of ethnic and religious minorities across Europe. This group of more recent Ahmadi migrants, attracted by the possibility of living near to their spiritual leader and with access to the flagship Baitul Futuh Mosque, has sought housing in the neighbourhood of the mosque visibly changing the make-up of the local population in some residential wards. As a community, therefore, the Ahmadis are a complex mixture of British-born Muslims and recent migrants some of whom may be seeking refugee status, middle-class professionals and an upwardly aspiring but presently less affluent and less formally well-educated majority. As Muslims in the UK, however, all constitute a minority and many are, in addition, ethnically marked as of South Asian heritage.

The post-industrial urban transformations represented by the Baitul Futuh Mosque can only be fully understood in the context of a longer history of mosque building in London dating back to the late colonial era. This history is briefly set out to contextualize the complex, and not always harmonious, local network of diasporic Muslim faith centres. Previous chapters have already outlined the polit-ico-religious history necessary to locate the sources of today's conflicts between the Ahmadi Muslims and Sunni Muslims in colonial India and, more particu-larly, after partition in Pakistan. As part of its account of the building of Ahmadi mosques in London, this chapter examines how the conflicts between local Mus-lim sects have been co-opted by local non-Muslim residents in their attempts to thwart Ahmadi Muslim mosque extension plans and how the local council has been embroiled in this as the authority empowered to adjudicate on plan-ning applications submitted to it. Needless to say, at least some of the issues that arose during the planning and building of the mosque mirror the experiences of other diaspora faith communities when dealing with the planning system, includ-ing the inevitable opposition of local residents as they seek to develop existing, or construct new, religious buildings (Nye 2000; Naylor and Ryan 2002, 2003; Gale 2004, 2005; Dunn 2005; McLoughlin 2005; Shah, Dwyer and Gilbert 2012). Throughout the chapter intersections of class, faith and ethnicity are brought to the fore as always relevant though in different ways at different times, to under-stand the shifting and evolving processes that become significant as individuals and groups seek to find ways to inhabit the post-industrial, suburban residential and urban landscapes in one part of a major global city.

A tale of two mosques

The Baitul Futuh Mosque which opened in 2003, boasts a gym, bookshop, library, television studio, homeopathic clinic, soundproof crèche for children (so that women are not disturbed while praying), and Merton's largest enclosed hall avail-able for hire by community organizations. These and a number of other features certainly make the mosque exceptional among European mosques.[6] However, what matters most for the present discussion is not the architectural distinctiveness of the building but the historical continuum and discursive network in which its formation needs to be understood. Had it not been for the refusal by Wandsworth Council to allow planning permission in the 1990s to expand the Fazl Mosque, which also belongs to the Ahmadiyya Muslim community, in neighbouring South-fields, the Merton mosque might not have been needed and the community would not have had to locate a new site on which to accommodate their increasing numbers in the area. The Merton mosque, therefore, represents the success of a town planning application to regenerate a derelict industrial site on the edge of London as a consequence, in part at least, of the failure to be granted planning permission to extend an already existing Ahmadiyya mosque in a suburban, middle class residential area in the neighbouring inner London Borough of Wandsworth.

These two mosques, the Fazl Mosque in Wandsworth and the Baitul Futuh Mosque in Merton, are only a few kilometres apart, both examples of minority faith construction in the suburbs, and yet their distinct histories mark the dramatic changes that have taken place in London over the last century as it has become a 'world capital' by 'virtue of [its] sizeable immigrant population' (Cesari 2005:1016). The first of these mosques, and the first purpose built mosque in London, was the Fazl Mosque constructed on orchard land, literally therefore a greenfield site, bought by the Ahmadiyya Muslim community in 1920 and officially opened in 1926 (Naylor and Ryan 2002:45).[7] In the 1920s, the area around the mosque was not the built-up and populated residential suburban location that it is today, and only a few residential buildings were located in the vicinity. Today it is a Grade II listed building of historic architectural value because of 'its gentle and harmonious fusion of formal and decorative traditions of mosque design with restrained 1920s British classicism, built using modern materials and construction methods; and as a neatly proportioned and delicately composed design by the nationally renowned firm TH Mawson and Sons' and as a 'British Islamic building influenced by contemporary trends deriving from the Arts and Crafts movement' which fused 'Mughal architectural forms with contemporary British stylistic trends' (Noakes 2018:13, 15). 'The Fazl Mosque therefore brought together distinct Indian and British architectural traditions, reflecting established mosque design without creating a structure ill-fitting of its location within a predominantly residential South London suburb setting' (Ibid.:15). In historical terms it is now valued as 'the first purpose-built mosque in London and only the second in Britain and: as an important manifestation of the Ahmadiyya Muslim Community's missionary activities in the early 20th century and for its significance as the centrepiece of the movement's international headquarters since 1984' (Ibid.:13–14). But in the 1920s the very existence of a mosque in the UK was so unusual that it was reported in the national press and a news film of the opening was screened around the country (Naylor and Ryan 2002:46). As Naylor and Ryan (2002) note, the Fazl Mosque was viewed in explicit orientalist terms by the British, as self-evidently a mosque and an example of the ornamental and exotic in the suburbs at a time when India was still part of the British empire, when the Muslim population of Britain[8] was far smaller as a proportion of the population than it is today, and when most Muslims were likely to use private spaces as mosques rather than worship in visible and public religious buildings or, to paraphrase Cesari, when Muslims constituted the private and invisible rather than today's public and unwanted (2005:1018).

The opening of the mosque attracted not only members of the British social and political elite but also many foreign dignitaries. The mosque was to be

Figure 5.2 Fazl Mosque

inaugurated by Prince Faisal of Saudi Arabia and, had this happened, it would have granted the Ahmadis a much sought-after legitimacy among Muslims. In the event, Prince Faisal did not attend the opening of the mosque and alerted the Ahmadis to this via telegram less than an hour before he was due to arrive (Basit 2012). The initial agreement officially to mark the opening of the mosque and the last minute failure to attend is significant given the later history of the Ahmadiyya Muslims.

The official exclusion of the Ahmadis from the Muslim *ummah* is directly relevant to the present discussion. Both these mosques, the earlier of the two billed as London's *first* purpose built mosque and the later one as Western Europe's *largest* mosque, are clearly by virtue of their domes and (non-functional) minarets, examples of Muslim religious architecture for the local non-Muslim populations. However, some other Muslim groups in the locality and beyond do not consider these buildings to be Muslim places of worship at all, and this perforce connects the two Ahmadiyya mosques to other mosques belonging to different Muslim sects in the area in a sometimes tense and uneasy relationship. It also connects the mosques of southwest London to local and national politics and also to the transnational political situation of Ahmadi Muslims in Pakistan and other Muslim nation states. The mosques and the communities they serve may in this respect be conceived of as a network of interrelated sites. It is to some of these matters that I now turn in order to show how religious and political conflicts which began in colonial India and continued in post-colonial Pakistan, together with the global rise of Islamic fundamentalism have shaped local perceptions and influenced the local practices of Muslim and non-Muslim groups and their efforts to make a home in the diaspora.

Books on British mosques and websites listing Muslim places of worship produced by Muslims do not routinely include Ahmadiyya mosques in their resources or show any hits when 'Ahmadiyya' is entered into searches on sites covering Muslim interests, groups and topics in the UK (e.g. Gailani 2000; Salatomatic 2014).[9] And while some British newspapers described Baitul Futuh when it officially opened in 2003 as Western Europe's largest mosque, one quoted a prominent British Muslim, Iqbal Sacranie, as saying the Ahmadis 'can call their place of worship by any name except for a mosque because that is for Muslims. . . . they are outside the fold of Islam' (Petre 2003).

Iqbal Sacranie, was at the time then General Secretary of the Muslim Council of Britain (MCB), which issued a press release on 2 October 2003 stating:

> In the light of much press interest, the Muslim Council of Britain wishes to make clear that the Qadiyani/Ahmadi Centre which has been constructed in Morden is not a Mosque. The Ahmadi community are regarded as non-Muslims by all Muslim scholars and groups world-wide because of the Ahmadi's central belief that Mirza Ghulam Ahmed (born in 19th century India) was a prophet and the promised Messiah. Ever since the days of British colonial rule in India, Muslim scholars have been united in rejecting Ghulam Ahmed's claim to prophethood and regard him as an imposter. . . . So, whilst we fully accept the right of Ahmadis to their own religion, it is clearly misleading to describe them as Muslims. They are not.[10]

This view, that Ahmadis are not really Muslim and therefore their places of worship are not really mosques, echoed the official Pakistani government position

and added both a sectarian and a transnational perspective to the local inaugura-
tion of a diasporic faith building. As the General Secretary of the MCB, an organization the British prime minister at the time, Tony Blair, was happy to do business
with and consider the voice of acceptable Islam in the UK, Sacranie's views may
have appeared as authoritative and mainstream. Yet, as Archer (2009:335) shows,
Sacranie's move into national level political circles began some years before the
formation of the MCB when he coordinated Muslim protests against Salman
Rushdie's 1988 book *The Satanic Verses* and brought 'sub-continental politics
into Britain, particularly the politics of the Pakistani revivalist Jamaat-e-Islami
party (JI), founded by Abul A'la Mawdudi in 1941'. Archer further notes that
'[m]any others within the group, like Sacranie, sympathized with the Pakistani Islamist tendency. . . . and Sacranie has made no secret of the influence of
Mawdudi on him, having for instance described him as a "renowned scholar" and
an "inspiration" to the BBC'. As already noted earlier in this book, the Maududi-
inspired Pakistani Jamaat-e-Islami party, together with other anti-Ahmadi groups,
led campaigns against the Ahmadiyya Muslim Community in Pakistan which
culminated in riots in 1953 in the Punjab, resulted in many deaths and led to the
imposition of martial law to restore order. That same year Maududi published
an anti-Ahmadi text, *The Qadiani Problem*, and later also another text targeting
Ahmadi beliefs (*The Finality of Prophethood* (1978)). As Sacranie and the MCB's
example shows, it is possible to play out old and distant conflicts of faith through
legitimate contemporary political channels in the UK and to use access to those
in government to advance one's own causes while impeding those of others. And
these causes have their roots in events that began over a hundred years ago in
South Asia.

While the influence of the MCB has somewhat waned since its formation in
1997 and heyday in the years that followed, the current local situation with the
Ahmadiyya Muslim community in southwest London is one where Sacranie
continues to hold positions of local significance as trustee and former chair
of the management committee of Balham Mosque and the Tooting Islamic
Centre.[11] It was while holding this position that Sacranie declared in 2007: 'I have
no problem with Qaderis [*sic*]. It is their religion they have the right to practice
it. But it is offensive to me when they say they are Muslims. They are not Muslims'.[12] Both Balham Mosque and Tooting Islamic Centre are located in southwest
London and in proximity to the two Ahmadiyya mosques discussed in this chapter. Representatives of both the Balham Mosque Sacranie is associated with, and
the London Mosque run by the Ahmadis meet in the inter-faith gatherings organized post-9/11 by Wandsworth Council,[13] and the tensions between them can on
occasion flare up and become matters that local council officials have to mediate
(Balzani 2014:116).

The politics of faith

Mosques are both religious and social centres for the communities that use them,
encouraging worshippers to gravitate towards them and so changing the local

population and landscape as they move into the neighbourhoods surrounding the mosques, set up local businesses and begin to shape the environment in new ways. In part, the public demonstration by Sunni Muslims of anti-Ahmadi sentiment in southwest London which I came across during fieldwork, and some of which I describe here, was a consequence of the success of local Ahmadis in redeveloping the post-industrial site of a disused dairy into a large and active mosque and the resulting inflow of Ahmadis to the area so that they now form a visible local minority. It is also, in part, the consequence of the greater visibility of Ahmadis in public life at both the local and national levels in politics, a visibility that is evidence of growing middle class aspirations within the Ahmadi community. Had the Ahmadis not become such a significant local population centred on the Baitul Futuh Mosque and had their numbers in some electoral wards not substantially increased over the years, the level of sustained hostility towards them might not have been quite so visible. But changes in local demographics and the presence of Ahmadis in public life were not the only causes of hostility directed against the Ahmadis.

Conflicts rooted in the politico-religious history and contemporary politics of the sub-continent have also been played out in southwest London where the local Muslim population, both Sunni and Ahmadi, go about their everyday lives. This happened very publicly during the 2010 national election campaign in Tooting in the Borough of Wandsworth and is illustrative of how Pakistani politics may directly impact UK Muslim communities and so also impact on British national elections.[14] On 29 March 2010 the Tooting Islamic Centre invited a speaker from the London branch of Khatm-e-Nabuwat, to give a talk. Khatm-e-Nabuwat, as previously noted, is an organization which exists solely to bring about the end of Ahmadiyya Islam and is today linked with the persecution of Ahmadis in Pakistan (Kennedy 1989:93ff). It was also listed on the Muslim Council of Britain's website as an affiliated organization until 2016 when it was suspended pending an inquiry by the MCB into allegations made in the media which centred on the discovery of leaflets encouraging violence against Ahmadis in one of their mosques. The Charity Commission for England and Wales also conducted an inquiry following a BBC news article 'dated 10 April 2016, that alleged that literature calling for the killing of members of the Ahmadi community was displayed at the [Khatm-e-Nabuwat] charity's premises, which is the mosque' (2019:3). The Charity Commission concluded that the trustees of the Khatm-e-Nubuwat Centre had not fulfilled 'their duties and responsibilities under charity law' and issued them an 'official warning' (2019:9–10).[15] But that is to jump ahead almost a decade from events that took place in Tooting, southwest London and just down the road from the Baitul Futuh Mosque.

From local and national newspaper and television reports, pro- and anti-Ahmadi websites, interviews with local council officials and members of the Ahmadi community, and debates held in the British Parliament, it appears that the 29 March 2010 talk at the Tooting Islamic Centre was at the root of the anti-Ahmadi leaflets (with titles such as 'Deception of the Qadiyani'), that were soon found on shop windows and reportedly also distributed on the streets in Tooting and other local areas. The leaflets urged Muslims to boycott Ahmadi businesses and to avoid interacting with Ahmadis. The local Wandsworth press reported that the Khatm-e-Nabuwat speaker had said:

> I don't know why our sisters or mothers are talking with these Qadiani and
> making friendships. . . . I know in this road, Tooting high street, all of the
> shops who are selling to Qadiani.
> Don't make friends with them. . . . they are trying to deceive you, they are
> trying to convert you from Islam to Qadianism.

(Oates 2010a)

These and other events, unsurprisingly, were reported to the local police, and under the supervision of the borough commander, the most senior police officer in Wandsworth, the speech given at the Tooting Islamic Centre by the Khatm-e-Nabuwat speaker, Abdul Rehman Bawa, was translated from Urdu to English to determine if there was sufficient evidence for a prosecution. While the speech was considered clearly unpleasant, it was eventually decided that while it had come close to inciting violence it had not actually done so explicitly enough to guarantee a reasonable likelihood of conviction under the Racial and Religious Hatred Act 2006. Therefore the police, after Crown Prosecution Service review, decided not to take the matter any further. But they did, I have been reliably informed, make clear to the Tooting Islamic Centre that they would be keeping a close eye on what happened there in future.[16] Attempts in the months that followed to mediate and reach some acceptable understanding, if only a local one between the Ahmadis and Tooting Islamic Centre, failed to reach a positive outcome. The MP for Tooting and shadow Justice Secretary, Sadiq Khan, organized a meeting at Wandsworth Town Hall on Monday, December 13 2010 to discuss the Ahmadis' concerns: 'It was attended by Mr Khan, Wandsworth police borough commander David Musker, Wandsworth Council Leader Edward Lister, four representatives from the TIC [Tooting Islamic Centre] and nine representatives from the Ahmadiyya Muslim Association (AMA)' (Oates 2010d). According to Oates, reporting in a local newspaper ten days later, a 'joint statement was due to be issued . . . on behalf of the TIC and the AMA, but so far no statement has been agreed and no further meetings have been planned' (Ibid.). As far as I am aware, no statement was ever issued.

It was also in 2010 that the the first Westminster Hall debate[17] on the Ahmadi issue in the UK took place, and an all-party parliamentary group for the Ahmadiyya community was established. And it was the year in which, in Lahore Pakistan, on 28 May, two mosques were attacked by members of Tehrik-e-Taliban Pakistan during the Friday prayers (Nijhawan 2010). As Nijhawan (2010:430) put it: 'Among recent attacks targeting other religious minorities . . . this was . . . the most spectacular and lethal assault in a post-Partition history of social and political mobilizations against Ahmadis in Pakistan'. It was in the aftermath of this attack that, as Jane Ellison the conservative MP for Battersea, noted:

> The Ahmadi Muslim community in the UK has noticed . . . [a] disturbing trend
> in the months since the Lahore massacres. . . . the persecution of Ahmadis has

intensified in tone and frequency around our country, particularly in south-west London. There have been the incidents . . . of intimidation during the general election [though this was before the Lahore killings], and posters and leaflets with aggressive and derogatory messages have appeared around the area. I have been shown images of posters put up in Scotland that denounce Ahmadis as infidels and publish their place of worship. That leaves those observing the poster to read between the lines.

(Westminster Hall Debate 2010)

One unexpected consequence of the anti-Ahmadi hostilities in southwest London that became a matter of urban planning concern, is that the acts of a small minority of extremist Muslims, prepared to use violence in Pakistan and to stir up hostility towards the Ahmadis in the UK, were strategically commandeered by non-Muslims in their attempts to foil planning permission for the building extension of the Fazl Mosque in Southfields. However, before I turn to the connection between mosques, town planning and the discourse of fundamentalism and terrorism as used by local non-Muslim residents in the Ahmadi case, I wish to suggest that the more typical forms of anti-mosque protests which take place across the UK and Europe may signify rather more than mere racism, fear of migrants or Islamophobia (e.g. Göle 2011; Allievi 2009). Rather, in many places what appear to be anti-mosque protests are, in fact, more than manifestations of simple anti-Muslim prejudice; they are often complex articulations of concerns about control of public space, social justice and changes in communal life. Such concerns may coalesce around plans by minority faith and ethnic groups to build places of worship because these buildings make public a minority's long-term goals in material form, require acceptance of a change in the urban built environment and compel local people to generate new discourses to accommodate changed realities (Astor 2012).

When the Baitul Futuh Mosque in Merton was in the planning stages, and as it was under construction from the late 1990s to its opening in 2003, the expected local response included residents writing to the Council to protest against the proposed mosque on the grounds that local amenities would be negatively impacted by the development. Some suggested that the derelict Dairy Express Plant not be turned into a mosque but into a residential home for the elderly instead. Others feared violence between Muslims and non-Muslims in the area and a local rise in Muslim fundamentalism. The British National Party (BNP), a right wing and anti-immigrant organization, went so far as to stage a protest outside the mosque site on 17 November 2002.[18] The ultra-nationalists who organized it argued that all mosques in the UK should be closed down to prevent 'terrorism by Islamic extremists worldwide' and were either ignorant of, or did not care about, the fact that the Ahmadis are themselves the victims, and not the perpetrators, of such violence.[19] The demonstration, however, failed to attract many people and the organizers were left to claim, somewhat unconvincingly, that although numbers at the protest itself were small, they had the support of many of the motorists driving past. Some of the residents I spoke with recalled posters opposed to the mosque on walls and lampposts and even in the windows of private houses at this time. And one person remembered thinking that a mosque on the derelict site would mean no partying, no drinking and no late-night music, all of which made her consider that it might not be such a bad idea after all, and certainly better than turning the site into a night club or rehabilitation centre for drug addicts which were also suggestions put forward for the redevelopment of the disused dairy. This same interviewee, however, did say that many people thought the neighbourhood would be fundamentally altered because of the mosque as the white population left to be replaced by South Asian Muslims. She considers that this has indeed happened over the last ten years and now believes some local schools cater mainly for children who are of South Asian Muslim heritage, and more specifically for Ahmadi Muslim children.

While some residents and right wing political groups use acts of violence by a minority as justification for their protests and Islamophobic attitudes, assuming that all Muslims are the same, others in southwest London used the same acts of violence in a more focused and distinctly targeted fashion to argue, not that Ahmadi Muslim mosques are the source of such violence and radicalization, but that they might attract such violence to the neighbourhood. In short, as potential victims of violence, Ahmadi Muslims should not be permitted to expand or build as this puts 'innocent' non-Ahmadis at risk of being caught up in sectarian Muslim-on-Muslim violence in an otherwise quiet and peaceful suburb. The approach taken by local residents opposed to mosque extension did not, in southwest London therefore, follow the more routine and familiar local resident concerns that the Ahmadiyya mosques, simply because they are mosques, would be institutions fomenting radicalization (Langer 2010; Shah, Dwyer and Gilbert 2012).

This line of thought and this strategic form of opposition to mosque development is certainly more sophisticated and clearly more knowledgeable of actual local and international Muslim factions and sects than many superficially similar anti-mosque protests. That such a strategy has been employed is clear from both interviews and a study of Wandsworth planning records for the Fazl Mosque in Southfields, and is one that has worked, up to a point. It is a strategy that has been organized and led by mainly white, non-Muslim, middle-aged and often retired middle class professionals who live in the streets that surround the mosque where a terraced family home now costs in the region of £1,250,000 and a semi-detached house in a neighbouring street sold for just under £3,000,000 in 2014.[20] It is clear, for example, from the many letters sent to Wandsworth Borough Planning Office over a period of years, that pro-forma letters have been designed and circulated for those who wish to protest but are less able to draft their own responses. This accounts not only for the lack of explicit racist and Islamophobic statements in letters to the Council about the mosque development plans, and which are more readily heard when speaking directly with local residents, but also for the persistence and organization of the protests over many years. One home I visited near the mosque had what amounted to an anti-mosque development coordination office in the front reception room of the house. Minutes of resident opposition group meetings, plans, letters, strategies, cuttings from newspapers, official documents and more were systematically organized and stored in a series of box files. And Wandsworth Council's own planning records have archived this opposition movement over the years. In the early 1990s planning applications to extend the Fazl Mosque and build residential accommodation for the Imam of the mosque were refused. Among the reasons cited for the rejection of the planning applications were: 'The changes which have occurred since the Imam arrived' and 'the changes which appear to have occurred in the nature of the activity [at the mosque]'.[21] Part of the mosque's problem was that from the time it was built in the 1920s to the application for expansion in the 1990s the area had become a predominantly middle class residential area and the Borough Plan recognized:

> [T]he importance of protecting and enhancing the environment seeking to control the nature and scale of non-residential development in predominantly residential areas so as to minimise noise, traffic and other intrusion. Non-residential uses will only be permitted if compatible with a residential envi-ronment, of a limited scale and of benefit to the local neighbourhood.
> (File no. 92/W/0503 The London Mosque, Wandsworth Council Planning Office [Microfiche])

In other words the Borough Planner had resorted to an argument based on the 'sub-jective problematic of amenity' to refuse planning permission (Naylor and Ryan 2002:52). Another reason given for the refusal of the planning application was that the khalifa had only relocated to southwest London in 1984 when it became impossible for him to continue to live in safety in Pakistan. Local residents, but not the Council, dated the increase in numbers attending the Fazl mosque from this time and considered that the arrival of the khalifa was responsible. In the early 1990s the Borough Planner's take on this, as the Council's Assessment of the Appeal Proposal (point 5.1) explaining why planning permission had not been granted makes clear, was that:

> The Council is concerned that the scale of the building proposed has arisen from the world leader locating at the premises. This may not be a permanent arrangement and the Council and neighbours are concerned that a permanent solution to a temporary problem is proposed.
> (File no. 92/W/0503 The London Mosque, Wandsworth Council Planning Office [Microfiche])

However, noting resident concerns that this local religious building was no longer just for local use, the Council also stated (point 5.5):

> Whilst the general level of worship and demand upon the site has increased over the years, there does not appear to have been a marked change since the world leader has made [. . . the mosque] effectively the world headquar-ters of the organisation. There has been an intensification of activity. Neigh-bours have expressed concern about this and that the emphasis of the site

has shifted with the site attracting a world-wide audience rather than a local congregation and that the on site activity has altered with greater emphasis on other activities associated with international organisational matters rather than local religious/community activity.

This change in use, if substantiated, it was further suggested, might even amount to 'a material change of use' (Ibid. point 5.9) with potentially significant consequences for the mosque itself if fresh permission had to be sought for the activities now taking place on the site.

The Ahmadis themselves made the case to the Borough Planner that the Imam had no choice but to live at the mosque for security reasons and confirmed that the 'present Imam is also the head of the international Ahmadiyya community'.[22] This situation was one that local residents themselves took up in the consultation on the mosque expansion to argue that the quiet and pleasant residential setting of the mosque made the location 'unsuitable as world headquarters of an international movement' and they objected to what they considered to be the 'fortress-like arrangements with sentries' arguing, contra to the Ahmadis, that they did not consider there was 'a "security risk" to the leader of the community [and] therefore no need for the world leader to be housed on site'. Yet, one well-informed local resident who wrote to oppose the expansion plan included in his 1992 letter a copy of an earlier letter he had sent in 1991 about a prior planning application in which he had written:

In 1924 when the mosque was first erected the Ahmadiyya movement was a relatively minor sect within the Islamic faith. It has since grown very considerably in size and importance, and its development in the UK has been helped by the considerable number of immigrants following its teachings. The presence of the Head of the Community since 1984 has led to increase in importance of the site and of the number of visitors who come to see him, as acknowledged in the Authorities [*sic*] letter to you.

It is unfortunate that the permission was given in 1969 for the creation of the ugly office/residential/hall block which conflicts with the residential nature of the neighbourhood. It is inevitable that the growth in size of the movement has led to further approaches for additional office/residential accommodation. This is firmly opposed by the local residential community. There is no reason why the administrative/organisational side of activities should be on the same site as the mosque: it is a convenience which is obtained at the expense of the neighbours. I urge that the Council press the movement to take all organisation and administrative matters away from the mosque site which be left solely as a place of worship.

The application cites the wish to provide more appropriate living conditions for the Head of the community and his family. His presence at . . . Road is a matter of considerable concern to local residents. As the position is understood, his life is under threat and he has bodyguards with him all the time. In addition there are security guards at the premises. I should like to know specifically what weapons the bodyguards and security guards carry and whether it has been agreed by the Council and the Wandsworth Police. I am sure you can appreciate the concern of surrounding residents on this issue.

Meetings held in the past have not been fruitful; they have degenerated into accusations of racial prejudice, religious feeling, etc. all untrue.[23]

This letter was part of the organized and systematic opposition to further extension or development of the Fazl Mosque in Wandsworth in the early 1990s. It is particularly interesting because it demonstrates just how much knowledge of Ahmadi Muslims local residents have and it notes the threat of violence *against* the khalifa which local residents were already aware of and used strategically, but at this point, not very directly, to make their case against the Ahmadi mosque extension planning proposal. The letter also demonstrates an awareness of the anti-Muslim sentiment, racism and inter-ethnic tensions discussed in my interviews but which the official planning documents contain very little explicit reference to.

More recently, in 2010, the Ahmadis again applied for planning permission to develop the Fazl Mosque. While a Wandsworth Council Committee recommended approval of the new application, councilors voted against it, once again on the grounds of amenity.[24] However, by 2013 planning approval, with some restrictions, had been granted by the Council and a modified redevelopment of the mosque site agreed. This 2013 planning agreement was not what the local residents, who by this time were also writing openly to state their fears of terrorist acts in the suburban streets of Wandsworth, wanted. The concerns of the residents were summarized by the Council in their committee minutes as: 'Security measures heavy handed and obtrusive, increase in security not acceptable. Chances of terrorist attack would increase, should disclose security risks'.[25] And in one letter, dated 14 February 2012, a local resident listed some 17 reasons for denying the Ahmadi mosque extension planning application, with point 16 reading:

Neither planning application [sic] show the intrusive use of CCTV, guard house complex fences / walls around the site which are viewed by residents as intrusive and threatening as well as out of keeping with a faith site. Given that other sites of this faith have been bombed in Lahore in 2010, any increase in size of this building will make this an even more attractive terrorist target and place residents and users at even more risk than present.

In this case Wandsworth Council appear to have used the persistent attempts by the Ahmadis to get planning permission for their mosque site, and the equally persistent opposition by the neighbours to prevent this, to reach a compromise which enabled the Council to enforce a rectification of planning contraventions that it had no other way of enforcing. Wandsworth Council had long been aware that about ten residential houses, owned by the Ahmadis immediately surrounding the mosque had been used as offices and guest accommodation for the community rather than as private residential homes. Local residents had complained of their occasional use as large-scale hostels with marquees straddling several back gardens set up to accommodate large numbers of guests as well as causing disruption to amenity with noise, lighting and cooking taking place for large numbers of visitors. As the buildings had been used as offices and guest accommodation for many years, in some cases since 1989, the council had no means of enforcing a change of use on the Ahmadis.[26] However, when planning permission was given to redevelop the mosque site, allowing for a new residence for the khalifa, new office space and a redesigned mosque space, the Council also included restrictions which require the Ahmadis to return the houses they own 'to residential use . . . with the integration of the office use into the site'.[27] By this means the Council, in effect, gave both sides something they wanted but neither side got everything they were after. The Ahmadis got better facilities for the khalifa and worshippers in their mosque, and the non-Ahmadi local residents got the houses owned by the Ahmadis returned to residential use thus improving this aspect of local amenity as these houses can no longer be used as offices or to house large numbers of visitors beyond the normal capacity of a small family home. It would appear that in this case it is the Council that has found the means to compel the Ahmadis to comply with planning regulations by permitting some of the planning application they had submitted to go forward and, at the same time, to improve local amenity for non-Ahmadi residents by restricting how the Ahmadis can, in future, use the houses they own close to the mosque.

In March 2018 the Fazl Mosque was listed as a Grade II listed building on the basis of its historical and architectural value and the impact of any future development now has to be considered in the light of this (Noakes 2018:8). A planning proposal from 2015 to redevelop the site to 'enhance and reveal the architectural significance of the Mosque and improve the physical and aesthetic links between the Mosque and the wider Site, thus enhancing the historical significance of the Mosque' (Noakes 2018:18) but which also included a new multi-function hall was again opposed by local residents. Opposition included the usual traffic and amenity concerns but, perhaps with an eye to increased attention to environmental concerns, also feared that the proposal to fell some trees on the mosque site might lead to an increase in levels of air pollution. And yet others stated they were happy to have a local mosque but not one which was viewed as the 'hub for a growing and international religion' and, utilizing the new Grade II listed status of the mosque, some also argued that the new development would be 'too high, too close and too bulky to show off and enhance the beauty of the listed asset' (Objection comment 5115344). The proposal for redevelopment of the Fazl Mosque site was approved by the Council in 2016 but because of the Grade II listing this had to be reconsidered and approved again on 27 March 2018 with conditions attached. Yet, some of the local residents' objections to the development of the Fazl mosque site, including improvements to residential accommodation for the khalifa, and the continued use of the site in a quiet residential area as the world headquarters of the Ahmadiyya Muslims themselves became matters of history when the khalifa, his administrative offices and hence the global headquarters, relocated to the Ahmadi site Islamabad, in Tilford, Surrey, on 15 April 2019.

Conclusion

The outcome of decades of planning applications to develop the Fazl Mosque and resident opposition to these has engaged the professional knowledge and cultural capital of both Ahmadis and local residents in their mostly polite and middle class interactions mediated by Wandsworth Council. This was a situation in which locals used the fear of violence to support their case against planning approval while the Ahmadis used this to argue their case for expansion and better security on the mosque site. In the process the Fazl Mosque, hidden away in a quiet residential suburb, demonstrates how all diasporic places of worship are, and have always been, what Massey (1994) calls 'extroverted spaces' linked to other faith sites in complex networks whose meanings change and are changed, often by events that take place far from the sites themselves. These sites are 'created and sustained through postcolonial networks and trajectories' (Shah, Dwyer and Gilbert 2012:80). The meaning of these interconnections may change over time, and for the Fazl Mosque this has meant a transformation from a unique and picturesque 'orientalist' building in colonial times to just one more mosque among many, now also associated with the risk of attracting fundamentalist violence in the minds of some locals who can plausibly use such fears strategically to limit the development of the mosque site. These local residents do not wish to have to live with any expansion of the mosque in their own back yard when they can now expect such expansions to take place in other backyards and particularly so in Morden where the much larger Ahmadi Baitul Futuh mosque opened in 2003. This latter mosque, as a post-industrial building project dating from the early years of the new millennium and supported by Merton Council to regenerate a derelict site in a less affluent part of the borough, has itself not been entirely free from local protest. For non-Muslims such protests have focused on the place of Islam locally and, for Muslims, on the particular sect of Muslims frequenting the mosque. They have also focused on concerns over the changing ethnic make-up of the borough and over non-Christian faith buildings seen, by the majority population, as somehow foreign to the area. This particular discourse has been expressed primarily in terms of amenity issues so as to fall within town planning regulations and avoid accusations of overt racism and Islamophobia.

The location of the large Baitul Futuh Mosque, however, fronting a main road with good local public transport and significant on-site parking space marks the physical location as very different to that of the Fazl Mosque which was built in the 1920s at a time when very few people owned cars and before the development of the residential suburb that has since grown up around it. This latter mosque is not so conveniently sited for public transport and is located in an affluent part of Wandsworth where, despite the arrival of some Ahmadi home-owner residents, a larger proportion of the local residents are not Ahmadi and not Muslim.

Aware of public concern about Islam in general in a post-9/11 context and to deal with local concerns, the Ahmadis running the Baitul Futuh Mosque instituted liaison committee meetings to bring together local non-Ahmadi residents, representatives of local organizations, police officers, elected councilors and faith leaders. These meetings have made considerable progress in planning ahead and preparing for large mosque events, alerting the mosque authorities to local concerns and ensuring a reasonable level of local acceptance, if not yet wholehearted support, for the mosque itself. Such initiatives demonstrate awareness of, and a desire to negotiate, the local complexities of faith, ethnicity and class to inform and, wherever possible, accommodate others in order to ensure the continued viability of the mosque and good relations with the local community. In addition, the more affordable properties in the neighbourhood of the Baitul Futuh Mosque, particularly when compared to the cost of similar housing in the vicinity of the Fazl Mosque in Wandsworth, has meant that over the last decade there has been an influx of Ahmadi residents, including more recent German-speaking migrants to the UK, and a corresponding exodus of the primarily white lower middle class population.

Yet such developments in London's suburban environment happen not only in local space but as a consequence of events that had their origin in nineteenth-century India as well as those that have taken place closer to the present but thousands of miles away. What such developments mean may always be a matter for local exegesis but they now inevitably involve local authorities, including council officials and the police, in learning about ethnic, religious and political matters far from their own jurisdictions. That all sides in these local interactions strategically use their knowledge to progress their own ends is inevitable; that the authorities are aware of this and also use it to pursue their goals, mediate between contesting factions, both Muslim contra Muslim and non-Muslim contra Muslim, speaks to the level of grounded expertise, knowledge of each other and skills selectively to use this knowledge that local individuals and groups now routinely possess in the global city.

Notes

1 Goodhart (2013).
2 'Mega mosque' is a media term used to describe places of worship that can accommodate several thousand worshippers. It is a short-hand term reflecting negative local reaction to planning applications for such buildings. It may also signal the increased confidence of Muslim groups to raise funds to pursue such projects and may, less positively also be a mark of competition between Muslim groups to stake a claim to authority on this basis e.g. Hough (2012) who also connects the Muslim group in this case to radicalization and terrorism and DeHanas and Pieri (2011) who link such developments to national identity, Islamophobia and governance. The term is also a consequence of sensationalized media attention (Poole 2002; Neal 2003).
3 Ibid.
4 Ibid.
5 www.merton.gov.uk/leisure/history-heritage/architecture/mordenmosque.htm describes the mosque as a: 'purpose-built mosque and the largest in Europe, with 15m diameter dome and minarets 36m and 23m high, and accommodating 1,600 worshippers in each of its two prayer halls. The building is a blend of Islamic and modern British architecture and incorporates much of the structure of an old dairy site. The building is a focal point for the Ahmadiyya Muslim Community. This is an international religious organisation with branches in over 176 countries and a membership of over 200,000,000

people worldwide [this statement is unlikely to be verifiable]. The foundation stone was laid by the spiritual leader, Hazrat Khalifatul Masih IV in 1999 and the building was inaugurated by Hadrat Mirza Masroor Ahmad, the Supreme Head of the Ahmadiyya community. . . . Voted one of top 50 buildings in the world by Spectator magazine'.

6 On 26 September 2015 a fire broke out at the Baitul Futuh Mosque destroying the hall at the front of the mosque and administration offices (www.bbc.com/news/uk-england-london-34369710). The MCB website posted a statement which read: 'We are deeply distressed to learn about the fire in Bait Ul Futuh, Morden. We pray no worshipper is hurt and that everyone is safe (www.mcb.org.uk/fire-at-bait-ul-futuh-in-morden/). The mosque is currently being rebuilt with a completion planned for the end of 2020. The community has taken this as an opportunity to redesign a section of the mosque. Merton Council Planning Office records detail this but I do not discuss these developments in this chapter.

7 The London Mosque needs to be viewed also in the context of Ahmadiyya mosque building in Germany at this time. Ahmadis supported British rule in India and were British colonial subjects but the internationalist outlook of the second khalifa also included Germany and the US. The London Mosque was built after plans to build a mosque in Berlin fell through. On Ahmadi mosques in Germany during this period, see Jonker (2005:1068).

8 With more than 11 million Muslims living in the major countries of the European Union, making up almost 3% of the population, Muslims are the largest religious minority in Western Europe (Cesari 2005:1015). For the UK Archer (2009:332) states: 'The majority of British Muslims are citizens, and "immigrant" is either not a relevant label for British-born Muslims (46% of Muslims in England and Wales in the 2001 census) or of secondary importance'. In St. Helier ward, Merton, where the Baitul Futuh Mosque is sited, the census shows that the BME population in the ward rose by 136% from 2001 to 2011 and that Pakistan was the second largest country of birth listed for residents (at 4% of the ward population, and after 65% for those born in England). Islam was listed as the third largest faith at 12% of all residents after Christianity (54%) and no religion (20%). Only 23% of the population in this ward had degree level education as compared with 62% for Wimbledon Village in the same borough. (www.merton.gov.uk/ward_profile_st_helier.pdf) and (www.merton.gov.uk/ward_profile_village.pdf).

9 A recent exception to this is Saleem 2018.

10 The press release 'Qadiyani Centre not Mosque' is no longer available on the MCB website. See: https://mcb.org.uk/mcb-updates/position-statement-the-muslim-council-of-britain-and-ahmadis/ for a 2016 more recent MCB statement on the Ahmadis.

11 www.progressonline.org.uk/2009/10/21/sir-iqbal-sacranie-correction-and-apology/. He is also listed as chairman, board of trustees, Balham mosque from 1986 in the *Independent* 2005 (Woolf 2005). The Balham Mosque charity report available via the Charities Commission, lists Sacranie as a Trustee in 2018 (https://beta.charitycommission.gov.uk/charity-details/?regid=271538&subid=0).

12 www.opendiscussions.com/index.php?option=com_content&task=view&id=3 (accessed January 14, 2013 but no longer works). 'An evening with Iqbal Sacranie', with a transcript of his talk and answers to questions. The meeting seems to have taken place in 2007 as the website www.shiachat.com/forum/topic/234926576-an-evening-with-sir-iqbal-sacranie/ has a poster inviting people to attend this event on 22 May 2007 at a venue in London.

13 WLSP Multi-Faith Group: www.wandsworth.gov.uk/info/200041/equality_and_diversity/60/faith_group.

14 See also Oates (2010b). These forms of everyday violence continue today with cases of primary age Ahmadi children being bullied by Sunni Muslim children or even thrown out of people's homes when they are found to be Ahmadi (Oates 2010c); see also Balzani 2014:120; personal communication Mr G., 18 July 2014 at Big Iftar (Merton)).

15 www.mcb.org.uk/about-mcb/affiliates/. The MCB interim report (2016:23) makes clear that the organization rejects all forms of violence against all religious groups including Ahmadis, who remain, nonetheless non-Muslim as far as the MCB is concerned. UK Khatm-e-Nabuwat mosque trustees maintain that the leaflets found on their premises did not belong to them. The Charity Commission for England and Wales *Decision on Khatme Nubuwat Centre*, published on 2 March 2019 can be found in full at: https://www.gov.uk/government/publications/charity-inquiry-khatmenubuwwat-centre/khatme-nubuwwat-centre

16 Personal communication with Wandsworth Council employees who wish to remain anonymous. See also the statement by Sadiq Khan in December 2010: 'The police complete a report to send to the CPS [Crown Prosecution Service] who will decide whether or not to prosecute. There's two criteria with the CPS. One, does it satisfy the evidential burden of more than 50 per cent chance of a successful prosecution? Two, is it in the public interest to prosecute. They have said it doesn't, so they're not going to prosecute. . . . To be fair, the police's hands are tied. They've done the investigation, and it's for the CPS to decide. The Borough Commander has invested a considerable number of police officers to look into the allegation, including having documents translated from Urdu into English' (Oates 2010c).

17 Held on 20 October 2010.

18 The BNP website (www.bnp.org.uk/policies/immigration) cites the following rationale for BNP anti-immigrant policies: 'Given current demographic trends, we, the indigenous British people, will become an ethnic minority in our own country well within sixty years – and most likely sooner. . . . Immigration is out of control. Britain's population is now over 60 million and rising, solely due to immigration. Not only is Britain increasingly overcrowded, but the fact is that a country is the product of its people and if you change the people you inevitably change the nature of the country. We want Britain to remain – or return to – the way it has traditionally been'.

19 www.nfse.co.uk/bermondsey_site/frame1.htm. For a similar BNP protest, this time against a Dawoodi Bohra mosque in London, see Crinson (2002:94). For a recent protest against an Ahmadi mosque see Massey (2014). And for Sunni Muslim protests against an Ahmadi mosque in Walsall in 2009 see Bunglawala (2009).

20 www.zoopla.co.uk/property/17-melrose-road/london/sw18-1nd/23371256. The rental value of this four-bedroom house in 2019 is estimated at £10,250 per calendar month.

21 File no. 92/W/0503 The London Mosque . . . Wandsworth Council Planning Office (Microfiche).

22 Paper 8925 Wandsworth Borough Council Planning Committee – 15th February 1993 Report of the Borough Planner on a planning application in respect of development at the London Mosque.

23 Letter dated 28 November 1992 including a copy of a letter to Wandsworth Council dated 9 July 1991.

24 2010/0486 Refusal of Permission for Development, dated 15 July 2011. (https://planning.wandsworth.gov.uk/WAM/doc/Decision%20Notice-2246700.pdf?extension=.pdf&id=2246700&location=VOLUME8&contentType=application/pdf&pageCount=1).

25 Planning applications committee ref:2011/4853 18 April 2012. (https://planning.wandsworth.gov.uk/WAM/doc/Committee%20Report-2347718.pdf?extension=.pdf&id=2347718&location=VOLUME8&contentType=application/pdf&pageCount=18).

26 Ibid.

27 https://planning.wandsworth.gov.uk/WAM/doc/Decision%20Notice-2529085.pdf?extension=.pdf&id=2529085&location=VOLUME8&contentType=application/pdf&pageCount=1

Postscript

There is no neat end to the narration of the events and histories set out in the chapters of this book. My ethnographic work with the Ahmadiyya community members continues and each day brings news of fresh initiatives, new setbacks, welcome achievements. And these open up more complex ways of thinking about how such matters might be conceptualised in relation to the materials stored in archives, in print and in memories, set, as they must be, within the framework of the broader contemporary socio-political context of the South Asian diaspora in the UK.

Each chapter in the book considers Ahmadiyya Muslims in the places where they have made their homes, exploring how this was achieved and what it meant to them and to others in colonial India, in Pakistan, and in the UK. Aspects of Ahmadi identity are therefore considered throughout in relation to places and times which are themselves interlinked in complicated and occasionally fortuitous ways, and seen as far as possible from the perspective of the Ahmadis themselves as well as from a host of other positions, neutral, supportive and hostile to the Ahmadis. Identity, as it is now commonplace to state, is not, despite the protestations of many who hold to the belief in an identity position as true and unchanging, fixed. For over a century the Ahmadis have responded to the ever shifting social and political world around them and developed institutionally in ways their founder, Ghulam Ahmad, could not have imagined, though, the Ahmadis believe, in ways he would have approved of. Ahmadis are in the UK today because the British were in India in the past. Decisions made by colonial rulers have played out and continue to play out in ways that no-one in nineteenth-century India could have imagined, and the ethnographer's task is to begin to unravel some of the distant and not so distant decisions and actions which help to make sense of how people today understand themselves, how they make their home in the diaspora, what being Ahmadi means, and how this is lived in a global city such as London.

Glossary

Achūt untouchable

'Alim (pl. 'ulamā) Muslim religious scholar

Amīr leader, often of local Aḥmadī group or community

Anjuman council, committee or administrative body

Ārya Samāj Hindu revivalist movement founded in the late nineteenth century

Auqaf pl. of waqf see *waqf*

Bai'at (bay'a) pledge of allegiance to religious saint, leader; initiation ceremony

Barzakh the liminal space in which spirits of the deceased dwell until Judgement Day

Bid'a improper innovation, acceptance of un-Islamic practice for which there is no precedent

Burūz manifestation, very close imitation of the original

Chandā charitable donation

Fatwā (pl. fatāwā) ruling by a religious scholar on a matter relating to Islamic law

Ḥadīth lit. speech, saying or act of the prophet as subsequently codified

Ḥaj/ḥajj Pilgrimage to the holy sites in Mecca, Saudi Arabia. One of the pillars of Islam.

Ishtihār written announcement

Istikhara form of divination usually following an istihkara prayer

Jalsa a gathering/convention

Jalsa sālāna annual convention

Jamā'at a congregation, community

Jihād literally 'struggle', with an inner spiritual dimension and outer dimension which may encompass struggles against injustice and holy war.

Kāfir infidel, unbeliever

Kalima Muslim profession of faith

Khalīfa Caliph. For the Aḥmadīs the caliph is the elected leader of the religious community and serves as deputy of the founder of Aḥmadīyya Islam, Ghulām Aḥmad.

Khātam-al-nabiyyīn seal of the prophets, in reference to the Prophet Muḥammad

Khilāfat the caliphate

Lajna Imaillah   Aḥmadīyya women's organization

Mahdī   the savior who will come before the Day of Judgement, the rightly guided one, a prophet.

Majlis Ansarullah   Aḥmadīyya men's organization (for men aged 40 and over)

Majlis Khuddam ul Aḥmadīyya   Aḥmadīyya men's organization (for men aged under 40)

Majlis-i shūrā   advisory council

Majlis Tahaffuz Khātam-e-Nabuwat   organization for the finality of prophethood

Masīḥ   the messiah

Masīḥ-i mau'ūd   promised messiah

Muḥaddath   a person spoken to by Allah or angels

Mujaddid (pl. mujaddidun)   renewer of the Muslim faith

Pīr   saint, ṣūfī, founder of religious order

Parda   veil, seclusion

Qadiani   derogatory term for Aḥmadīs derived from the birth place of Ghulām Aḥmad in Qadian, India

Qu'rān   Islamic sacred book

Tabarruk   food that has been blessed – remnant of food or other gifts to *walī* and family, similar to relics

Tablīgh   missionary work, preaching

Tajdīd   renewal of Islam

Tarbiyyat   spiritual and moral training

'Ulamā (pl. of 'alim)   religious scholars, particularly in matters of Islamic jurisprudence

Umma   the global community of Muslims united beyond national, ethnic and sectarian divides

'Umrah   non-mandatory lesser pilgrimage made by Muslims to Mecca

Wāqifāt-e-nau   lit. new endowment, when children are given in service to the jama'at either pre-birth or in infancy

Waqf (pl. Auqaf)   pious endowment

Walī (pl. awliyā)   saint

Ẓillī   shadowy, reflective

Bibliography

National archives – UK

CO. 1935. CO (Colonial Office) 323/1346/4 *Ahmadiyya Movement: C.O. Representative at Annual Festival in London Mosque.*

DO. 1947. 142/323 *Ahmadiyya Community.*

FCO. 1984. 37/3833 *Qadianis in Pakistan.*

FCO. 1988. 37/5244 *Ahmadiyya Muslim Community.*

HO. 1984–5. HO 325/617 *The Ahmadiyya Community in Pakistan.*

Country guidance – legal determinations

KK (Ahmadi, Unexceptional, Risk on Return) Pakistan CG [2005] UKIAT 00033 (04 February 2005). www.bailii.org/uk/cases/UKIAT/2005/00033.html

MJ and ZM (Ahmadis, Risk) Pakistan CG [2008] UKAIT 00033. www.bailii.org/uk/cases/UKIAT/2008/00033.html

MN and others (Ahmadis – Country Conditions – Risk) Pakistan CG [2012] UKUT 00389 (IAC). www.bailii.org/uk/cases/UKUT/IAC/2012/00389_ukut_iac_2012_mn_ors_pakistan_cg.html

Published and online texts

Adamson, I. 1991. *A Man of God: The Life of His Holiness Khalifatul Masih IV.* Bristol: George Shepard Publishers.

Ahmad, Bashir-ud-Din. February 2008. 'The truth about the split.' *Review of Religions,* 10–46.

Ahmad, Bashir-ud-Din. 2013. *Blessings of Khilafat: Address Delivered at Annual Convention 1914.* www.alislam.org/library/books/Blessings-of-Khilafat.pdf

Ahmad, Ghulam. 2004 [1976]. *Tadhkirah: English Rendering of the Dreams, Visions and Verbal Revelations Vouchsafed to Hazrat Mirza Ghulam Ahmad, the Promised Messiah and Mahdi (on Whom be Peace).* Islamabad, Surrey: Islam International Publications Ltd.

Ahmad, Ghulam. 2016 [1899]. *Jesus in India: Jesus' Deliverance from the Cross & Journey to India.* Qadian, India: Islam International Publications Ltd.

Ahmad, Irfan. 2010. 'Genealogy of the Islamic state: Reflections on Maududi's political thought and Islamism.' F. Osella and B. Soares, eds., *Islam, Politics, Anthropology,* Oxford: Wiley-Blackwell, 138–155.

Ahmad, Ishtiaq. 1999. 'The 1947 partition of Punjab: Arguments put forth before the Punjab boundary commission by the parties involved.' I. Talbot and G. Singh, eds., *The Partition of India*. Cambridge: Cambridge University Press, 116–167.

Ahmad, Khurshid. n.d. *A Brief History of Ahmadiyya Muslim Community*. www.alislam. org/library/book/brief-history-ahmadiyya-muslim/international-baiat/

Ahmad, Masroor. June 2008. 'Khilafat centenary message.' *Review of Religions*.

Ahmad, Masroor. 2014a. 'Friday sermon: A conference on some living religions.' February 28. www.alislam.org/friday-sermon/printer-friendly-summary-2014-02-28.html

Ahmad, Masroor. 2014b. 'Friday sermon: Conference of world religions 2014.' March 7. www.alislam.org/friday-sermon/printer-friendly-summary-2014-03-07.html

Ahmad, Mubasher. 2008. *Approaching the West*. www.alislam.org/library/books/Appro aching-the-West.pdf

Ahmad, Nakasha. 2018. 'Unveiling the mysteries of the past: The Turin Shroud.' *Review of Religions* 113/1:30–38.

Ahmad, S. S., ed. 2008. *Al-Nahl* 19/2 www.alislam.org/alnahl/an2008v19-no2.pdf

Ahmad, Safeer. 2004. 'My life with Huzur.' Souvenir Issue. *Tariq Magazine*, 50–56.

Ahmad, Tariq. 2008. 'Editorial.' Khalifat Centenary Souvenir Issue. *Tariq Magazine*, 18–31.

Ahmad, Tufail. 2017. At Anti-Ahmadi conferences in Pakistan, Islamic clerics declare: '[Ahmadi Muslims are] Brokers of the Zionist and imperial powers, and agents of Israel'; '[They] should be removed from all important positions [In the military and government of Pakistan].' *MEMRI*. www.memri.org/reports/anti-ahmadi-conferences-pakistan-islamic-clerics-declare-ahmadi-muslims-are-brokers-zionist

Ahmad, W. 2008. 'Letter: Preaching hatred was a flagrant misuse of airwaves.' *Birmingham Post*, September 18.

Ahmadiyya Muslim Jamaat International Desk. 2012. 'Muslims respond to mosque attack in Virginia: Attack will not deter Muslims from completing the Mubarak mosque.' 1 February. https://www.alislam.org/press-release/muslims-respond-to-mosque-attack-in-virginia/

Ahmadiyya Muslim Press Release. 23 March 2013. 'National symposium to mark centenary of one of Britain's oldest established Muslim communities.' Ahmadiyya Muslim Association UK, Press and Media Desk.

Ahmadiyya Muslim Press Release. 18 May 2017. *Historic Reception Held to Mark 25th Anniversary of MTA International Held in London*. www.khalifaofislam.com/ press-releases/mta-dinner-2017/

Ahmadiyya Muslim Association, UK. 2018. *Jalsa Salana Programme and Information Booklet*. https://www.jalsasalana.org.uk/information-booklet-2018/

AHRC and IHRC. 2015. *Report of the Fact Finding Mission to Pakistan, on the Rising Persecution of the Ahmadiyya Muslim Community, A Beleaguered Community*. http:// hrcommittee.org/wp-content/uploads/2017/05/IHRC-2015-Report.pdf

Ali, Maulana Muhammad. 1992. *The Antichrist and Gog and Magog*. Columbus, OH: Ahmadiyya Anjuman 'Isha'at Islam Lahore Inc.

All Party Parliamentary Group. 2016. *Freedom of Religion or Belief in Pakistan & UK Government Policy: APPG for International Freedom of Religion or Belief*. https:// appgfreedomofreligionorbelief.org/media/APPG-Pakistan-Inquiry-Full-Report-March-2016.pdf

All Party Parliamentary Group. 2018. *International Freedom of Religion or Belief*. https:// appgfreedomofreligionorbelief.org/house-of-commons-debates-the-persecution-of-ahmadis/

Allievi, Stefano. 2009. *Conflicts over Mosques in Europe: Policy Issues and Trends*. London: Alliance Publishing.

Al-Nahl. June 1990. 'A brief history of Majlis Ansarullah.' *4–7 and 16.* Publication of Majlis Ansarullah, USA.

Amanullah, Muhammad. 2009. 'Islamic dreaming: An analysis of its truthfulness and influence.' Kelly Bulkeley, Muhammad Amanullah, Kate Adams, Patricia Davis, Lee Butler, Bart Koet, Bonnelle Strickling, Geoff Nelson, Patricia Bulkley and Hidayet Aydar, eds., *Dreaming in Christianity and Islam: Culture, Conflict, and Creativity.* Brunswick, NJ: Rutgers University Press, 98–110.

Anon. 1947. *Qadian: A Test Case.* Lahore. In DO. 1947. 142/323 Ahmadiyya Community.

Ansari, Humayun. 2004. *The Infidel Within: Muslims in Britain Since 1800.* London: C. Hurst & Co.

Ansari, Humayun. 2008. 'Making transnational connections: Muslim networks in early twentieth-century Britain.' N. Clayer and E. Germaine, eds., *Islam in Inter-war Europe.* London: Hurst & Co., 31–63.

Anwar, Muhammad. 1998. *Between Cultures: Continuity and Change in the Lives of Young Asians.* London: Routledge.

Appadurai, Arjun. 2006. *Fear of Small Numbers: An Essay in the Geography of Anger.* Durham and London: Duke University Press.

Archer, John Clark. 1946. *The Sikhs in Relation to Moslems, Christians, and Ahmadiyyas.* Princeton: Princeton University Press.

Archer, Toby. 2009. 'Welcome to the Umma: The British state and its Muslim citizens since 9/11.' *Cooperation and Conflict: Journal of the Nordic International Studies Association,* 44/3:329–347.

Arendt, Hannah. 1967. *The Origins of Totalitarianism.* London: Allen and Unwin.

Arjana, Sophia Rose. 2017. *Pilgrimage in Islam: Traditional and Modern Practices.* St Ives: Oneworld Academic.

Arnold, Thomas. 1913 [1896]. *The Preaching of Islam: A History of the Propagation of the Muslim Faith.* London: Constable and Company Ltd.

Asad, Ahmed. 2006. *Adjudicating Muslims: Law, Religion and the State in Colonial India and Postcolonial Pakistan.* Chicago: PhD Chicago University.

Ashraf, Ajaz. 2018. 'Historian Ayesha Jalal interview: Why Pakistan is vulnerable to military rule but India isn't.' *Scroll.in.* https://scroll.in/article/887803/historian-ayesha-jalal-interview-why-pakistan-not-india-is-vulnerable-to-military-rule

Asian Human Rights Commission. 2016. *Pakistan: September 7: One of the Darkest Days in the History of Pakistan.* www.humanrights.asia/news/ahrc-news/AHRC-STM-137-2016

Asian Human Rights Commission and International Human Rights Committee. 2015. *Report of the Fact Finding Mission to Pakistan. A Beleaguered Community: On the Rising Persecution of the Ahmadiyya Muslim Community.* UK: International Human Rights Committee. http://stopthepersecution.org/wp-content/uploads/2016/02/IHRC%202015%20Report.pdf

Astor, Avi. 2012. 'Memory, community, and opposition to mosques: The case of Badalona.' *Theory and Society* 41:325–349.

Awan, Muhammad, Rizwan Kokab and Rehana Iqbal. 2013. 'Jama'at-i-Islami: Movement for Islamic constitution and anti-Ahmadiyya campaign.' *Asian Culture and History* 5/2:181–187.

Awan, Samina. 2009. 'Muslim urban politics in colonial Punjab: Majlis-i-Ahrar's early activism.' *Journal of Punjab Studies* 16/2:235–258.

Awan, Samina. 2010. *Political Islam in Colonial Punjab: Majlis-i-Ahrar 1929–1949.* Oxford: Oxford University Press.

Aydar, Hidayat. 2009. 'Istikhara and dreams: Learning about the future through dreaming.' Kelly Bulkeley, Muhammad Amanullah, Kate Adams, Patricia Davis, Lee Butler, Bart Koet, Bonnelle Strickling, Geoff Nelson, Patricia Bulkley and Hidayet Aydar, eds., *Dreaming in Christianity and Islam: Culture, Conflict, and Creativity*. Brunswick, NJ: Rutgers University Press, 123–136.

Bajwa, Lubna and Shaheer Khan. 2015. *Exploring Rabwah as an Identity Marker for the Ahmadiyya Community: A Baseline Qualitative Study*. Islamabad: Pakistan Association of Anthropology.

Ballard, Roger. 1987. 'The political economy of migration: Pakistan, Britain and the middle East.' Eades Jeremy, ed., *Migrants, Workers and the Social Order*. London: Tavistock, 17–41.

Ballard, Roger. 2003. 'The South Asian presence in Britain and its transnational connections.' Bhikhu Parekh, et al., eds., *Culture and Economy in the Indian Diaspora*. London: Taylor & Francis, 197–222.

Ballard, Roger. 2005. 'Remittances and economic development in India and Pakistan.' Maimbo, Samuel and Dilip Ratha, eds., *Remittances: Development Impact and Future Prospects*. Washington, DC: World Bank, 103–118.

Ballard, Roger. 2006. 'On the consequences of migration from below: Ethnic colonization and the dynamics of transnational networks.' *Paper Presented at Conference on Migration and the State: Network Formation in the Indian Diaspora*, University of Inchon, South Korea.

Balzani, Marzia. 2011. 'Constructing victims, construing credibility: Forced marriage, Pakistani women and the UK asylum process.' A. Gill and S. Anitha, eds., *Forced Marriage: Introducing a Social Justice and Human Rights Perspective*. London: Zed Books, 200–220.

Balzani, Marzia. 2014. 'An ethnographer among the Ahmadis: Learning Islam in the suburbs.' G. Marranci, ed., *Islam in Practice*. London, New York: Routledge, 110–123.

Balzani, Marzia. 2015. 'Old industrial space, new suburban uses: The Ahmadiyya mosque.' *Special Issue of Laboratorium: Russian Review of Social Research* 7/3:49–71.

Basit, Asif. June 2012. 'London's first Mosque – A study in history and mystery.' *Review of Religions*, 30–46.

Bates, Stephen. 2016. 'Lord Avebury obituary.' *The Guardian*, 14 February.

Bausani, A. 1985. 'I sogni nell'Islam.' G. Tullio, ed., *I Sogni nel Medioevo*. Roma: Edizioni dell'Ateneo, 25–36.

Bax, Mart. 1995. *Medjugorje: Religion, Politics, and Violence in Rural Bosnia*. Amsterdam: VU Uitgeverij.

Belokrenitsky, Vyacheslav and Vladimir Moskalenko. 2013. *A Political History of Pakistan 1947–2007*. Oxford: Oxford University Press.

Bennett, Jane. 2001. *The Enchantment of Modern Life: Attachments, Crossings, and Ethics*. Princeton and Oxford: Princeton University Press.

Berliner, David. 2005. 'The abuses of memory: Reflections on the memory boom in anthropology.' *Anthropological Quarterly* 78/1:197–211.

Bhachu, Parminder. 1986. *Twice Migrants: East African Sikh Settlers in Britain*. London: Routledge, Kegan and Paul.

Bhachu, Parminder. 2016. 'Twice migrants and multiple migrants.' John Stone, Rutledge Dennis, Polly Rizova, Anthony Smith and Xiaoshuo Hou, eds., *The Wiley Blackwell Encyclopedia of Race, Ethnicity, and Nationalism*. New Jersey, Oxford: John Wiley & Sons, Ltd, 1–4.

Bilu, Yoram and Eyal Ben-Ari. 1992. 'The Making of Modern Saints: Manufactured Charisma and the Abu-Hatseiras of Israel.' *American Ethnologist* 19/4:672–687.

Blank, Jonah. 2001. *Mullahs on the Mainframe: Islam and Modernity Among the Daudi Bohras*. Chicago: University of Chicago Press.

Blinder, Scott. 2017. *Non EU-Migration to the UK: Family and Dependents*. The Migration Observatory, Oxford University. http://migrationobservatory.ox.ac.uk/resources/briefings/non-european-migration-to-the-uk-family-unification-dependents/

Blom, Amélie. 2008. 'The 2006 anti-"Danish Cartoons" Riot in Lahore: Outrage and the emotional landscape of Pakistani politics.' *South Asia Multidisciplinary Academic Journal* 2:1–32.

Brass, Paul. 2003. 'The partition of India and retributive genocide in the Punjab, 1946–1947: Means, methods and purposes 1.' *Journal of Genocide Research* 5/1:71–101.

Brush, S. E. 1955. 'Ahmadiyyat in Pakistan: Rabwah and the Ahmadis.' *The Muslim World* 45/2:145–171.

Bulkeley, Kelly. 2002. 'Reflections on the dream traditions of Islam.' *Sleep and Hypnosis* 4/1:4–14.

Bunglawala, Inayat. 2009. 'Freedom of worship for Ahmadis.' *The Guardian*, 8 December.

Butterworth, Jonathan. 2012. 'Human rights, human principles, and the case of derogatory cartoons.' *Review of Religions*, February 38–49.

Cabinet Office. 2007. *Security in a Global Hub: Establishing the UK's New Border Arrangements*. London: Cabinet Office.

Cantwell Smith, Wilfred. 1943. *Modern Islām in India: A Social Analysis*. Lahore: Minerva Book Shop.

Carrell, Severin. 2016. 'Man who murdered Glasgow shopkeeper Asad Shah in sectarian attack jailed.' *The Guardian,* 9 August.

Carver, Natasha. 2016. '"For her protection and benefit": The regulation of marriage-related migration to the UK.' *Ethnic and Racial Studies* 39/15:2758–2776.

Cesari, Jocelyne. 2005. 'Mosque conflicts in European cities: Introduction.' *Journal of Ethnic and Migration Studies* 31/6:1015–1024.

Charity Commission for England and Wales. 2019. *Khatme Nubuwwat Centre: Decision*. www.gov.uk/government/publications/charity-inquiry-khatmenubuwwat-centre/khatme-nubuwwat-centre.

Charsley, Katherine and M. Benson. 2012. 'Marriages of convenience, and inconvenient marriages: Regulating spousal migration to Britain.' *Immigration, Asylum and Nationality Law* 26/1:10–26.

Charsley, Simon. 1996. '"Untouchable": What's in a name?' *Journal of the Royal Anthropological Institute* 2/1:1–23.

Chattha, Ilyas. 2011. *Partition and Locality: Violence, Migration and Development in Gujranwala and Sialkot 1947–1961*. Oxford: Oxford University Press.

Chaudhary, Aziz Ahmad. 1996. 'Khilafat-e-Ahmadiyya.' *The Promised Messiah and the Mahdi*. Islamabad, Surry: Islam International Publications, 227–231.

Chawla, Muhammad Iqbal. 2011. 'Role of the Majilis-i-Ahrar Islam-Hind in the Kashmir movement of 1931.' *Pakistaniaat: A Journal of Pakistan Studies* 3/2:82–102.

Chester, Lucy. 2009. *Borders and Conflict in South Asia: The Radcliffe Boundary Commission and the Partition of Punjab*. Manchester: Manchester University Press.

Clayton, John. 2009. 'Thinking spatially: Towards an everyday understanding of inter-ethnic relations.' *Social and Cultural Geography* 10/4:481–498.

Coates, Andrew. 2016. *Sectarian Hatred Reaches Britain as Muslims Picket Ahmadi Mosque*. https://tendancecoatesy.wordpress.com/2016/02/16/sectarian-hatred-reaches-britain-as-muslims-picket-ahmadi-mosque/

Cole, Tim. 2003. *Holocaust City: The Making of a Jewish Ghetto*. London: Routledge.

Copland, Ian. 1981. 'Islam and political mobilization in Kashmir, 1931–1934.' *Pacific Affairs* 54/2:228–259.

Corbin, H. 1966. 'The visionary dream in Islamic spirituality.' G. E. Von Grunebaum and R. Caillois, eds., *The Dream and Human Societies*. Berkeley: University of California Press 381–408.

Cornwall, Paige. 2017. 'Monroe mosque vandalized; "maybe the person who did this just doesn't understand Islam".' *Seattle Times*, 15 September.

Council on American Islamic Relations (CAIR), 2005. *Women Friendly Mosques and Community Centers: Working Together to Reclaim Our Heritage*. www.isna.net/assets/ildc/documents/womenandmosquesbooklet.pdf

Craig, Tim. 2015. 'Karachi's downtrodden Christians get a towering if contentious symbol of hope.' *The Guardian*, 19 May.

Cranmer, T. 2018. 'Advertising standards authority probes billboards declaring "The Messiah has come".' *Archbishop Cranmer*, 20 February. http://archbishopcranmer.com/advertising-standards-authority-billboards-messiah-has-come/

Crinson, M. 2002. 'The mosque and the metropolis.' Jill Beulieu and Mary Roberts, eds., *Orientalism's Interlocutors: Painting, Architecture, Photography*. Durham: Duke University Press, 79–101.

Dard, A. R. 2008. *Life of Ahmad[as]: Founder of the Ahmadiyya Movement*. Islamabad, Surrey: Islam International Publications Limited.

Das, Veena. 1996. *Critical Events: An Anthropological Perspective on Contemporary India*. Oxford: Oxford University Press.

Davis, Kingsley. 1949. 'India and Pakistan: The demography of partition.' *Pacific Affairs* 22/3:254–264.

Dawn Newspaper. 2010. 'PML-N defends Nawaz's remarks about Ahmadis.' 10 June. www.dawn.com/news/850096

Dawn Newspaper. 2014. 'Police rapped for gravestones removal.' 14 March. www.dawn.com/news/1092998/police-rapped-for-gravestones-removal

Dawn Newspaper. 2018. 'Declaration of faith compulsory before joining civil, armed services and judiciary: Islamabad high court.' 9 March. www.dawn.com/news/1394175/declaration-of-faith-compulsory-before-joining-civil-armed-services-and-judiciary-islamabad-high-court

Deeb, Lara. 2006. *An Enchanted Modern: Gender and Public Piety in Shi'i Lebanon*. Princeton: Princeton University Press.

DeHanas, Daniel and Zacharias Pieri. 2011. 'Olympic Proportions: The expanding scalar politics of the London "Olympics mega-mosque" controversy.' *Sociology* 45/5: 798–814.

Del Re, Emanuela. 2014. 'Approaching conflict the Ahmadiyya way: The alternative way to conflict resolution of the Ahmadiyya community in Haifa, Israel.' *Contemporary Islam* 8:115–131.

DFID. 2017. *Pakistan Profile Report*. https://assets.publishing.service.gov.uk/government/uploads/system/uploads/attachment_data/file/636548/Pakistan1.pdf

Di Giovine, Michael. 2011. 'Pilgrimage: Communitas and contestation, unity and difference.' *Tourism Review* 59/3:247–269.

Douglas, Mary. 1984 [1966]. *Purity and Danger: An Analysis of Concepts of Pollution and Taboo*. London: Routledge.

Dunn, Kevin M. 2005. 'Repetitive and troubling discourses of nationalism in the local politics of mosque development in Sydney, Australia.' *Environment and Planning D: Society and Space* 23/1:29–50.

Durrani, Saeed. 1991. 'Sir Thomas Arnold and Iqbal.' *Iqbal Review: Journal of the Iqbal Academy Pakistan* 32/1.

Edgar, Iain. 2007. 'The inspirational night dream in the motivation and justification of Jihad.' *Nova Religio: The Journal of Alternative and Emergent Religions* 11/2:59–76.

Edgar, Iain. 2010. 'Istikhara: The guidance and practice of Islamic dream incubation through ethnographic comparison.' *History and Anthropology* 21/3:251–262.

Edgar, Iain. 2016. *The Dream in Islam: From Qur'anic Tradition to Jihadist Inspiration.* Oxford: Berghahn Books.

Evans, Nicholas. 2017. 'Beyond cultural intimacy: The tensions that make truth for India's Ahmadi Muslims.' *American Ethnologist* 44/3:490–502.

Ewing, Katherine. 1983. 'The politics of Sufism: Redefining the saints of Pakistan.' *The Journal of Asian Studies* 42:251–268.

Ewing, Katherine. 1994. 'Dreams from a saint: Anthropological atheism and the temptation to believe.' *American Anthropologist* 96/3:571–583.

The Express Tribune. 2010. 'Sharif's statement on Ahmadis angers clerics.' 7 June. https://tribune.com.pk/story/19379/sharifs-statement-on-ahmadis-angers-clerics/

Fabian, Johannes. 1966. 'Dream and charisma "Theories of dreams" in the Jamaa-movement (Congo).' *Anthropos* 61:544–560.

Farhat, Amtul. 2013. 'Kababir, home of Israel's Muslim Ahmadiyya.' *The Muslim Times*, 28 June.

Farley, Harry. 2018. 'Advertising standards authority assesses dozens of complaints over "Messiah has come" billboards.' *Christian Today*, 19 February.

Faruqui, N. A. 1999. 'Dreams.' *The Light*. http://alislam.org/text/articles/ light/dreams.shtml

Freedman, Samuel. 2010. 'Grief links members of a persecuted Muslim sect.' *New York Times*, 11 June.

Friedmann, Yohanan. 1989. *Prophecy Continuous: Aspects of Ahmadi Religious Thought and Its Medieval Background.* Berkeley: University of California Press.

Full, Fact. 2018. *UK Spending on Foreign Aid.* https://fullfact.org/economy/uk-spending-foreign-aid/

Gabrielatos, Costas and Paul Baker. 2008. 'Fleeing, sneaking, flooding: A corpus analysis of discursive constructions of refugees and asylum seekers in the UK press 1996–2005.' *Journal of English Linguistics* 36/1:5–38.

Gailani, Fatima. 2000. *The Mosques of London.* Henstridge: Elm Grove Books Limited.

Gale, Richard. 2004. 'The multicultural city and the politics of religious architecture: Urban planning, mosques and meaning making in Birmingham, UK.' *Built Environment* 30/1:18–32.

Gale, Richard. 2005. 'Representing the city: Mosques and the planning process in Birmingham.' *Journal of Ethnic and Migration Studies* 31/6:1161–1179.

Galtung, Johann. 1969. 'Violence, peace, and peace research.' *Journal of Peace Research* 6:167–191.

Germain, Eric. 2008. 'The first Muslim missions on a European scale: Ahmadi-Lahori networks in the inter-war period.' N. Clayer and E. Germain, eds., *Islam in Inter-War Europe*. New York: Columbia University Press, 89–118.

Gerth, Hans and C. Wright Mills 1946. *From Max Weber: Essays in Sociology.* Oxford: Oxford University Press.

Geschiere, Peter. 2009. *The Perils of Belonging: Autochthony, Citizenship, and Exclusion in Africa and Europe.* Chicago: Chicago University Press.

Gillani, Waqar. 2018. 'A night of trouble in Sialkot.' *The News on Sunday*, 3 June.

Gilmartin, David. 1998. *Empire and Islam: Punjab and the Making of Pakistan.* Berkeley: University of California Press.

Göle, Nilüfer. 2011. 'The public visibility of Islam and European politics of resentment: The minarets-mosques debate.' *Philosophy and Social Criticism* 37/4:383–392.

Good, Anthony. 2007. *Anthropology and Expertise in the Asylum Courts.* Oxford: Routledge-Cavendish.

Good, Anthony. 2011. 'Witness statements and credibility assessments in the British asylum courts.' Livia Holden, ed., *Cultural Expertise and Litigation: Patterns, Conflicts, Narratives.* London: Routledge, 95–122.

Goodhart, David. 2013. 'A mega mosque in a suburb that was 90 per cent white 30 years ago and the polite apartheid dividing Britain.' *Daily Mail,* 24 March.

GOV.UK 2017. *Immigration Statistics, October to December 2016.* www.gov.uk/government/statistics/immigration-statistics-october-to-december-2016

Gower, Melanie and Terry McGuinness. 2018. *The UK's Refugee Family Reunion Rules: Striking the Right Balance?* House of Commons Library Briefing paper number 07511, 1 March.

Graeber, David. 2012. 'Dead zones of the imagination: On violence, bureaucracy, and interpretive labor.' *HAU: Journal of Ethnographic Theory* 2/2:105–128.

Hadi, Abdul. 2015. 'Injustice and persecution: Forced migration of Sindhi Hindus in Pakistan' *Mediterranean Journal of Social Sciences* 6/2:11–14.

Hadi, Sheikh Abdul. 1997. *Basics of Religious Education.* Islamabad and Tilford, Surrey: Islam International Publications Ltd.

Hamdani, Yasser, L. 2012. 'Do Ahmadis deserve to live in Pakistan?' *The Friday Times,* August 31 September 2006, XXIV:29. www.thefridaytimes.com/beta3/tft/article.php?issue=20

Hamid, Mohsin. 2018. 'Mohsin Hamid on the rise of nationalism: "In the land of the pure, no one is pure enough".' *The Guardian,* 27 January.

Hansard, UK Parliament. 2010. *Westminster Hall Debate: Ahmadiyya Community.* https://hansard.parliament.uk/Commons/2010-1020/debates/10102039000002/AhmadiyyaCommunity

Hansard, UK Parliament. 2018. *House of Commons Debate: Ahmadiyya Muslim Community,* 24 May. https://hansard.parliament.uk/Commons/2018-05-24/debates/B2B8FC6E-7F7F-4BFC-8C7A-107F94D1B9FB/AhmadiyyaMuslimCommunity

Hanson, James. 2005. 'Was Jesus a Buddhist?' *Buddhist-Christian Studies* 25:75–89.

Hare, William Loftus. 1924. 'An account of the "Conference on some living religions within the empire", Held at the imperial institute, London, September 22nd to October 3rd, 1924.' *The Open Court,* 707–759.

Hare, William Loftus, ed. 1925. *Religions of the Empire: A Conference on Some Living Religions with the Empire.* London: Duckworth.

Harris, Ruth. 1999. *Lourdes: Body and Spirit in a Secular Age.* London: Penguin.

Hayat, Meliha Rafiq. 2014. 'Religious teachings: A vehicle for peace.' *Review of Religions* June 18–24.

Heijnen, Adriënne and Iain Edgar. 2010. 'Imprints of dreaming.' *History and Anthropology* 21/3:217–226.

Heo, Angie. 2012. 'The virgin made visible: Intercessory images of Church territory in Egypt.' *Comparative Studies in Society and History* 54/2:361–391.

Hermansen, Marcia. 1997. 'Visions as "good to think": A cognitive approach to visionary experience in Islamic Sufi thought.' *Religion* 27:25–43.

Hermansen, Marcia. 2001. 'Dreams and dreaming in Islam.' K. Bulkeley, ed., *Dreams: A Reader on Religious, Cultural and Psychological Dimension of Dreaming*. New York: Palgrave Macmillan, 73–91.

Hirschkind, Charles. 2006. *The Ethical Soundscape: Cassette Sermons and Islamic Counterpublics*. New York: Columbia University Press.

Hirschkind, Charles. 2012. 'Experiments in devotion online: The YouTube Khutba.' *International Journal of Middle East Studies* 44:5–21.

Hoag, Colin. 2011. 'Assembling partial perspectives: Thoughts on the anthropology of Bureaucracy.' *PoLAR: Political and Legal Anthropology Review* 34/1:81–94.

Hodges, Matt. 2008. 'Rethinking time's arrow: Bergson, Deleuze and the anthropology of time.' *Anthropological Theory* 8/4:399–429.

Hoffman, Valerie. 1997. 'The role of visions in contemporary Egyptian religious life.' *Religion* 27:45–64.

Holmes, Kristin. 2018. *The Ahmadiyya Muslim Community's "Pope" Visits to Dedicate a Mosque in North Philadelphia*. http://www2.philly.com/philly/news/ahmadiyya-muslim-philadelphia-mirza-masroor-ahmad-20181018.html. *The Inquirer*, 18 October.

The Holy Qur'ān, Arabic text with English Translation and short commentary. 2016 [1969]. Islam International Publications Ltd. www.alislam.org/quran/Holy-Quran-Short-Commentary.pdf

Home Office. 2002. *Secure Borders, Safe Haven: Integration with Diversity in Modern Britain*. Parliamentary White Paper. London: HMSO.

Home Office. 2015. *Country Information and Guidance Pakistan: Ahmadis*. https://www.refworld.org/publisher,UKHO,,,54ef2a7e4,0.html

Home Office. 2016. *Country Information and Guidance Pakistan: Ahmadis*. https://assets.publishing.service.gov.uk/government/uploads/system/uploads/attachment_data/file/566234/Pakistan-_Ahmadis.pdf

Home Office. 2017. *Humanitarian Protection*. https://assets.publishing.service.gov.uk/government/uploads/system/uploads/attachment_data/file/597377/Humanitarian-protection-v5_0.pdf

Home Office. 2018. *Country Policy and Information Note, Pakistan: Ahmadis*. https://assets.publishing.service.gov.uk/government/uploads/system/uploads/attachment_data/file/717821/CPIN-Pakistan-Ahmadis-v3.0-June_2018.pdf

Hoodbhoy, Pervez. 2007. 'Jinnah and the Islamic state: Setting the record straight.' *Economic and Political Weekly* 42/32:3300–3303.

Hough, Andrew. 2012. 'Plans for new east London "mega-mosque" rejected by local council.' *The Telegraph*, December 5.

House of Commons Culture, Media and Sport Committee. 2013. *Written Evidence Submitted by the Ahmadiyya Muslim Community UK*. https://publications.parliament.uk/pa/cm201314/cmselect/cmcumeds/729/729vw55.htm

Howard, Thomas Albert. 2017. '"A remarkable gathering": The conference on living religions within the British empire (1924) and its historical significance.' *Journal of the American Academy of Religion* 1–32.

HRC. 2015. *Submission to the All Party Parliamentary Group for International Religious Freedom or Belief, Parliamentary Inquiry, Freedom of Religion or Belief in Pakistan and UK Government Policy*. https://freedomdeclared.org/media/APPG-UK-Submission.pdf

Hull, Matthew. 2012. 'Documents and bureaucracy.' *Annual Review of Anthropology* 41:251–267.

Human Rights Watch. May 2010. *Pakistan: Massacre of Minority Ahmadis*. www.hrw.org/en/news/2010/05/31/pakistan-massacre-minority-ahmadis

Human Rights Watch. 2018. *Pakistan: Ensure Ahmadi Voting Rights Repeal Discriminatory Laws Against Religious Community*. www.hrw.org/news/2018/06/28/pakistan-ensure-ahmadi-voting-rights

Husain, Soheil. 2011. 'Cartoons of the prophet Muhammad.' Letters, *New York Times*, 6 November.

Hussain, Azhar and Ahmad Salim with Arif Naveed. 2011. *Connecting the Dots: Education and Religious Discrimination in Pakistan: A Study of Public Schools and Madrassas*. Washington, DC: United States Commission on International Religious Freedom.

Idara, Dawat-O-Irshad. n.d. *Mirza Ghulam's Knowledge and Practice of Islam*. www.irshad.org/exposed/knowledge.php

IHRC. 2017. *Ahmadis in Pakistan Face an Existential Threat: The Growing Violence, Legal Discrimination and Social Exclusion Since 2015*. http://hrcommittee.org/wp-content/uploads/2017/06/Persecution-2017-Final-PRINT-COPYV2-.pdf

Inayat, Naila. 2018. 'Pakistani court ruling aims to publicly identify all religious minorities.' *Religion News Service*, 27 March. https://religionnews.com/2018/03/27/pakistani-court-ruling-aims-to-publicly-identify-all-religious-minorities/

Iqbal, Muhammad. 1900. 'The doctrine of absolute unity, as expounded by Abdu-l-Karim Al-Jilani.' *The Indian Antiquary*, 237–246.

Iqbal, Muhammad. 1944 [1934]. 'Qadianis and orthodox Muslims.' Shamloo, ed., *Speeches and Statements of Iqbal*. Lahore: Al-Manar Academy.

Iqbal, Muhammad. 1995 [1936]. 'Introduction.' *Islam and Ahmadism*, edited by Zafarul-Islam Khan. New Delhi: Media and Publishing.

IRB Canada. 11 January 2013. *Responses to Information Requests. Pakistan-Ahmadi Membership Verification*. http://irb-cisr.gc.ca/Eng/ResRec/RirRdi/Pages/index.aspx?doc=454344

IRB Canada. 2013. *Responses to Information Requests. Pakistan: Registration Procedures and Documents of the Ahmadiyya Muslim Jama'at in Canada, the US and the UK*. www.irb-cisr.gc.ca/Eng/ResRec/RirRdi/Pages/index.aspx?doc=454346&pls=1

Islam, Shamsul. 2011. 'Ahmadis expelled from school: 10 students, teacher forced out of schools because of their faith.' *The Express Tribune*, 8 October.

Islam, Shamsul. 2012. 'Police remove Quranic verses from Ahmadi graves to 'avert clashes.' *The Express Tribune with the International Herald Tribune*, August 18.

Ispahani, Farahnaz. 2013. *Cleansing Pakistan of Minorities*. Hudson Institute. www.hudson.org/research/9781-cleansing-pakistan-of-minorities.

Jalal, Ayesha. 2014. *The Struggle for Pakistan: A Muslim Homeland and Global Politics*. Cambridge, MA: Belknap Press.

Jenkins, Richard. 2000. 'Disenchantment, enchantment and re-enchantment: Max Weber at the millennium.' *Max Weber Studies* 1/1:11–32.

Jones, Garth. 1986. 'The Ahmadis of Islam: A Mormon encounter and perspective.' *Dialogue: A Journal of Mormon Thought* 19:39–54.

Jones, Kenneth. 2008. *The New Cambridge History of India: Socio-religious Reform Movements in British India*. Cambridge: Cambridge University Press.

Jones, Lewis Bevan. 2010 [1932]. *The People of the Mosques: The Study of Islam with Special Reference to India*. Whitefish, MT: Kessinger Publishing.

Jonker, Gerdien. 2005. 'The Mevlana mosque in Berlin-Kreuzberg: An unsolved conflict.' *Journal of Ethnic and Migration Studies* 31/6:1067–1081.

Joseph, Simon. 2012. 'Jesus in India? Transgressing social and religious boundaries.' *Journal of the American Academy of Religion* 80/1:161–199.

Kalberg, Stephen. 1980. 'Max Weber's types of rationality: Cornerstones for the analysis of rationalization processes in history.' *American Journal of Sociology* 85/5:1145–1179.

Kamran, Tahir. 2013. 'Majlis-i-Ahrar-i-Islam: Religion, socialism and agitation in action.' *South Asian History and Culture* 4/4:465–482.

Kamran, Tahir. 2015. 'The pre-history of religious exclusionism in contemporary Pakistan: Khatam-e-Nubuwwat 1889–1953.' *Modern Asian Studies* 1–35.

Kapferer, Bruce. 2010. 'In the event – Toward an anthropology of generic moments.' *Social Analysis* 54/3:1–27.

Katz, Jonathan. 1997. 'An Egyptian Sufi interprets his dreams: 'Abd al-Wahhab al-Shar'rani 1493–1565.' *Religion* 27:7–24.

Kaul, Harikishan. 1912. *Census of India, 1911*. Vol. XIV. Punjab Part 1, Report. Lahore: Civil and Military Gazette Press.

Kelly, Tobias. 2006. 'Documented lives: Fear and the uncertainties of law during the second Palestinian intifada.' *Journal of the Royal Anthropological Institute* 12:89–107.

Kennedy, Charles. 1989. 'Towards the definition of a Muslim in an Islamic state: The case of the Ahmadiyya in Pakistan.' D. Vajpeyi and Y. Malik, eds., *Religious and Ethnic Minority Politics in South Asia*. New York, NY: The Riverdale Company, 71–108.

Kennedy, Charles. 1992. 'Repugnancy to Islam – who decides? Islam and legal reform in Pakistan.' *International and Comparative Law Quarterly* 41/4:769–787.

Khan, Adil Hussain. 2012. 'The Kashmir crisis as a political platform for Jama'at-i Ahmadiyya's entrance into South Asian politics.' *Modern Asian Studies* 46/5:1398–1428.

Khan, Adil Hussain. 2015. *From Sufism to Ahmadiyya: A Muslim Minority Movement in South Asia*. Bloomington and Indianapolis: Indiana University Press.

Khan, Amjad Mahmood. 2003. 'Persecution of the Ahmadiyya community in Pakistan: An analysis under international law and international relations.' *Harvard Human Rights Journal* 16:217–244.

Khan, Arif. 2010. 'The shroud of Turin.' *Review of Religions* 105/8.

Khan, Arif. 2015. 'The sudarium of Oviedo & The shroud of Turin.' *Review of Religions* 110/5:40–53.

Khan, Chaudhry Zafrulla. 2008. 'Hadhrat Khalifatul Masih II(ra) – A personal memoir.' *Review of Religions* February 63–79.

Khan, Muhmmad Ismail. 2011. 'The assertion of Bareli extremism.' *Hudson Institute*. www.hudson.org/research/9848-the-assertion-of-barelvi-extremism

Khokhar, Tooba. 2014. 'The enchanting story of Guildhall.' *Maryam: Taleem and Tarbiyyat Magazine for Waaqifaat-e-Nau* April–June 10:16–17.

Kilborne, Benjamin. 1981. 'Moroccan dream interpretation and culturally constituted defence mechanisms.' *Ethos* 9/4:294–312.

Kinberg, Leah. 1985. 'The legitimation of the madhahib through dreams.' *Arabica* 32:47–79.

Kinberg, Leah. 1993. 'Literal dreams and prophetic hadits in classical Islam: A comparison of two ways of legitimation.' *Der Islam* 70/2:279–300.

Krenkow, F. 1912. 'The appearance of the prophet in dreams.' *Journal of the Royal Asiatic Society* 77–79.

Kublitz, Anja. 2010. 'The cartoon controversy: Creating Muslims in a Danish setting.' *Social Analysis* 54/3:107–125.

Laegaard, Sune. 2007. 'The cartoon controversy: Offence, identity, oppression?' *Political Studies* 55:481–498.

Lall, M. 2009. 'Education dilemmas in Pakistan: The current curriculum reform.' M. Lall and E. Vickers, eds., *Education as a Political Tool in Asia*, London: Routledge, 179–197.

Lamoreaux, John. 2002. *The Early Muslim Tradition of Dream Interpretation*. New York: SUNY Press.

Langer, Lorenz. 2010. 'Panacea or pathetic fallacy? The swiss ban on minarets.' *Vanderbilt Journal of Transnational Law* 43, 1–62.

Lavan, Spencer. 1974. *The Ahmadiyya Movement: A History and Perspective*. Delhi: Manohar.

Leirvik, Oddbjørn. 2008. 'Religion in school, interreligious relations and citizenship: The case of Pakistan.' *British Journal of Religious Education* 30/2:143–154.

Leudar, Ivan, Jacqueline Hayes, Jirí Nekvapil and Johanna Turner Baker. 2008. 'Hostility themes in media, community and refugee narratives.' *Discourse Society* 19/2:187–221.

Lewin, Carroll. 2002. 'Ghettos in the Holocaust: The improvisation of social order in a culture of terror.' Carol J. Greenhouse et al., eds., *Ethnography in Unstable Places: Everyday Lives in Contexts of Dramatic Political Change*. Durham, NC: Duke University Press, 37–60.

Love, Brian. 2011. 'French paper reprints Mohammad cartoon after fire-bomb.' *World News*. https://www.reuters.com/article/us-france-fire-magazine/french-paper-reprints-mohammad-cartoon-after-fire-bomb-idUSTRE7A26MO20111103

Luhrmann, Tanya. 2012. *When God Talks Back: Understanding the American Evangelical Relationship with God*. New York: Alfred Knopf.

Mahmood, Saba. 2005. *Politics of Piety: The Islamic Revival and the Feminist Subject*. Princeton: Princeton University Press.

Majoka, Muhammad Luqman. 2017. 'The Berlin mosque plan of 1923.' *Review of Religions* 24–38 March.

Malik, Iftikhar. 2002. *Religious Minorities in Pakistan*. London: Minority Rights Group International.

The Manchester Guardian. 1924. 'Religions of the empire: Islam's day. Prophet of a new sect at London conference.' 24 September.

Mandaville, Peter et al. 2010. *Muslim Networks and Movements in Western Europe*. Pew Forum on Religion and Public Life. http://pewforum.org/Muslim/Muslim-Networks-and-Movements-in-western-Europe.aspx

Maryam: Taleem and Tarbiyyat Magazine for Waaqifaat-e-Nau. 2014. April–June, Issue 10.

Massey, Doreen. 1994. 'A global sense of place.' *Space, Place and Gender*. Minneapolis: University of Minnesota Press, 146–156.

Massey, Doreen. 2005. *For Space*. London: Sage.

Massey, Lizzie. 2014. 'Police investigating after Britain First go to two Gillingham Mosques objecting to planning application for a new place of worship.' *Kent Online*, 3 July. www.kentonline.co.uk/medway/news/right-wing-group-threaten-to-19501

McClenaghan, Maeve. 2018. 'Young asylum seekers face "blanket study ban".' *The Guardian*, 8 April.

McDonald, K. 2006. 'Islamic makings of the self.' *Global Movements: Action and Culture*. Oxford: Blackwell Publishing, 184–208.

McLoughlin, Seán. 2005. 'Mosques and the public sphere: Conflict and cooperation in Bradford.' *Journal of Ethnic and Migration Studies* 31/6:1045–1066.

Menski, Werner. 1999. 'South Asian women in Britain, family integrity and the primary purpose rule.' Barot, Rohit, Harriet Bradley and Steve Fenton, eds., *Ethnicity, Gender and Social Change*. Basingstoke: Palgrave Macmillan, 81–98.

Metcalf, Barbara. 1990. 'The pilgrimage remembered: South Asian accounts of the *hajj*.' Dale F. Eickelman and James Piscatori, eds., *Muslim Travellers: Pilgrimage, Migration and the Religious Imagination*. London: Routledge, 169–202.

Meyer, Birgit and Annelies Moors, eds. 2005. *Religion, Media, and the Public Sphere*. Bloomington and Indianapolis: Indiana University Press.

Michael, S. M. 2010. 'Dalit encounter with Christianity: Change and continuity.' Robinson Rowena and Joseph Marianus Kujur, eds., *Margins of Faith: Dalit and Tribal Christianity in India*. London: Sage, 51–74.

Minattur, Joseph. 1962. *Martial Law in India, Pakistan and Ceylon*. The Hague: Martinus Nijhoff.

Mittermaier, Amira. 2010. *Dreams That Matter: Egyptian Landscapes of the Imagination*. Berkeley: University of California Press.

Moin, Azfar. 2012. *The Millennial Sovereign: Sacred Kingship and Sainthood in Islam*. New York: Columbia University Press.

Moles, Tarje. 2009. *The Evolution of the Ahmadiyya Muslim Community of the UK, 1913–2003*. Department of History, Royal Holloway, University of London. Unpublished PhD.

Monier Monier-Williams, M. 1899. *Sanskrit – English Dictionary*. Oxford: Oxford University Press.

Morris, Isabel. 2018. 'PakSoc criticised for neglecting to screen documentary.' *The Cherwell*, 18 May. http://cherwell.org/2018/05/18/paksoc-criticised-for-neglecting-to-screen-documentary/

Mortimer, Caroline. 2016. 'Charity commission opens formal inquiry into mosque where 'Kill Ahmadis' leaflets were allegedly found.' *The Independent*, 1 October. www.independent.co.uk/news/uk/home-news/muslim-islam-kill-ahmadi-leaflet-found-charity-commission-investigation-stockwell-green-mosque-hate-a7340911.html

Munn, Nancy. 1992. 'The cultural anthropology of time: A critical essay.' *Annual Review of Anthropology* 21:93–123.

The Nation. 2014. 'Geo clarifies its position on anti-Ahmadiyya content.' 30 December. http://nation.com.pk/national/30-Dec-2014/geo-clarifies-over-offensive-content

Naylor, Simon and James Ryan. 2002. 'The mosque in the suburbs: Negotiating religion and ethnicity in South London.' *Social and Cultural Geography* 3/1:39–59.

Naylor, Simon and James Ryan. 2003. 'Mosques, temples and gurdwaras: New sites of religion in twentieth-century Britain.' D. Gilbert, D. Matless and J. Short, eds., *Historical Geographies of Twentieth Century Britain*. Oxford: Blackwell, 168–183.

Neal, Sarah. 2003. 'The Scarman report, the Macpherson report and the media: How newspapers respond to race centred social policy interventions.' *Journal of Social Policy* 32/1:55–74.

Nijhawan, Michael. 2010. ' "Today we are all Ahmadi': Configurations of heretic otherness between Lahore and Berlin.' *British Journal of Middle Eastern Studies* 37/3:429–447.

Noakes, Helen. 2018. *The Fazl Mosque: Heritage Impact Assessment*. Salisbury: Wessex Archaeology.

Nomani, Asra. 2006. *Standing Alone: An American Woman's Struggle for the Soul of Islam*. San Francisco: Harper Collins.

Nora, Pierre. 1989. 'Between memory and history: Les Lieux de Mémoire.' *Representations* 28:7–24.

Nye, Malory. 2000. *Multiculturalism and Minority Religions in Britain: Krishna Consciousness, Religious Freedom and the Politics of Location*. Richmond: Curzon Press.

Oates, Omar. 2010a. 'Worshippers told at Tooting Islamic centre to boycott Ahmadiyya shops.' *Wimbledon Guardian*, October 14.

Oates, Omar. 2010b. 'Tooting election race infected by anti-Ahmadiyya hate campaign.' *Wimbledon Guardian*, October 14.

Oates, Omar. 2010c. 'Interview: Sadiq Khan on the Ahmadiyya hate campaign.' *Wandsworth Guardian*, 25 November.

Oates, Omar. 2010d. 'Meeting between Ahmadiyya community and Tooting Islamic centre ends in silence.' *Wimbledon Guardian*, December 23.

O'Collins, Gerald. 2008. 'The hidden story of Jesus.' *New Blackfriars* 89/1024:710–714.

Ofcom. 2010. *Broadcast Bulletin*. Issue 167. www.ofcom.org.uk/__data/assets/pdf_file/0031/45499/issue167.pdf

Pannick, D., N. Blake, S. Persaud, D. Rose, M. Shaw and R. Singh. 1993. *The Primary Purpose Rule: A Rule with No Purpose*. London: Young Justice.

Parish, Debra. 1992. 'The power of female pietism: Spiritual authorities and religious role models in seventeenth-century England.' *The Journal of Religious History* 17/1:33–46.

Parliamentary Human Rights Group. Ensor, Jonathan, ed. 2007. 'Rabwah: A place for Martyrs?' *Report of the Parliamentary Human Rights Group Mission to Pakistan Into Internal Flight for Ahmadis*. www.thepersecution.org/dl/rabwah_report.pdf

Petre, Jonathan. 2003. 'Fellow Muslims criticise opening of large mosque.' *The Telegraph*, 3 October. www.telegraph.co.uk/news/uknews/1443123/Fellow-Muslims-criticise-opening-of-large-mosque.html

PHRG. 2010. *Report of the PHRG Fact Finding Mission to Pakistan to Examine the Human Rights Situation of the Ahmadiyya Community*. London: PHRG.

PHRG. 2015. *A Beleaguered Community: On the Rising Persecution of the Ahmadiyya Muslim Community*. London: PHRG.

PHRG. 2017. *Ahmadis in Pakistan Face an Existential Threat: The Growing Violence, Legal Discrimination and Social Exclusion Since 2015*. London: PHRG.

Pierucci, Antônio. 2000. 'Secularization in Max Weber: On current usefulness of re-accessing that old meaning.' *Brazilian Review of Social Sciences* 1:129–158.

Piovanelli, Pierluigi. 2005. 'What is a Christian apocryphal text and how does it work? Some observations on apocryphal hermeneutics.' *Nederlands Theologisch Tijdschrift* 59:31–40.

Poole, Elizabeth. 2002. *Media Representations of British Muslims*. London: I. B. Tauris.

Porter, Tom. 2016. 'Birmingham council "Endorsed Muslim Sectarianism" against persecuted Ahmadi sect.' *International Business Times*. www.ibtimes.co.uk/birmingham-council-endorsed-muslim-sectarianism-against-persecuted-ahmadi-sect-1577946

Powell, Avril. 2000. '"Duties of Ahmadi women": Educative processes in the early stages of the Ahmadiyya movement.' Antony Copley, ed., *Gurus and Their Followers: New Religious Reform Movements in Colonial India*. Oxford: Oxford University Press, 128–158.

Price, Simon. 1987. 'The future of dreams: From Freud to Artemidorus.' *Past and Present* 113:3–37.

Punjab Government. 1954. *Report of the Court of Inquiry Constituted Under Punjab Act ii of 1954 to Enquire into the Punjab Disturbances of 1953*. Lahore: Government Printing, Punjab.

Qureshi, Zayn. 2016. *Emergence of Sectarianism in the Diaspora: The Case of Anti-Ahmadiyya Discrimination with the United Kingdom*. Unpublished MA Utrecht University, Netherlands.

Rabwah Times, 18 March 2017. 'Indonesia shuts down Ahmadiyya Mosque in Depok.' www.rabwah.net/indonesia-shuts-ahmadiyya-mosque-depok/

Rafiq, B. A. 'Jihad against the British government in India? Opinion of the Muslim scholars of that time.' *Truth About Ahmadiyyat*. www.alislam.org/jihad/muslim-scholars.html

Rahimian, Parisa. 2009. 'Women and dream interpretation in contemporary Iran.' Kelly Bulkeley, Muhammad Amanullah, Kate Adams, Patricia Davis, Lee Butler, Bart Koet,

Bonnelle Strickling, Geoff Nelson, Patricia Bulkley and Hidayet Aydar, eds., *Dreaming in Christianity and Islam: Culture, Conflict, and Creativity*. Brunswick, NJ: Rutgers University Press, 155–164.

Rahman, Mujeeb Ur. 2015. 'Apartheid of Ahmadis in Pakistan.' Part 1. *Review of Religions*. www.reviewofreligions.org/12287/apartheid-of-ahmadis-in-pakistan/

Rahman, Mujeeb Ur. 2016. 'Apartheid of Ahmadis in Pakistan.' Part 2. *Review of Religions*. www.reviewofreligions.org/12427/apartheid-of-ahmadis-in-pakistan-2/

Railton, Nicholas. 2003. 'Gog and Magog: The history of a symbol.' *The Evangelical Quarterly* 75/1:23–43.

Raja, Masood. 2010. *Constructing Pakistan: Foundational Texts and the Rise of Muslim National Identity 1857–1947*. Oxford: Oxford University Press.

Ramji, Hasmita. 2006. 'Journeys of difference: The use of migratory narratives among British Hindu Gujaratis.' *Ethnic and Racial Studies* 29/4:702–724.

Redding, Jeffrey. 2004. 'Constitutionalizing Islam: Theory and Pakistan.' *Virginia Journal of International Law* 44/3:459–827.

Rehan, Ehsan. 2018. 'Bilawal Bhutto deletes tweet endorsing Ahmadi rights.' *Rabwah Times*, 8 May.

Rehman, Hina. 2014. 'The conference of great religions 1896.' *Maryam: Taleem and Tarbiyyat Magazine for Waaqifaat-e-Nau* April–June 10:33–36.

Review of Religions, February 2008. Khilafat Centenary Special Edition.

Reynolds, Sile and Helen Muggeridge. 2008. *Remote Controls: How UK Border Controls are Endangering the Lives of Refugees*. London: Refugee Council.

Robbins, J. 2003. 'Dreaming and the defeat of charisma: Disconnecting dreams from leadership among the urapmin of Papua New Guinea.' R. Lohmann, ed., *Dream Travellers: Sleep Experiences and Culture in the Western Pacific*. New York: Palgrave Macmillan, 19–41.

Robinson, Francis. 2003. 'Islam and the impact of print in South Asia.' *Islam and Muslim History in South Asia*. Oxford: Oxford University Press, 66–104.

Robinson, Francis. 2005. *Khilafat*. https://pure.royalholloway.ac.uk/portal/files/889318/khilafat1.pdf

Robinson, Vaughn. 1988. 'The new Indian middle class in Britain.' *Ethnic and Racial Studies* 11/4:456–473.

Rudee, Eliana. 2018. 'Ahmadi Muslims, among persecuted Mideast minorities finding religious freedom in Israel, promote a message of peace.' *Jewish News Syndicate*. www.jns.org/ahmadi-muslims-among-persecuted-mideast-minorities-finding-religious-freedom-in-israel-promote-a-message-of-peace/

Rudolph, Lloyd and Susanne Rudolph. 1979. 'Authority and power in bureaucratic and patrimonial administration: A revisionist interpretation of Weber on bureaucracy.' *World Politics* 31/2:195–227.

Sadiq, Imran. 2018. 'Historic building demolished, Ahmadiyya place of worship vandalised in Sialkot.' *Dawn*, 24 May. www.dawn.com/news/1409714

Saeed, Sadia. 2010. *Politics of Exclusion: Muslim Nationalism, State Formation and Legal Representations of the Ahmadiyya Community in Pakistan*. PhD Dissertation. The University of Michigan.

Salaam, Amtul. 2008. 'The dervishes of Qadian: An historical perspective.' *Al Nusrat*, November. www.lajna.org.uk/index.php/articles-by-lajna/110-lajna-imaillah-uk-articles-derveshes-of-qadian-

Salatomatic. 2014. *The Most Comprehensive Guide to Mosques and Islamic Schools*. www.salatomatic.com/sub/United-Kingdom/London/Merton/OwjXfyWubG.

Saleem, Sana. 2010. 'A muted response to minority killings.' *Dawn*. www.dawn.com/news/813276/a-muted-response-to-minority-killings

Saleem, Shahed. 2018. *The British Mosque: An Architectural and Social History*. Swindon: Historic England.

Salem, Sara. 2016. 'Intersectionality and its discontents: Intersectionality as traveling theory.' *European Journal of Women's Studies* 1–16.

Sallnow, Michael. 1981. 'Communitas reconsidered: The sociology of Andean pilgrimage.' *Man* 16/2:163–182.

Sayeed, Saad. 2017. 'Pakistan's long-persecuted Ahmadi minority fear becoming election scapegoat.' *Reuters. World News*, 16 November. www.reuters.com/article/us-pakistan-election-ahmadis/pakist . . . ted-ahmadi-minority-fear-becoming-election-scapegoat-idUSKBN1DG04H

Sevea, Iqbal. 2012. *The Political Philosophy of Muhammad Iqbal: Islam and Nationalism in Late Colonial India*. Cambridge: Cambridge University Press.

Shah, Bindi, Claire Dwyer and David Gilbert. 2012. 'Landscapes of diasporic religious belonging in the edge-city: The Jain temple at potters bar, outer London.' *South Asian Diaspora* 4/1:77–94.

Shah, Zia. 2014. 'Is Ahmadiyya in the asylum business? A strong Rebuttal by Ahmadiyya Muslim Jamaat Germany.' *The Muslim Times*, 25 November. https://themuslimtimes.info/2014/11/25/is-ahmadiyya-in-the-asylum-business-a-strong-rebuttal-by-ahmadiyya-muslim-jamaat-germany/

Shahid, Kunwar Khuldune. 2018a. 'Pakistan High Court judge calls for "termination" of Ahmadiyyas.' *Asia Times*, 27 March. www.atimes.com/article/pakistan-high-court-judge-calls-termination-ahmaddiyas/

Shahid, Kunwar Khuldune. 2018b. 'How Pakistan weaponized "Love for Prophet Muhammad".' *The Diplomat*, May 8. https://thediplomat.com/2018/05/how-pakistan-weaponized-love-for-prophet-muhammad/

Shaw, Alison. 2001. 'Kinship, cultural preference and immigration: Consanguineous marriage among British Pakistanis.' *Journal of the Royal Anthropological Institute* 7:315–334.

Shaw, Alison. 2004. 'Immigrant families in the UK.' Jacqueline Scott, Judith Treas and Martin Richards, eds., *The Blackwell Companion to the Sociology of Families*. Oxford: Blackwell Publishing Ltd, 270–285.

Shaw, Alison. 2006. 'The arranged transnational cousin marriages of British Pakistanis: Critique, dissent and cultural continuity.' *Contemporary South Asia* 15/2:209–220.

Shearmur, Jeremy. 2014. 'The Woking mosque: British Islam in the early twentieth century.' *Journal of Muslim Minority Affairs* 34/2:165–173.

Spate, O. H. K. 1947. 'The partition of the Punjab and of Bengal.' *The Geographical Journal* 110/4–6:201–218.

Speier, Jackie and Peter King. 2018. 'With religious freedom ministerial, an opportunity to act on behalf of oppressed Ahmadi Muslims.' *The Hill*. http://thehill.com/blogs/congress-blog/foreign-policy/399771-with-religious-freedom-ministerial-an-opportunity-to-act

Stewart, Charles. 2016. 'Historicity and anthropology.' *Annual Review of Anthropology* 45:79–94.

Sutherland, Robert. 2009. 'Expert evidence – the role, duties and responsibilities of the expert witness in litigation.' *Presentation Delivered at an Expert Witness Training Seminar Hosted by Terra Firma Chambers on 20 April*. www.terrafirmachambers.com/articles/ExpertEvidenceRoleDutiesandResponsibilitiesoftheExpertWitnessinCourtProceedings.pdf

Swatos, William, ed. 1998. 'Routinization.' *Encyclopedia of Religion and Society*. Lanham, MD: Rowman Altamira Press.

Tahir, Kholood. 2018. 'The purpose of Ba'ait.' *JalsaConnect*. www.mta.tv/jalsaconnect/purpose-baait

Talbot, Ian and Gurharpal Singh, eds. 2009. *The Partition of India*. Cambridge: Cambridge University Press.

Tanveer, Rana. 2016. 'Enshrined discrimination: No Ahmadis for Chenab Nagar plots.' *The Express Tribune*, March 18. https://tribune.com.pk/story/1067763/enshrined-discrimination-no-ahmadis-for-chenab-nagar-plots/

Tarikh-e-Ahmadiyyat. 2018. 'History of Majlis Ansarullah.' *Al Hakam*, 9 September. www.alhakam.org/history-of-majlis-ansarullah/

Taylor, Jerome. 2008a. 'A pilgrimage to the end of the Northern line; Persecuted in Pakistan, followers of the 70-million strong Ahmadi Muslim sect will gather in London for the centenary of their leader's death.' *The Independent*, 24 July.

Taylor, Jerome. 2008b. 'Islamic sect complaint highlights Ofcom's increasing impotence.' *The Independent*, 6 October.

The Times of India. 1924a. 'Empire religions: The Wembley conference.' 30 June.

The Times of India. 1924b. 'The Ahmadiyya movement: Coming of the Khalifa.' September 6.

Tinker, Hugh. 1977. 'Pressure, persuasion, decision: Factors in the partition of the Punjab, August 1947.' *The Journal of Asian Studies* 36/4:695–704.

Tobitt, Charlotte. 2019. 'Ofcom fines UK Urdu-language news channel £75,000 for "hate speech" against Muslim group.' *Pressgazzette UK*. www.pressgazette.co.uk/ofcom-fines-channel-44-city-news-network-75000-for-hate-speech-against-ahmadiyya-community/

Tong, Joy Kooi-Chin and Bryan Turner. 2008. 'Women, piety and practice: A study of women and religious practices in Malaya.' *Contemporary Islam* 2:41–59.

Toth, Michael. 1972. 'Toward a theory of the routinization of charisma.' *Rocky Mountain Social Science Journal* 9/2:93–98. http://web.pdx.edu/~tothm/essays/essays/toward_a_theory_of__the_routiniz.htm

Tsangarides, Natasha. 2010. *The Refugee Roulette: The Role of Country Information in Refugee Status Determination*. London: Immigration Advisory Service.

Turner, Victor. 1969. *The Ritual Process: Structure and Anti-Structure*. London: Routledge & Kegan Paul.

Turner, Victor. 1973. 'The center out there: Pilgrim's goal.' *History of Religions* 12/3: 191–230.

UNCHR. 2010. *Convention and Protocol Relating to the Status of Refugees*. www.unhcr.org/3b66c2aa10.pdf

UNHCR. 2017. *Eligibility Guidelines for Assessing the International Protection Needs of Members of Religious Minorities from Pakistan*. HCR/EG/PAK/17/01.

UNHCR. 2018. *Resettlement Handbook, Country Chapter UK*. www.unhcr.org/40ee6fc04.pdf

USSD. 2006. *International Religious Freedom Report, Pakistan*. www.state.gov/j/drl/rls/irf/2006/71443.htm

USSD. 2009. *International Religious Freedom Report, Pakistan*. https://2009-2017.state.gov/j/drl/rls/irf/2009/127370.htm

USSD. 2017. *Country Report on Human Rights Practices for 2016 – Pakistan*. www.state.gov/j/drl/rls/hrrpt/humanrightsreport/index.htm?year=2016&dlid=265546.

USSD. 2018. *Pakistan International Religious Freedom.* www.state.gov/wp-content/uploads/2019/05/PAKISTAN-2018-INTERNATIONAL-RELIGIOUS-FREEDOM-REPORT.pdf

Vatuk, Sylvia. 2011. 'South Asian Muslims and country expertise in the American Immigration Courts.' Holden Livia, ed., *Cultural Expertise and Litigation: Patterns, Conflicts, Narratives.* London: Routledge, 13–34.

Veninga, Jennifer. 2016. 'Echoes of the Danish cartoon crisis 10 years later: Identity, injury and intelligibility from Copenhagen to Paris and Texas.' *Islam and Christian-Muslim Relations* 27/1:25–34.

Visram, Rozina. 1986. *Ayahs, Lascars and Princes: The Story of Indians in Britain 1700–1947.* London: Pluto Press.

Wadud, Amina. 2006. *Inside the Gender Jihad: Women's Reform in Islam.* Oxford: Oneworld.

Walsh, Declan. 2011. 'Pakistan minister Shahbaz Bhatti shot dead in Islamabad.' *The Guardian*, 2 March.

Walter, Howard A. 1916. 'The Ahmadiyya movement to-day.' *The Moslem World* 66–78.

Weber, Max. 1978 [1922]. *Economy and Society: An Outline of Interpretive Sociology.* G. Roth and C. Wittich, eds. Berkeley, CA: University of California Press.

Weber, Max. 1989 [1918]. 'Science as a vocation.' P. Lassman and I. Velody, eds., *Max Weber's Science as a Vocation.* London: Unwin Hyman.

Weber, Max. 2005. *Readings and Commentary on Modernity.* Stephen Kalberg, ed. Oxford: Blackwell.

Weber, Max. 2011 [1920]. *The Protestant Ethic and the Spirit of Capitalism.* Stephen Kalberg, trans. Oxford: Oxford University Press.

Weinbaum, Marvin and Abdullah Khurram. 2014. 'Pakistan and Saudi Arabia: Deference, dependence, and deterrence.' *Middle East Journal* 68/2:211–228.

Werbner, Pnina. 2003. *Pilgrims of Love: The Anthropology of a Global Sufi Cult.* Bloomington and Indianapolis: Indiana University Press.

Westminster Hall Debate. 2010. 'Ahmadiyya community.' 20 October. https://hansard.parliament.uk/Commons/2010-10-20/debates/10102039000002/AhmadiyyaCommunity

Westminster Hall Debate. 2016. *Backbench Business: Persecution of Religious Minorities, Pakistan.* https://publications.parliament.uk/pa/cm201516/cmhansrd/cm160211/halltext/160211h0001.htm#16021142000331

Woolf, Marie. 2005. 'Sir Iqbal Sacranie: "There can never be justification for killing civilians".' *The Independent*, 18 July. www.independent.co.uk/news/people/profiles/sir-iqbal-sacranie-there-can-never-be-justification-for-killing-civilians-299817.html

Zaheer, Ehsan Elahi. 1984. *Qadiyaniat: An Analytical Survey.* Lahore, Pakistan: Idara Tarjuman Al-Sunnah.

Zaidi, Akbar. 1988. 'Religious minorities in Pakistan today.' *Journal of Contemporary Asia* 18/4:444–457.

Zaidi, Akbar. 2017. 'Authoritarianism and the downfall.' *Dawn.*

Index

Note: *Italic* page numbers refer to figures and tables.